Super-Diversity in Everyday Life

Presenting several in-depth studies, this book explores how super-diversity operates in everyday relations and interactions in a variety of urban settings in Western Europe and the USA.

The contributors raise a broad range of questions about the nature and effects of super-diversity. They ask if a quantitative increase in demographic diversity makes a qualitative difference in how diversity is experienced in urban neighborhoods, and what are the consequences of demographic change when people from a wide range of countries and social backgrounds live together in urban neighborhoods. The question at the core of the book is to what extent, and in what contexts, super-diversity leads either to the normalization of diversity or to added hostility towards and amongst those in different ethnic, racial, and religious groups. In cases where there is no particular ethno-racial or religious majority, are certain long-established groups able to continue to exert economic and political power, and is this continued economic and political dominance actually often facilitated by super-diversity?

With contributions from a number of European countries as well as the USA, this book will be of interest to researchers studying contemporary migration and ethnic diversity. It will also spark discussion amongst those focusing on multiculturalism in urban environments.

This book was originally published as a special issue of *Ethnic and Racial Studies*.

Jan Willem Duyvendak is a Distinguished Research Professor of Sociology at the University of Amsterdam, the Netherlands, and the Director of the Netherlands Institute for Advanced Study in the Humanities and Social Sciences.

Nancy Foner is a Distinguished Professor of Sociology at Hunter College and the Graduate Center of the City University of New York, New York City, USA.

Philip Kasinitz is a Presidential Professor of Sociology at the Graduate Center of the City University of New York, New York City, USA.

Ethnic and Racial Studies
Series editors:
Martin Bulmer, *University of Surrey, UK*, and
John Solomos, *University of Warwick, UK*

The journal *Ethnic and Racial Studies* was founded in 1978 by John Stone to provide an international forum for high quality research on race, ethnicity, nationalism and ethnic conflict. At the time the study of race and ethnicity was still a relatively marginal sub-field of sociology, anthropology and political science. In the intervening period the journal has provided a space for the discussion of core theoretical issues, key developments and trends, and for the dissemination of the latest empirical research.

It is now the leading journal in its field and has helped to shape the development of scholarly research agendas. *Ethnic and Racial Studies* attracts submissions from scholars in a diverse range of countries and fields of scholarship, and crosses disciplinary boundaries. It is now available in both printed and electronic form. Since 2015 it has published 15 issues per year, three of which are dedicated to *Ethnic and Racial Studies Review* offering expert guidance to the latest research through the publication of book reviews, symposia and discussion pieces, including reviews of work in languages other than English.

The *Ethnic and Racial Studies* book series contains a wide range of the journal's special issues. These special issues are an important contribution to the work of the journal, where leading social science academics bring together articles on specific themes and issues that are linked to the broad intellectual concerns of *Ethnic and Racial Studies*. The series editors work closely with the guest editors of the special issues to ensure that they meet the highest quality standards possible. Through publishing these special issues as a series of books, we hope to allow a wider audience of both scholars and students from across the social science disciplines to engage with the work of *Ethnic and Racial Studies*.

Most recent titles in the series include:

Migration and Race in Europe
Edited by Martin Bulmer and John Solomos

Race and Crisis
Edited by Suman Gupta and Satnam Virdee

Why Do We Still Talk About Race?
Edited by Martin Bulmer and John Solomos

Islamophobia and Surveillance
Genealogies of a Global Order
Edited by James Renton

The Mechanisms of Racialization Beyond the Black/White Binary
Edited by Bianca Gonzalez-Sobrino and Devon R. Goss

Super-Diversity in Everyday Life
Edited by Jan Willem Duyvendak, Nancy Foner and Philip Kasinitz

Super-Diversity in Everyday Life

Edited by
Jan Willem Duyvendak, Nancy Foner
and Philip Kasinitz

First published 2020
by Routledge
2 Park Square, Milton Park, Abingdon, Oxon, OX14 4RN

and by Routledge
52 Vanderbilt Avenue, New York, NY 10017

Routledge is an imprint of the Taylor & Francis Group, an informa business

First issued in paperback 2021

Introduction, Chapters 1–3, 6 © 2020 Taylor & Francis
Chapter 4 © 2017 Paul Mepschen. Originally published as Open Access.
Chapter 5 © 2017 Fenneke Wekker. Originally published as Open Access.
Chapter 7 © 2017 Steven Vertovec. Originally published as Open Access.

With the exception of Chapters 4, 5 and 7, no part of this book may be reprinted or reproduced or utilised in any form or by any electronic, mechanical, or other means, now known or hereafter invented, including photocopying and recording, or in any information storage or retrieval system, without permission in writing from the publishers. For details on the rights for Chapters 4, 5 and 7, please see the chapters' Open Access footnotes.

Trademark notice: Product or corporate names may be trademarks or registered trademarks, and are used only for identification and explanation without intent to infringe.

British Library Cataloguing-in-Publication Data
A catalogue record for this book is available from the British Library

ISBN13: 978-0-367-27315-6 (hbk)
ISBN13: 978-1-03-208880-8 (pbk)

Typeset in Myriad Pro
by codeMantra

Publisher's Note
The publisher accepts responsibility for any inconsistencies that may have arisen during the conversion of this book from journal articles to book chapters, namely the inclusion of journal terminology.

Disclaimer
Every effort has been made to contact copyright holders for their permission to reprint material in this book. The publishers would be grateful to hear from any copyright holder who is not here acknowledged and will undertake to rectify any errors or omissions in future editions of this book.

Contents

Citation Information		vi
Notes on Contributors		viii
	Introduction: super-diversity in everyday life Nancy Foner, Jan Willem Duyvendak and Philip Kasinitz	1
1	Pioneer migrants and their social relations in super-diverse London Susanne Wessendorf	17
2	Coming of age in multi-ethnic America: young adults' experiences with diversity Van C. Tran	35
3	Super-diversity as a methodological lens: re-centring power and inequality Sofya Aptekar	53
4	A discourse of displacement: super-diversity, urban citizenship, and the politics of autochthony in Amsterdam Paul Mepschen	71
5	"We have to teach them diversity": on demographic transformations and lived reality in an Amsterdam working-class neighbourhood Fenneke Wekker	89
6	What about the mainstream? Assimilation in super-diverse times Richard Alba and Jan Willem Duyvendak	105
7	Talking around super-diversity Steven Vertovec	125
Index		141

Citation Information

The chapters in this book were originally published in *Ethnic and Racial Studies*, volume 42, issue 1 (January 2019). When citing this material, please use the original page numbering for each article, as follows:

Introduction
Introduction: super-diversity in everyday life
Nancy Foner, Jan Willem Duyvendak and Philip Kasinitz
Ethnic and Racial Studies, volume 42, issue 1 (January 2019) pp. 1–16

Chapter 1
Pioneer migrants and their social relations in super-diverse London
Susanne Wessendorf
Ethnic and Racial Studies, volume 42, issue 1 (January 2019) pp. 17–34

Chapter 2
Coming of age in multi-ethnic America: young adults' experiences with diversity
Van C. Tran
Ethnic and Racial Studies, volume 42, issue 1 (January 2019) pp. 35–52

Chapter 3
Super-diversity as a methodological lens: re-centring power and inequality
Sofya Aptekar
Ethnic and Racial Studies, volume 42, issue 1 (January 2019) pp. 53–70

Chapter 4
A discourse of displacement: super-diversity, urban citizenship, and the politics of autochthony in Amsterdam
Paul Mepschen
Ethnic and Racial Studies, volume 42, issue 1 (January 2019) pp. 71–88

Chapter 5
"We have to teach them diversity": on demographic transformations and lived reality in an Amsterdam working-class neighbourhood
Fenneke Wekker
Ethnic and Racial Studies, volume 42, issue 1 (January 2019) pp. 89–104

Chapter 6
What about the mainstream? Assimilation in super-diverse times
Richard Alba and Jan Willem Duyvendak
Ethnic and Racial Studies, volume 42, issue 1 (January 2019) pp. 105–124

Chapter 7
Talking around super-diversity
Steven Vertovec
Ethnic and Racial Studies, volume 42, issue 1 (January 2019) pp. 125–139

For any permission-related enquiries please visit:
http://www.tandfonline.com/page/help/permissions

Contributors

Richard Alba is a Distinguished Professor at the Graduate Center at the City University of New York, New York City, USA.

Sofya Aptekar is an Associate Professor in the Department of Sociology at the University of Massachusetts Boston, USA.

Jan Willem Duyvendak is a Distinguished Research Professor of Sociology at the University of Amsterdam, the Netherlands, and the Director of the Netherlands Institute for Advanced Study in the Humanities and Social Sciences.

Nancy Foner is a Distinguished Professor of Sociology at Hunter College and the Graduate Center of the City University of New York, New York City, USA.

Philip Kasinitz is a Presidential Professor of Sociology at the Graduate Center of the City University of New York, New York City, USA.

Paul Mepschen is a Postdoctoral Researcher in the Department of Sociology at the University of Amsterdam, the Netherlands.

Van C. Tran is an Associate Professor of Sociology at the Graduate Center at the City University of New York, New York City, USA.

Steven Vertovec is the Founding Director of the Max-Planck-Institute for the Study of Religious and Ethnic Diversity and an Honorary Joint Professor of Sociology and Ethnology at the University of Göttingen, Germany.

Fenneke Wekker is the Head of Academic Affairs at the Netherlands Institute for Advanced Study in the Humanities and Social Sciences (NIAS-KNAW), the Netherlands.

Susanne Wessendorf is an Assistant Professorial Research Fellow at the International Inequalities Institute (III) at the London School of Economics, UK.

Introduction: super-diversity in everyday life

Nancy Foner, Jan Willem Duyvendak and Philip Kasinitz

ABSTRACT
In the introduction to this special issue, we consider a number of questions central to the study of super-diversity in urban contexts in Western Europe and the United States. We begin with a discussion of why the super-diversity concept has had more impact on scholarship in Western Europe than the United States, where it has had much less resonance. We explore the nature and effects of super-diversity for ongoing social relations in everyday life, considering both the positive and negative consequences. And we conclude with a consideration of some unfulfilled promises of super-diversity, including integrating the dimension of power into the analyses as well as finding ways to examine the many bases and intersections of different forms of diversity, while at the same time not downplaying the role of continued and long-term inequalities, such as race and class, that typically remain of primary importance in super-diverse settings.

The concept of super-diversity has captured the imagination of social scientists who study contemporary immigration and ethnic diversity, especially in Western Europe. The term was coined, and the concept put forward, by Vertovec (2007) a decade ago in an *Ethnic and Racial Studies* article, "Super-diversity and its Implications", which has turned out to be the most highly cited article in the journal's forty year history. Over the past ten years, super-diversity has become a buzzword among scholars, policymakers, urban planners, and social workers, at least in Western Europe, and has begun to have some impact on migration studies on the other side of the Atlantic, as well. Indeed, Western European scholars and social policy analysts concerned with immigration, integration, and ethnic diversity who fail to explicitly take into account the notion of super-diversity run the risk of being reproached for neglecting the "new multicultural condition of the twenty-first century" (Sarah Neal and Allan Cochrane cited in Meissner and Vertovec 2015, 542).

The basic argument advanced for coining the term and developing the concept is that it describes changing patterns of global migration flows of the post-World War II decades that have entailed the movement of people from more varied national, ethnic, linguistic, and religious backgrounds, who occupy more varied legal statuses, and who bring a wide range of human capital (education, work skills, and experience). Super-diversity, as Wessendorf (2014, 2) puts it, is a lens to describe "an exceptional demographic situation characterized by the multiplication of social categories within specific localities". The notion of super-diversity has been presented as challenging dominant approaches in "conventional migration studies" by moving beyond an "ethno-focal lens" (or "groupism", to borrow Brubaker's [2004] term) and calling for greater attention to other bases of differentiation – such as gender, social class, sexual orientation, age, legal status, and language – *within* each ethnic or national origin group to better understand the dynamics of their inclusion or exclusion (Vertovec 2007, 1025, 1039).

One of the great benefits of a super-diversity lens is that, like other new sociological concepts, it has the virtue of bringing new perspectives to familiar issues and advancing our understanding of social processes by reconstituting our perceptual field and identifying connections not previously seen or emphasized (cf. Portes 1997). The concept, however, is still in its infancy, and in this special issue, we heed Vertovec's explicit call to "critically interrogate, refine and extrapolate" the notion of super-diversity (Meissner and Vertovec 2015, 542). We do this by bringing together a series of in-depth studies on how super-diversity unfolds and operates in concrete every-day relations and interactions in a variety of settings in Western Europe as well as the United States.

The articles raise a broad range of questions about the nature and effects of super-diversity. One basic question is whether a quantitative increase in demographic diversity, marked, for example, by a growing number of ethno-racial groups, makes a qualitative difference in how diversity is experienced in urban settings. Or to put it another way: what are the actual consequences and outcomes of demographic change when people from a wide range of countries and social backgrounds now live together in urban neighborhoods? A central issue is the extent to which, and in what contexts, super-diversity leads to the normalization of diversity or, alternatively, to added hostility to and conflicts among those in different ethnic, racial, and religious groups. Another analytic dimension is also pertinent. Although no one ethno-racial or religious group may numerically dominate in particular areas or cities, are certain long-established groups able to continue to exert economic and political power? Indeed, and perhaps paradoxically, is this continued economic and, especially political, dominance actually often facilitated by super-diversity?

As for what might be called the "diversification of diversity", an analytic concern is to what degree, and under what circumstances, certain bases of social differentiation which cross-cut national origin or ethnic group affiliation (especially class and race) remain central in super-diverse settings. All differences or bases of diversity, in other words, are not equal, and how and why they vary in significance and impact are an important subject for analysis. Then, too, there is the fact that even scholars concerned with super-diversity who start out writing about different forms of diversity in contemporary global cities, such as generation, sexuality, gender, legal status, and class, often end up focusing on ethnicity, or even crude proxies for ethnicity, in their work – for instance, using national origin groups as the key units of analysis or characterizing cities as majority–minority, that is, those where whites are no longer a majority in the United States or long-established natives a majority in Europe.

Finally, there are questions about the broader societal impact of super-diversity. If scholars of super-diversity generally focus on racial and ethnic minorities, and even more specifically, immigrants and their children, a critical issue is what impact the super-diversity of cities and nations has for the so-called "native" population. To put it in rather stark terms: is the incorporation of an array of new ethnic and racial minorities leading to a redefining of the societal mainstream or what it means to be "native"?

The introduction begins to tackle these questions while, in the process, drawing on and highlighting key points in the articles in this special issue. We start out with an intriguing transatlantic question: why has the super-diversity concept had more impact on scholarship in Western Europe than the United States, where it has had much less resonance? We consider, among other things, how much this has to do with the historical experience of immigration and urban diversity on the two sides of the Atlantic as well as earlier models of or theories about diversity that have been dominant there. Next, we explore the nature and effects of super-diversity for ongoing social relations in everyday life, considering both the positive and negative consequences. We conclude with a consideration of some as yet unfulfilled promises of super-diversity, including integrating the dimension of power into the analyses as well as finding ways to examine the many bases and intersections of different forms of diversity, while at the same time not downplaying the role of continued and long-term inequalities, such as race and class, that typically remain of primary importance in super-diverse settings.

Super-diversity on the two sides of the Atlantic

The speed with which the concept of super-diversity has been embraced by students of the migrant-receiving societies of Western Europe has been truly impressive. It has been used far less often by students of diversity in the

United States (as noted by Tran, this issue). This is striking, in part, because the demographic preconditions for super-diversity – migration from a wide variety of source countries and the creation of "no majority" cities, as well as increasing internal diversity among migrant and ethnic groups – are at least as common in the United States today as in Europe. Some of the difference may simply reflect the fact that Americans have used other terminology and concepts to do at least some of the "work" super-diversity does in Europe. However, we argue that it also reflects the different histories and different traditions of urban politics in Western Europe and the United States that analysts bring to their scholarship on the two sides of the Atlantic.

Writings on urban diversity in the United States, for one thing, inevitably have been influenced by the presence of and barriers facing African Americans – a historical legacy, of course, of African slavery on U.S. soil, legal segregation, and ghettoization. American urban scholars have long recognized that social and political life works differently in places divided between two or three clearly bounded and unequal ethnic or racial groups, on the one hand, and places in which there are a variety of groups with what Alba (2009) terms more blurred and porous boundaries, on the other. The classic example of the former would be rigidly racially segregated cities in the early and mid-twentieth century United States in which the population was comprised of blacks and whites who were sharply (and in the case of the southern U.S., legally) separated from each other and lived most of their lives among those in their own racial group. Of course, as observers have long pointed out, both the black and white communities were internally diverse in terms of class, gender, ethnic origin, and so on (see Du Bois 1899; Drake and Cayton 1945). But particularly for African Americans, that fact did not matter very much. Race remained the "master status" in shaping most important aspects of social life. Class, educational status, even ethnicity all paled in comparison.

At the same time, the long and continuous history of immigration to and ethnic diversity in northern cities and the taken-for-granted legitimacy and central role of urban ethnic politics have also shaped scholarly thinking about urban diversity in the United States (see Foner 2017). In *Beyond the Melting Pot*, Glazer and Moynihan (1963), writing about mid-twentieth century urban America, suggested that urban politics operated differently in cities characterized by a two-group black/white divide and strict black/white segregation, what they termed the "southern model", than in cities like New York, characterized by what they called the "northern model", in which a wide variety of ethnic (immigrant-origin) groups contested for power, with no one-group permanently dominant. Their claim for such hurly-burly pluralist competition and cross-cutting alliances between and across ethnic groups in northern immigrant cities was clearly overly rosy, ignoring, among other things, the continued high degree of black–white residential segregation there. Yet it is worth remembering that Glazer and Moynihan saw cities that lacked a clear ethnic majority, of which New York was offered as the premier example, as very different in their politics and intergroup relations than cities in which social and institutional life was organized around a central power cleavage between blacks and whites. Skerry (1993) has made a similar argument in his comparison of Mexican Americans in cities like San Antonio, Texas, in which power was historically divided between highly segregated Mexican and Anglo communities, and immigrant cities with a greater variety of ethnic and class communities such as Los Angeles.

More recent analyses have built on the long concern in American urban politics with ethnic diversity, but with new twists and turns. In the wake of the enormous post-1965 immigration and increased ethnic diversity it has brought, John Mollenkopf has argued that the wide variety of ethnic groups and lack of demographic dominance by any one group in electoral politics in contemporary New York (and a number of other "no majority" cities) has led to a situation where shifting ethnic boundaries and cross-ethnic alliances promote a more complex and multi-faceted politics than is typical in cities with a few large and clearly bounded groups. Paradoxically, in highly diverse American cities, the lack of a unified nonwhite group – which is splintered by ethnic divisions – has at times allowed native whites to continue domination of many aspects of political and social life long after they have become a numerical minority (Mollenkopf 2003, 2014).

Another concept competing at least to some degree with super-diversity is the notion of intersectionality. While this concept is widely used on both sides of the Atlantic, particularly among feminist scholars, it has probably had broader acceptance in the United States (see, for example, Patricia Hill Collins's American Sociological Association presidential address, Collins 2015). The intersectionality approach highlights the fact that no person is reducible to a single identity. Despite the centrality of race and ethnicity in social life, these identities are experienced in interaction with other identities such as gender, sexual orientation, and religion. Or to put it another way, individuals stand at the intersection of multiple identities, despite the tendency of some social scientists, and sometimes ethnic group leaders, to reduce people to a single identity. Indeed, like super-diversity, the intersectionality perspective provides a critique of the ways in which racial and ethnic diversity is generally studied in the United States, particularly in quantitative analysis that emphasizes group comparisons ("the Mexicans do this, the Chinese do that") to such an extent that other possibly more important identities can be obscured.

As for the European side, no doubt some of the appeal of the super-diversity concept is that it provides an alternative to the increasingly politically unpopular notion of multiculturalism. The (false) belief that multiculturalism has been a failure has become a cliché in European policy discussions, far more so than in the United States. In part, this has to do with the very meaning of the term on the two sides of the Atlantic. In Western Europe, multiculturalism is often associated with state policies supporting the political accommodation of cultural practices, traditions, and identities among immigrant origin groups, policies which often have proved unpopular. In the United States, by contrast, multiculturalism is often associated with a vague cultural orientation favouring inclusion and diversity and attempts in the post-civil rights era to recognize the experiences and contributions of African Americans, non-white immigrants, and other previously marginalized groups in American history and national identity, especially in schools. While much of the attack on multiculturalism in Europe is simply a mask for intolerance and bigotry, it is also true, as Sen (2006) notes, that in practice some versions of multiculturalism have the potential to reinforce what he labels "plural monoculturalism" (or what also might be called hard boundary multiculturalism) in which different ethnic communities may be encouraged to remain largely separate culturally, socially, and geographically or, as he puts it, different traditions live side by side without the twain meeting. The fear then is that multiculturalism is a threat to social cohesion. Another fear is that the tolerance of ethnic group differences can go hand in hand with intolerance of other forms of difference *within* ethnic or religious communities – traditional Muslim intolerance of homosexuals or Orthodox Jewish intolerance of feminists, for example.

In contrast to multiculturalism, super-diversity seems more a descriptive than a normative concept, not associated with any specific government policy or policies; it is also closer to and has come to be associated with descriptions of a soft boundary multiculturalism, in which individuals of diverse backgrounds may come together and form bonds based on a variety of identities or interests. This is partly a result of new demographic realities. In cities and communities with a huge variety of internally varied groups, interactions and experiences in everyday life are likely to cut across group boundaries. A degree of integration emerges, not necessarily because newcomers share social and institutional spaces with long time natives but because diverse newcomers inevitably share them with each other (Crul 2016). There are strong forces pushing for a "lingua franca" (both literally and figuratively). While these dynamics are usually put forward as a description of demographic reality, super-diversity can sometimes take on a normative dimension, particularly in discussions of public policy. In this regard, super-diversity clearly is a more reassuring and more optimistic vision than the political caricature of a "failed multiculturalism" of socially isolated groups suggests. As such the super-diversity concept might provide a chance to envision a kind of street-level cosmopolitanism in which different cultures can be appreciated without making allegiance to one group mandatory.

Does European style super-diversity add a dimension to the analysis of the experience of highly diverse settings that goes beyond the insights of American studies of urban politics or those emphasizing intersectionality? When it comes to understanding, and indeed bidding us to focus on, the everyday life experiences and social relations of those living in increasingly diverse cities, we think that it does. It is important, however, not to romanticize super-diverse communities as (to borrow the title of one study of Queens, New York) "the future of us all" (Sanjek 1999). As both recent history and some of the articles in this issue (e.g. Wekker) show, extreme diversity is no guarantee of a more cosmopolitan outlook on either side of the Atlantic.

The effects of super-diversity on everyday interactions

Ultimately, a key issue is what consequences super-diversity has for everyday interactions and relationships. How has the diversification of diversity in many urban areas around the world affected social life on the local level? How do people get along in contexts where almost everyone comes from somewhere else? (Wessendorf 2014, 2).

Because the study of super-diversity is relatively new, we know little about how super-diversity affects day-to-day intergroup relations, including how, and why, these effects differ in cities and countries or varied contexts within them. The research that is available on super-diversity in particular places also typically examines the impact of one kind of diversity, ethnoracial, and is related to migration flows, although ethnoracial origin is often used as a proxy for other differences such as language, culture, and religion. The studies, moreover, do not always agree on the impacts. On one side, are analyses emphasizing the positive consequences of super-diversity for intergroup relations; on the other, are studies that stress negative effects. To some degree, these different emphases echo an earlier divide in the literature on diversity and intergroup contact, with a meta-analysis of hundreds of intergroup contact studies supporting the "contact hypothesis", showing that contact diminishes intergroup prejudice (Pettigrew and Tropp 2008); in contrast, Putnam (2007) has argued that greater ethnic diversity reduces social solidarity so that in ethnically and racially diverse neighbourhoods people tend to "hunker down" – withdrawing from collective life and distrusting their neighbours – and stick to their own kind in mutually antagonistic sub-communities.

Perhaps the best-known examination of super-diversity at the local level is Wessendorf's (2014) ethnography on London's borough of Hackney, which comes down squarely on the positive side. Hackney, one of Britain's most ethnically diverse boroughs, is about a third white British, with other residents having origins in more than 100 countries and speaking more than 100 languages, including significant numbers of West Africans, Afro-Caribbeans, and South Asians as well as Turks, Chinese, and Poles. Far from hunkering down in the face of super-diversity, Hackney residents have learned to live with it. Diversity has become normal, taken for granted, and unsurprising – or, in Wessendorf's phrase, commonplace in public space, such as in street markets, libraries, hospitals, supermarkets, post offices, and banks as well in the parochial realm of schools, for example, and associations. Indeed, an ethos of mixing has developed in which it has come to be expected that people should mix and interact with residents of other backgrounds in public space and associations (Wessendorf 2013). At the same time, however, in the private realm of friends and relatives, people's closest ties are with those most like themselves in terms of ethnicity, race, and class.

Is Hackney an unusual case of commonplace diversity? Wessendorf (2014) thinks not. Yes, it has a long history of ethnic diversity, a public and political discourse that celebrates diversity, and like other European cities, a culture of walking, public transport, and sharing of public (and often publicly funded) spaces and organizations that attract and reach out to a broad spectrum of the population. But conditions associated with super-diversity itself, she argues, where multiple dimensions of difference are not perfectly correlated, can reduce the potential for polarizing loyalties along any one single fault line, thereby increasing acceptance of social diversity. As Coser (1956, 77) put it many years ago, when the lines of conflict between groups in a society, or we would add an urban neighbourhood, do not converge, no one single cleavage is likely to endanger its stability. Moreover, in Wessendorf's (2014) analysis, the unavoidability of encounters in super-diverse urban localities with others who are different fosters a practical need to get along, at least on a superficial level, in public spheres, and a civility to diversity.

One feature of Hackney and other super-diverse areas that may be especially likely to lead to positive intergroup social relations is the absence of any one majority national origin or ethnoracial group that dominates numerically, culturally, and politically. Indeed, a question that arises from the articles in this issue that requires further discussion concerns the very definition of super-diversity: should the term only be applied to cities or neighbourhoods where no single ethnic group is a numerical majority – and as Fenneke Wekker (2017) puts it, dominates the public or semi-public sphere through sheer numbers – or is this majority–minority condition just one type of super-diversity?

Demography may operate in other positive ways in some neighbourhood institutions and associations in which people develop sustained and longer-term relationships. For example, the great diversity of ethnic groups in schools in many urban communities on both sides of the Atlantic encourages the development of interethnic friendships, since, among other things, at least some students have only a few members of their national origin group (who have the same homeland language) in their classes and grade (on relations among parents of students in ethnically diverse London schools see Neal, Vincent, and Iqbal 2016). Friendships among classmates are an example of what Richard Alba and Jan Willem Duyvendak (this issue) call horizontal interpersonal relations, in which imbalances of authority and power are relatively minimal; they suggest that the very tendency of research on super-diverse neighbourhoods to focus on these kind of relations has ended up highlighting contexts where interactions are likely to be less fraught and openly conflictual.

The articles in this issue also point to other factors that may lead to positive attitudes to diversity and to amicable relations among those in different ethnic groups in super-diverse settings. Among the highly educated pioneer migrants Wessendorf (2017) studied in East London, their educational and occupational backgrounds and ability to speak English enabled them to build networks and form friendships with people with similar backgrounds in different ethnic groups. The young white adults from Iowa and Minnesota discussed in Van Tran's article (2017) were directly exposed to and became more comfortable with racial and ethnic diversity on college campuses; going to school or college together and intermingling in workplaces provided opportunities for members of the second generation in the New York area and San Diego, whom Tran also discusses, to develop friendships with, and more positive attitudes to, those from different ethnic, racial, and religious backgrounds.

Super-diversity, to be sure, is not synonymous with amicable intergroup relations. Social relations in super-diverse neighbourhoods and institutional settings are not always positive, and tensions and conflicts may arise along some dimensions of difference. Diversity, moreover, is not just about difference but about inequalities based on these differences, and these too often have a significant – and often adverse – impact on interactions. Much as Wessendorf (2014) emphasizes commonplace diversity in her study of Hackney, she also makes clear that racial divisions between disadvantaged black youngsters and the rest of the borough's population were a significant fault line: black youth were seen as threatening in public space and were involved in the riots that occurred in 2011. In general, commonplace diversity and negative attitudes toward and tensions with a particular group or groups in an urban community are not mutually exclusive but can go hand in hand.

It is not surprising that, as Back and Sinha (2016) put it, racism and multiculture coexist in London given its large black population, centrality of color-coded race, and history of racial inequalities and strained race relations between blacks and whites. It is also not surprising, given America's dark history of slavery and racism, that divisions based on race are so prominent in American cities, including New York, which is a subject in two of the articles in the issue. New York City's remarkably diverse post-1965 immigrant population with no one, or even two or three, numerically dominant national origin groups, its long history of successfully incorporating immigrants, and public discourse of tolerance, indeed celebration of ethnic diversity, has led to a great deal of optimism about and support for ethnic diversity among young adult second-generation New Yorkers, native white and nonwhite alike, as well as many friendships, positive interactions at work, and even romantic relationships that bring together individuals in different ethnic and racial groups. At the same time, racial inequalities remain entrenched in the city (Foner 2005, 2007, 2013; Kasinitz et al. 2008). New York City "remains deeply unequal in terms of race, highly [residentially] segregated, and occasionally hostile" (Waters 2014, 145). A large-scale study of the young adult second generation in the New York metropolitan area found that native blacks and West Indians reported the most discrimination; native blacks and West Indians also tended to work in predominantly black work sites. By contrast, many members of Hispanic groups and most Chinese respondents worked in racially mixed workplaces (Kasinitz et al. 2008).

In her analysis of a community garden and public sculpture park in the super-diverse New York City neighbourhood of Astoria, Queens, Sofya Aptekar (2017) argues that while they might seem at first to be multicultural havens of super-diversity – bringing together people speaking different languages and of different ages, ethnicities, religions, and socio-economic status – these sites are, in fact, divided by racial (as well as class) inequalities that shape interactions in ways that can be disempowering and exclusionary for some community residents. Although people worked on projects in the community garden with others very different from themselves, Aptekar describes interactions that empowered better-off whites who, owing to their class and race, were able to impose their aesthetic sensibilities, including what plants would be cultivated and how the garden would look. As for the public sculpture park, African Americans felt uncomfortable going there on their own even though it was a three-minute walk from the predominantly African American public housing where they lived; in contrast, more affluent, mostly white visitors, living locally or visiting, used the park more openly and freely. Events at the park to celebrate the diversity of the borough of Queens emphasized immigration-driven diversity, leaving African Americans, especially the lower-class African Americans who lived nearby, out of the loop.

Although not a matter of daily interactions in urban communities, it is worth mentioning the impact of super-diversity on the political sphere in New York since research indicates that, at least up until now, super-diversity has not prevented whites (now only a third of the population) from continuing to hold the top elected position of mayor (excluding one term in the early 1990s when an African American, David Dinkins, held this office). At least so far, the difficulties of assembling alliances with a wide array of ethno-racial groups now necessary to win mayoral office have been greater for ethnic minorities – and super-diversity is part of the problem. It has, as we suggested earlier, contributed to whites' ability to maintain mayoral political control in a kind of divide-and-rule manner, given that no racial/national-origin group in New York City is a clear majority and divisions among non-white ethnic minority groups have impeded them from uniting politically (e.g. Mollenkopf 2014). Nor has super-diversity averted political conflicts between immigrant-origin groups and native minorities (African Americans and Puerto Ricans) at lower levels of the city's political system which have arisen, for example, when an African American and West Indian are vying for office in a district housing blacks of different national origins or a Dominican and Puerto Rican are competing for votes among a broad range of Latinos.

Across the Atlantic, the two articles in this issue drawing on ethnographic research in Amsterdam suggest some of the ways that public discourse and government policies in national and urban contexts, as well as the particular demographic configuration of local associations, can create or accentuate intergroup tensions and hostilities in super-diverse urban areas. Although Amsterdam can now be considered a majority–minority city (Crul 2016) – migrants and people with foreign-born parents are slightly more than half of the population – this has not necessarily translated into amicable relations, tolerance, and accommodation in local communities. At the national society level, Dutch political and public debate has been dominated by a harsh xenophobic discourse; a significant proportion of the native majority population sees cultural diversity as a growing problem, with an aggressive emphasis on the need for immigrants and their children, especially Muslims, to adopt "Judeo-Christian" or "Dutch" values and progressive ideals on such issues as gender equality, abortion, and sexuality (Alba and Duyvendak, 2017; Duyvendak 2011). The political discourse stigmatizing people of migrant background has had an impact at the neighbourhood level where, as Paul Mepschen argues in the case of the multi-ethnic area he studied, it has become entangled with another development: competition for scarce resources triggered by government urban policies. Specifically, he points to government urban renewal plans to demolish existing social housing and build new owner-occupied and high-rent homes leading to resentments among local native majority residents – who, following widespread use in the Netherlands, see themselves as "autochthones" or, literally, those born from the soil. Even before these plans have been carried out, middle-aged, native majority neighbourhood residents have felt that those of recent migrant origin (whom they view as *allochthones* or strangers and cultural outsiders) have been favoured in the distribution of social housing.

Fenneke Wekker's article brings out another dynamic when it comes to associations and organizations in super-diverse areas: those that *lack* diversity can provide an environment that allows members to voice negative comments about – and even strengthen hostility toward and exclude – ethnic minority groups. Far from seeing diversity as commonplace or normal, the virtually all native white Dutch (and mostly elderly) visitors to the state-supported community centre she studied in a working-class super-diverse area of Amsterdam regularly and openly disparaged ethnic, racial, and religious others. Indeed, the centre ended up reinforcing hostile sentiments to these "others" and informally keeping out ethnic, racial, and religious "outsiders" who would feel uncomfortable and out of place there. Shared class, age, and generation, as well as race, ethnicity, and religion, fortified the centre regulars' sense of "we". In this regard, Wekker's account leads to general questions about the way divisions along age, generational, and class lines can feed into and affect attitudes toward and relations with those in different ethnic and racial groups. The fact that the older white Amsterdammers who came to the community centre grew up in a much less ethnically, racially, and religiously diverse city no doubt played a role in their negative views of post-World II immigration-created diversity. At the same time, the centre's middle-class management's preaching of tolerance for ethnic and racial differences fell on deaf ears partly because of a class divide: the white native working class Dutch were aware of the manager's and social workers' disdain for them and resisted the notion that they had to change.

We have identified some of the sources of civility as well as tension and conflict among ethnoracial groups in super-diverse locales, but this is, admittedly, a beginning attempt. Clearly, the value of super-diversity as a concept depends, in good part, on understanding and specifying its consequences for social relations in urban communities, including the conditions under which it leads to social harmony as opposed to tension, topics on which we still have a lot to learn.

Unfulfilled promises of super-diversity

One of these decisive conditions, as argued by Alba and Duyvendak (this issue), might be the broader context in which neighbourhood relations are embedded. This wider, "vertical" context not only includes formal and informal institutions present in local settings (for example, schools and their curricula), but also a country's discursive climate. At least to judge by the research the super-diversity concept has so far inspired, it seems best attuned to the normalized everyday diversity that sometimes characterizes horizontal interpersonal interactions in micro-settings with a very substantial immigrant presence. However, the concept often overlooks power differentials at a level beyond the neighbourhood. Or to phrase it somewhat differently, the super-diversity lens has so far been less able to capture the vertical phenomena that reflect the social, economic, and political power of the native majority. This may be partly because this would require a lens operating on a macro scale, rather than a micro one. To be sure, writings on super-diversity have hardly ignored mainstream institutions. In fact, since one of the goals of the super-diversity concept in its original formulation by Vertovec is to offer guidance to social service practitioners, the mainstream or dominant societal institutions that interact with immigrants have come within the concept's field of vision. But the emphasis is on the need for these institutions to adapt to the new super-diverse condition rather than the power they exert in shaping the experiences of immigrants and their children.

For some observers, the diversification of diversity and existence of no-majority cities puts into question the very existence of a societal "mainstream" (Crul 2016). Alba and Duyvendak, however, argue that in many diverse settings long-dominant groups continue to define the social and cultural mainstream even after they have ceased to be the demographic majority. These groups may – or can at least try to – set the rules for culturally accepted behaviour, and their mainstream status can even become a political resource or a way to legitimize their superior position. Political structure also plays a role. Legal status and the structure of political institutions may effectively exclude many newcomers from meaningful political and civic participation (Waters and Kasinitz 2015), thereby contributing to the mainstream minority's ability to exercise power over a diverse majority.

Taking macro-processes into consideration highlights that in countries of Western Europe such as the Netherlands members of the long-established native population have been drawing sharper immigrant/native boundaries in recent years than before. Culturalized and homogenized versions of citizenship have become hegemonic in the Netherlands over the past decade(s), as they have in many West European countries. Quite surprisingly, these new ethnic hierarchies and sensitivities – which can have a huge impact on social relations at the micro-level, as the articles by Wekker and Mepschen show – have not been taken into account by most scholars studying super-diversity. This may help to explain why super-diversity is often conceptualized as a form of rather peaceful co-existence. Incorporating the vertical dimension of the mainstream or dominant native population, as Alba and Duyvendak's article (this issue) suggests, would enrich the analytical power of the super-diversity concept. Indeed, as they also argue, assimilation and super-diversity are not mutually exclusive. Assimilation actually produces heterogeneity and diversification, if only because national origin groups become increasingly diversified over time as immigrants and their children adapt to dominant norms, values, and practices in different ways and rates and have different experiences of mobility. These processes of acculturation and assimilation may intensify the experiences of super-diversity for both migrants and natives.

This leads to another area for further reflection and study, what we might call adding more diversity to super-diversity research. Despite the stress on many types of diversity and difference inherent in the notion of super-diversity as laid out by Vertovec, the empirical literature using the concept remains overwhelmingly focused on one type of difference, namely *ethnic* differences (for a promising exception see Wessendorf 2014). The call to move beyond the ethno-focal lens has the potential to widen possibilities for individuals with migrant backgrounds to be acknowledged as human beings with a plurality of affiliations – and could encourage policymakers, service providers and scholars to recognize that members of "migrant communities, just like the settled population, can 'cohere' to different social worlds and communities simultaneously" (Zetter et al. cited in Vertovec 2007, 1049). Still, because much of the rapidly growing literature that uses the term super-diversity has yet to significantly move beyond an ethno-racial lens, the theoretical promise of Vertovec's formulation often goes unfulfilled, as do some important implications for public policy (see Hall 2017 on connecting super-diversity to migration border issues).

Just how various bases of diversity intersect in different super-diverse contexts also requires analysis. This includes understanding the conditions under which particular differences – race and class, to mention two critical ones – acquire more significance in some locations, institutions, and situations than others, and may produce or reproduce exclusionary forms of inequality and power imbalances. The articles in this issue grapple with many of these topics as they expand our appreciation of how super-diversity operates in every-day life and as they point to questions that call for further research, elaboration, and development on both sides of the Atlantic. The super-diversity concept has already stimulated new ways of thinking in the scholarly literature about changed realities, especially in Western Europe, and the articles in this issue can, we believe, help to advance us further in this endeavour.

Disclosure statement

No potential conflict of interest was reported by the authors.

References

Alba, Richard. 2009. *Blurring the Color Line: The New Chance for a More Integrated America*. Cambridge: Harvard University Press.
Back, Les, and Shamser Sinha. 2016. "Multicultural Conviviality in the Midst of Racism's Ruins." *Journal of Intercultural Studies* 37: 517–532.
Brubaker, Rogers. 2004. *Ethnicity Without Groups*. Cambridge: Harvard University Press.
Collins, Patricia. 2015. "Intersectionality's Definitional Dilemmas." *Annual Review of Sociology* 41: 1–20.
Coser, Lewis. 1956. *The Functions of Social Conflict*. New York: The Free Press.
Crul, Maurice. 2016. "Super-Diversity vs. Assimilation: How Complex Diversity in Majority–Minority Cities Challenges the Assumptions of Assimilation." *Journal of Ethnic and Migration Studies* 42: 54–68.
Drake, St. Claire, and Horace R. Cayton. 1945. *Black Metropolis: A Study of Negro Life in a Northern City*. New York: Harcourt, Brace, Jovanovich.

Du Bois, W. E. B. 1899. *The Philadelphia Negro*. New York: Cosimo Classics.

Duyvendak, Jan Willem. 2011. *The Politics of Home: Nostalgia and Belonging in Western Europe and the United States*. Basingstoke: Palgrave Macmillan.

Foner, Nancy. 2005. *In a New Land: A Comparative View of Immigration*. New York: New York University Press.

Foner, Nancy. 2007. "How Exceptional Is New York? Migration and Multiculturalism in the Empire City." *Ethnic and Racial Studies* 30: 999–1023.

Foner, Nancy, ed. 2013. *One Out of Three: Immigrant New York in the Twenty-first Century*. New York: Columbia University Press.

Foner, Nancy. 2017. "A Research Comment: What's New About Super-diversity?" *Journal of American Ethnic History* 36: 49–57.

Glazer, Nathan, and Daniel Patrick Moynihan. 1963. *Beyond the Melting Pot*. Cambridge: MIT Press.

Hall, Suzanne M. 2017. "Mooring 'Super-diversity' to a Brutal Migration Milieu." *Ethnic and Racial Studies* 40: 1562–1573.

Kasinitz, Philip, John Mollenkopf, Mary C. Waters, and Jennifer Holdaway. 2008. *Inheriting the City: The Children of Immigrants Come of Age*. New York: Russell Sage Foundation and Harvard University Press.

Meissner, Fran, and Steven Vertovec. 2015. "Comparing Super-Diversity." *Ethnic and Racial Studies* 38: 541–555.

Mollenkopf, John. 2003. "New York: The Great Anomaly." In *Racial Politics in American Cities*. 3rd ed., edited by Rufus Browning, Dale Marshall, and David Tabb, 115–142. New York: Longman.

Mollenkopf, John. 2014. "The Rise of Immigrant Influence in New York City Politics." In *New York and Amsterdam: Immigration and the New Urban Landscape*, edited by Nancy Foner, Jan Rath, Jan Willem Duyvendak, and Rogier van Reekum, 203–229. New York: New York University Press.

Neal, Sarah, Carol Vincent, and Humera Iqbal. 2016. "Extended Encounters in Primary School Worlds: Shared Social Resource, Connective Spaces and Sustained Conviviality in Socially and Ethnically Complex Urban Geographies." *Journal of Intercultural Studies* 37: 464–480.

Pettigrew, Thomas, and Linda Tropp. 2008. "How Does Intergroup Contact Reduce Prejudice? Meta-analytic Tests of Three Mediators." *European Journal of Social Psychology* 38: 922–934.

Portes, Alejandro. 1997. "Immigration Theory for a New Century: Some Problems and Opportunities." *International Migration Review* 31: 799–825.

Putnam, Robert. 2007. "E Pluribus Unum: Diversity and Community in the Twenty-first Century The 2006 Johan Skytte Prize Lecture." *Scandinavian Political Studies* 30: 137–174.

Sanjek, Roger. 1999. *The Future of Us All*. Ithaca, NY: Cornell University Press.

Sen, Amartya. 2006. "The Uses and Abuses of Multiculturalism." *The New Republic*, February 27.

Skerry, Peter. 1993. *Mexican Americans: The Ambivalent Minority*. Cambridge: Harvard University Press.

Vertovec, Steven. 2007. "Super-diversity and Its Implications." *Ethnic and Racial Studies* 30: 1024–1054.

Waters, Mary C. 2014. "Nativism, Racism, and Immigration to New York." In *New York and Amsterdam: Immigration and the New Urban Landscape*, edited by Nancy Foner, Jan Rath, Jan Willem Duyvendak, and Rogier van Reekum, 143–169. New York: New York University Press.

Waters, Mary C., and Philip Kasinitz. 2015. "The War on Crime and the War on Immigrants: Racial and Legal Exclusion in the Twenty-first Century United States." In *Fear, Anxiety, and National Identity: Immigration and Belonging in North America and Western Europe*, edited by Nancy Foner and Patrick Simon, 115–144. New York: Russell Sage Foundation.

Wessendorf, Susanne. 2013. "Commonplace Diversity and the 'Ethos of Mixing': Perceptions of Difference in a London Neighbourhood." *Identities* 20: 407–422.

Wessendorf, Susanne. 2014. *Commonplace Diversity: Social Relations in a Super-diverse Context*. Basingstoke: Palgrave Macmillan.

Pioneer migrants and their social relations in super-diverse London

Susanne Wessendorf

ABSTRACT
Urban areas in Europe and beyond have seen significant changes in immigration patterns, leading to profound diversification characterized by the multiplication of people of different national origins, migration histories, religions, educational backgrounds, legal statuses and socio-economic backgrounds, a condition now commonly described as super-diversity. An important part of this super-diversity is individual migrants who do not follow established chain migrations. Little is known about processes of settlement of migrants who do not form part of larger migration movements and might not be able to draw on the support of others of the same national, ethnic, linguistic, religious and socio-economic background. This article describes patterns of settlement of such individual migrants in London. Drawing on the notion of "pioneer migration", the article focuses on social networks, examining the kinds of social relations pioneer migrants form in the course of settlement and showing that many migrants strive to form social relations beyond co-ethnics.

Urban diversity has taken on new forms in recent years. Not only has the nature of immigration been changing globally, but over the past two decades, the demographic changes brought by immigration have accelerated. In the case of the UK, people have been arriving under various legal categories such as work schemes, economic migrants, students, asylum seekers, undocumented persons and more, and they have been coming from a range of countries of origin, doing a broader range of jobs and for more varied lengths of stay than before (Vertovec 2007). These new patterns of immigration have resulted in super-diversity, a condition of more mixed origins, ethnicities, languages, religions, work and living conditions, legal statuses, periods of stay and transnational connections than many cities have ever faced (Meissner and Vertovec 2015; Vertovec 2007).

An important part of the dynamics of super-diversity in many urban communities is the presence of many migrants who arrive individually and do not follow established chain migrations. Migration scholarship generally focuses on large migration movements. However, many initial migration movements do not involve, or even evolve into, migrations of much larger numbers of people (de Haas 2010). Little is known about processes of settlement of individual migrants who might not be able to draw on the support of people with whom they share the same national, religious, linguistic, ethnic and socio-economic background and who have preceded them in undertaking the same migration journey during a similar time period. How do these migrants settle in a super-diverse context? What kinds of networks of support do they form? Where do they get information about settlement, and how do they make friends?

This article describes patterns of settlement among a diverse group of such individual migrants, here conceptualized as pioneer migrants. The paper focuses on one crucial aspect of settlement, namely social networks, looking at the kinds of social relations pioneer migrants form upon arrival and in the course of settlement.

Social networks have long been recognized as key to understanding both migration and migrant settlement, with a large body of literature analysing their role in various stages of the migration process (Boyd 1989; Massey et al. 1998). Migration literature on early settlement generally assumes that migrants will gravitate towards co-ethnics with whom they share a language, similar cultural values and religious beliefs. In her review of the social scientific literature on transnational and local migrant networks, Moroşanu (2010) shows how this literature has been dominated by a focus on specific ethnic groups, interpreting migrant networks as ethnic networks so that "mixed networks never achieve prominence or are altogether ignored" (Moroşanu 2010, 6). This orientation has been changing in the context of work attempting to shed light on other-than-ethnic factors in shaping migrants' social relations (Moroşanu 2013; Ryan 2011; Williams 2006), some of which draws on scholarship in urban sociology and anthropology (Blokland 2003; Glick Schiller and Çağlar 2013; Glick Schiller, Çağlar, and Guldbrandsen 2006; Wimmer 2004).

The research on which this article is based did not focus on migrants from a specific country of origin, but on a broad range of countries of origin and migrants with various educational backgrounds, legal statuses, religions and other social characteristics. The research participants had migrated individually and lacked social capital when arriving, and had arrived within the last ten years. The aim of the research was to move away from the assumption that country of origin or ethnicity are the main factors shaping settlement, also critiqued as methodological nationalism (Fox and Jones 2013; Glick Schiller, Çağlar, and Guldbrandsen 2006; Wimmer and Glick Schiller 2002). Looking at the role of other-than-ethnic factors in migrant settlement enables us to analyse whether, when, how and why ethnicity or national origin can become salient or not (Brubaker 2004; Glick Schiller and Çağlar 2013; Wessendorf 2013; Wimmer 2004). Approaching the field without assuming specific sociological categories to be more relevant than others could also be described as a super-diversity lens which does not assume ethnicity and nationality to be the determining factors in migrant settlement (but see Aptekar, this issue). Pioneer settlement in twenty-first century London is considerably different to the settlement of migrants after the Second World War when migrants came from a smaller number of (mostly post-colonial) countries of origin, often shared common histories and aspirations, and settled in areas characterized by much less previous immigration than current super-diverse neighbourhoods.

This article draws on Bourdieu's differentiation between economic, cultural and social capital to illustrate variations in settlement patterns. Economic capital refers to economic resources and assets, while social capital refers to the resources gained from "durable networks of more or less institutionalized relationships of mutual acquaintance or recognition" (Bourdieu 1986, 248). Social capital is thus defined by its "ability to secure benefits by virtue of membership in social networks" (Portes 1998, 6). Cultural capital consists of a person's collection of knowledge and skills, including formal education (also referred to as institutionalized cultural capital or human capital), IT literacy, as well as, in the case of migrants, knowledge of the majority language (Bourdieu 1986). It also includes knowledge of the local habitus in terms of taste, dress, style, etc. (Bourdieu 1990). Cultural capital proved to be crucial in regards to the research participants' social network formation. As I will discuss below, one of the characteristics of pioneer migrants is that they often have higher cultural capital than those who follow established migration patterns. In fact, eighteen out of the twenty-three pioneer migrants who participated in the research had high cultural capital when arriving in London, including knowledge of English and IT skills, institutionalized forms of capital such as higher education, as well as knowledge of the local habitus in terms of taste, dress, style, etc. (Bourdieu 1986). This enabled them to form social relations with people of similar educational backgrounds. Elsewhere, I have shown how high cultural capital also made a difference in the kinds of social relations and social capital undocumented migrants and asylum seekers build during initial settlement (Wessendorf 2017). Among the study participants presented here, high cultural capital seemed to facilitate the formation of social networks beyond their "ethnic group", whereas the (minority of) research participants with low cultural capital more heavily relied on co-ethnic and religious social networks upon arrival. Even if only in small numbers, the pioneers with limited education or knowledge of English tended to cluster together and form stronger ethnic ties. Both historical research on immigrant settlement as well as more recent research have shown that during the early stages of settlement, such co-ethnic networks can be crucial in accessing resources and information (Cheung and Phillimore 2013). The co-ethnic social networks of the research participants with low cultural capital might thus be related to their newcomer status. Over time, and with increased knowledge of English, they might well build networks beyond co-ethnics. In fact, a range of studies indicates that migrants with lower cultural capital build alliances across ethnic differences, in neighbourhoods, workplaces, religious sites and political associations (e.g. Hudson, Phillips, and Ray 2009; Lamont and Aksartova 2002; Moroşanu 2013; Werbner 1999).

The article is based on qualitative research in East London from 2014 to 2015, including twenty-three in-depth interviews as well as four focus groups with recent migrants, and eighteen interviews with people working in the migrant sector such as English teachers and social workers, altogether involving a total of sixty-nine respondents. Respondents (including those who participated in focus groups) came from thirty-one countries of origin including Chechnya, Uzbekistan, Senegal, Ivory Coast, Argentina, Chile and Southern Azerbaijan. Sixteen of the twenty-three interviewees were female and research participants' ages ranged from twenty-three to forty-seven. At the time of writing this article, a comparative study was undertaken in Birmingham, with twenty-five research participants. Preliminary results reflect patterns of settlement and social network formation similar to those found in East London. This paper, however, only draws on the interviews with the London research participants. Research participants were found through personal social networks formed during previous fieldwork in the area (Wessendorf 2014), snowball sampling, through religious and voluntary organizations, English classes and serendipitous encounters, for example on playgrounds. Interviews were conducted in English, French, Italian and Spanish, transcribed and coded in NVivo. The author lived in the area where research was conducted and, on some occasions, had the opportunity to see research participants beyond a one-off interview, thus extending her knowledge about their life-worlds. East London could be described as a typical immigrant reception area, with a long-standing history of immigrant succession, especially since the Second World War (Butcher 2017; Butler and Hamnett 2011; Neal et al. 2015; Wessendorf 2014).

The research participants had various legal statuses, ranging from EU citizenship to work visas, asylum seekers and refugees. What became clear is that legal status determined all other aspects of settlement, although it is not, I should note, a focus in this article. UK asylum dispersal policies mean that asylum seekers are housed in places not of their choice (Hynes and Sales 2010), and asylum seekers are not allowed to work. The six asylum seekers and undocumented migrants in the study were by far the most disadvantaged among the research participants due to their legal status. I address the impact of, among other things, the prohibition to work and resulting social isolation elsewhere (Wessendorf 2017).

I begin by providing a short overview of the literature on pioneer migration, considering how it relates to super-diversity in terms of differentiation within groups as well as the formation of social networks which go beyond co-ethnics. I link this literature with scholarly discourses concerning cohesion and social capital, which often assume that migrants draw on bonding social capital with co-ethnics. The empirical section describes how initial social contacts are often with co-ethnics, but that most research participants soon developed different kinds of networks with people who shared similar interests or the same language, although they were not necessarily from the same country or region of origin. I discuss the reasons for this lack of interest in co-ethnic social networks, ranging from political tensions to gender differences and issues of social control.

Pioneer migrants and social networks

Bertin from Spain arrived in London some ten years ago, aged 22. He knew no one. He came with his girlfriend, and they first stayed in a hostel in central London. Although he had high cultural capital in terms of his education and previous work in the film industry in Spain, he was forced to start from scratch in London because of his limited knowledge of English. He spent the first weeks walking around central London, handing out his CV in cafes and bars. By chance, he bumped into a Spanish-speaking woman in a cinema, who gave him the telephone number of an acquaintance who was renting a room in North East London. Despite finding housing, Bertin and his girlfriend did not manage to get work and establish themselves in London, and after only a few months moved to Dublin, where a friend of his girlfriend's cousin was living. They obtained accommodation through this contact and found work with a builder through an advertisement on Gumtree, a website advertising accommodation, employment and goods. After about ten months in Dublin, their English had improved and they had saved enough money to return to London and try again. This time, Bertin managed to find (badly paid) work in the film industry, and slowly worked his way up the ladder. Today, Bertin is well established in the film industry as a digital composer, although it took him ten years to get to this position. In the meantime, he also helped about fifteen friends from Spain settle in London, providing them with initial accommodation and information about jobs, housing and other practicalities.

Bertin is a true pioneer, starting off with no contacts in London. But he slowly established himself both professionally and socially, to the point that when Spain faced a severe economic crisis, he was able to help friends follow in his footsteps. He thus turned from a pioneer to a gatekeeper.

What makes Bertin a pioneer migrant? Bertin was pioneering in that he migrated as an individual and not as part of a group, and he did not follow an established path of migration. He also exemplifies that migration at the initial or pioneer stage is an innovative process. Pioneer migrants have been recognized as taking higher risks than subsequent migrants; they are often entrepreneurial, relatively well off and better educated than later migrants (Browning and Feindt 1969; de Haas 2010; MacDonald and MacDonald 1964; Petersen 1958). This was confirmed in the project represented here, where three-quarters of the research participants came with high cultural capital, even if many had limited financial resources on arrival.

Migration scholars have identified different stages of migration processes to describe how migration from a sending to a destination country changes and becomes established over time (Lindstrom and López Ramírez 2010). Migration has been, for example, divided into three periods: the initial or pioneer stage, the early adopter or group migration stage and the mature or mass migration stage (Jones 1998; Petersen 1958). An established flow of people, goods, services and information between two places or a set of places has also been described as a migration system which emerges as a result of initial pioneer migration coupled with feedback mechanisms consisting of information travelling back from the destination country, which leads to further migration (Bakewell, de Haas, and Kubal 2012; Mabogunje 1970).[1] An important element of migration systems is chain migration, a process by which potential migrants find out about opportunities and are provided with help for transportation, accommodation and employment by previous migrants (MacDonald and MacDonald 1964).

In the context of research into super-diversity, differentiations within migrant groups have recently gained increasing attention (Meissner and Vertovec 2015; Vertovec 2007). Pointing to the danger of methodological nationalism when studying migrants based on country of birth or citizenship, Bakewell, de Haas, and Kubal (2012, 424) emphasize that groups from specific nations "can generally be broken down into several subgroups, periods of arrival, and modes of and reasons for migrating". National origin groups can thus consist of several subgroups originating from different regions, cities, ethnic, religious or class groups, migrating at different times and receiving different legal statuses in the settlement destination (see also Berg 2011). Migrant flows are often differentiated by class and education, and early pioneers in many cases are distinct from later arrivals. For example, initial labour migration to Western Europe after the Second World War was often followed by family migration, student migration or the migration of high-skilled professionals (Kubal, Bakewell, and de Haas 2011a, 2011b). Early and later arrivals from the same nation of origin need not have much contact, as shown by the case of Indian migrants who came to Britain in the 1950s and 1960s and current arrivals (Visram 2002). In general, according to Bakewell, de Haas, and

Kubal (2012, 426), the notion of "pioneer" should be contextualized "with regard to the specific group, time-frame and locality (of origin, and settlement), and type of migration".

According to Dekker and Engbersen (2012), much of the migration literature, which focuses on established migration movements, understands migrants' networks as consisting of what have also been described as strong ties (Granovetter 1973) such as family relations or close friendships and tight co-ethnic networks. However, the case of pioneer migrants demonstrates how, as has been shown more generally in urban contexts, many people today do not form part of dense and close communities, but develop a variety of changing and loose networks consisting of weak ties (Dekker and Engbersen 2012; Granovetter 1973; Wellman 1999). These weak ties can be crucial for migrants who are pioneering in their movement to a new place and cannot draw on existing and established social networks in the immigration context.

Much of the literature on migrant settlement has used Bourdieu's (1986) notion of social capital to describe the role of social relations in regards to the integration of migrants (e.g. Cheung and Phillimore 2013; Goodson and Phillimore 2008). Pioneer migrants usually arrive with limited social capital when settling in London. However, few migrants arrive unconnected, and most new arrivals have at least one connection with someone from their country of origin. These "foundation networks" (Phillimore, Humphris, and Khan 2014) are often characterized by weak ties (Granovetter 1973).

Putnam's (2000) differentiation between bonding social capital, referring to social relations within groups, and bridging social capital to refer to social relations across groups has been crucial in thinking about the role of social relations in migrant settlement. Academic and policy literature on migrant integration has emphasized the merit of bridging social capital both for migrant integration as well as social cohesion (Commission on Integration and Cohesion 2007), although the notion has come in for criticism for putting the burden of cohesion and bridging social capital on migrants rather than the majority society (see, among many others, Cheong et al. 2007; Hickman, Mai, and Crowley 2012; Portes and Vickstrom 2011). The policy literature on cohesion in particular has assumed that ethnicity and religion define the boundaries within and beyond which migrants build bonding and bridging social capital. In her critical review of the use of the social capital concept, Ryan (2011) shows how Polish migrants consciously extended their friendship networks beyond co-ethnics, but with people of similar educational backgrounds in order to learn more about the place of settlement. Rather than nationality, factors such as shared interests, similar careers and educational backgrounds shaped social relations during initial settlement. They were thus bridging beyond ethnicity, but bonding with migrants in similar social positions (see also Meissner 2016; Ryan 2011).

Foundation contacts

How do pioneer migrants settle in a new place? What is the role of social networks in the settlement process? How do pioneer migrants access practical and emotional support when they arrive? Initially, most migrants rely on foundation networks, meaning pre-existing networks of acquaintances, friends or family (Phillimore, Humphris, and Khan 2014). Foundation networks that develop out of initial contacts are key for pioneers, and as they root themselves in London, they create further social networks which are characterized by a combination of co-ethnics and others and, interestingly, in some cases by an attempt to distance themselves from co-ethnics. Although pioneer migrants cannot dock onto already established ethnic communities, almost all of my research participants had at least one contact when they arrived. Indeed, in the case of pioneer migrants, the notion of "foundation networks" is better termed "foundation contacts", because the initial contacts are often characterized by a single connection, rather than a connection to a network of people. Among my research participants, these connections were often with a co-ethnic (Bertin, the Spanish migrant in the film industry, was an exception to this generalization.) Apart from research participants who came to London to study and had thus set up a University place prior to arrival, including accommodation through the university, most other participants stated that one reason they came to London was that they had one contact there. "I wouldn't have come without knowing at least one person" was a common statement. Importantly, however, these contacts were not necessarily characterized by close ties, but were often weak or indirect.

For example Aika from Kyrgyzstan, who came to London when she was 22, had one contact via someone in her home town who had given her a package for a Kyrgyz acquaintance in London.

> I arrived here, and somebody asked me if I could pass on a parcel to somebody who lived in London; I didn't know anybody at all when I was coming. I booked a room for 2 weeks in Wimbledon. I didn't know how to get there, you know, but because I was passing on this parcel I was hoping that they can tell me, direct me, how to get there.... So the friend of a friend was kind enough to show me all the way to Wimbledon.

Aika did not like the room in Wimbledon nor the area, and instead found a shared house with other people from Kyrgyzstan in Hackney through the same person to whom she had brought the package. Especially in regards to housing, foundation contacts were crucial for all of my research participants.

First, contacts are sometimes made on the way to the UK. An undocumented migrant from Mali arrived at Heathrow airport with an address on a piece of paper of someone he did not know, but whose contact information he was given en route while waiting for his tourist visa in the Ivory Coast. Through this initial contact, he found both housing and work. Similarly, Alp, aged 34, from Southern Azerbaijan (an area in northern Iran) had met other Southern Azerbaijanis in Calais before he crossed to England on the back of a lorry in 2006, and he contacted these people again once he had arrived in London. Those whose asylum claim was successful were able to give him information about solicitors and legal advice centres to help with his asylum claim. After living in the UK for nine years, and after finally getting limited leave to remain in 2010, he continues to have this network of friends who speak the same language, although he also has a group of friends of other national backgrounds, some of them neighbours, others fellow students.

For migrants who might not bump into other people on the street from their country of origin or who speak the same language, the internet can play an important role during settlement. In their study of Brazilian, Ukrainian and Moroccan migrants in Dutch cities, Dekker and Engbersen (2012) show how social media not only facilitate continuing relationships with those left behind but can also lead to social contacts in the immigration context. This was exemplified by an Argentinean research participant who found out via Facebook that some of her friends from back home were in London. There are also numerous internet platforms where migrants can find assistance in practical aspects of settlement, as well as emotional support. For example, the research participant from Georgia (aged 34) found a Facebook site of Russian-speaking mothers who share information online about settling and raising children in London. Not only do they share the same language, but also the experience of motherhood and similar educational backgrounds. Some of these mothers sometimes meet for picnics and thus form new, pan-ethnic friendships.

Another example of social networks based on language is those of Spanish speakers; many have formed social relations with people from other Latin American countries or Spain with whom they share similar educational backgrounds. There is also a network of Malinke-speaking Muslims from West Africa who regularly meet at an Ivorian Muslim community centre for worship and socializing. Language and religion are thus important factors linking people pan-ethnically and potentially leading to networks of support (Wessendorf forthcoming). Sometimes, religious affiliations override the importance of language, as in the case of an illiterate Orthodox Jewish Yemeni refugee woman who spoke no English upon arrival at the age of 22. When she arrived in London with her husband, their only contact was one uncle. Their settlement was entirely shaped and supported by the network of the international Orthodox Jewish community within which her uncle was embedded.

Alisher from Uzbekistan, who came to London as a student in his early twenties, had one Uzbek contact in London with whom he shared a flat for two weeks after his arrival. He then found a room through an advertisement in a free Russian newspaper which he had picked up in central London. Since then, he has not had any Uzbek friends but developed friendships with people from many different national and ethnic backgrounds. His experiences indicate that just because people speak the same language, have the same religion or come from the same country of origin does not mean that they will end up socializing – or even want to socialize – with each other. To come back to the notion of methodological nationalism (Wimmer and Glick Schiller 2002) and the assumption that individuals gravitate towards co-ethnics, what is clear is that migrants from specific countries cannot simply be lumped together: they are divided by time of arrival and participation in different waves of migration, but also region of origin, educational background and class position, among other characteristics (Bakewell, de Haas, and Kubal 2012; Berg 2011; Meissner 2016). Moreover, some migrants are not interested in keeping ties to co-ethnics (Moroşanu 2010; Ryan 2011).

It should be noted that many crucial encounters during the early stages of settlement are serendipitous and unexpected, but end up providing support and resources or simply making the pioneer migrants feel more comfortable in London. For example, Hamam, the Orthodox Jewish woman from Yemen mentioned above, spent the first three years in London without any knowledge of English but got support from a Jewish nurse after the birth of her third child. Only through this nurse did she find out about English classes. Gaining access to these classes was not only a huge step towards learning English and finally feeling less isolated but also represented her first opportunity to obtain formal education and access to literacy. For Hamam, this was a life-changing experience.

Aika from Kyrgyzstan, quoted earlier, told me how her life changed thanks to an English friend's mother who, when struggling to find out what to do with her life, provided her with materials for sewing and advised her to open her own business. She now earns a living by selling children's clothes she makes. And Gabriela from Brazil moved in with an Italian young man who was renting a room in his flat. Through her new Italian housemate, she met many other people who shared similar interests and through whom she finally felt a sense of home and belonging in London. They did not share any ethnic or class background, but these friendships were based on shared experiences of being migrants as well as common interests.

Beyond co-ethnic networks

Aika from Kyrgyzstan was initially grateful for finding a house so easily, but she was soon unhappy to be sharing this house with other Kyrgyz.

> A: After staying there for 3 months I decided that it was like not leaving Kyrgyzstan.

S: Because the whole house was other people from Kyrgyzstan?
A: Yes, and it wasn't what I wanted. I was totally against that because I said I didn't come here to experience you guys, because I know what you're like, it was, I mean [laughs] I have Kyrgyz friends, don't get me wrong, you miss your home, you miss the people, but it was completely, it wasn't what I wanted. So my friend, one of my best friends came three months later and when she came I said to her "let's move, because now it's two of us we can move somewhere else", so we moved to Old Street and lived there together for a year.

Aika represents a common example of pioneer migrants who, drawing on foundation contacts with (a limited number of) co-ethnics upon arrival, actively attempted to build networks with people who are not from the same country. Some actually distance themselves from co-ethnics. Moroşanu (2013), in her study of Romanians' social networks in London, noted how students and professionals in particular showed a specific cosmopolitan outlook and consciously attempted to meet non-Romanians. Similarly, although they lacked explicit cosmopolitan orientations, low-skilled Romanian migrants formed relations beyond co-ethnics, which were sometimes nurtured by a shared situation of precariousness. Among my research participants, it was mainly those with high cultural capital who spoke the majority language and were able to navigate the local system by way of obtaining information about settlement on the internet, and gaining access to the labour market, who were keen to form social relations beyond co-ethnics. Migrants who spoke limited English, including those with high educational backgrounds, relied more on co-ethnic social networks. There were different reasons why pioneer migrants attempted to build networks with people of other national and ethnic backgrounds, ranging from political tensions in their countries of origin to issues around social control, as well as lack of shared educational and class backgrounds. For example Amina, a Woman's Rights Activist from Chechnya (aged 32) who had been granted refugee status, preferred to limit her relations with other Chechens for fear of information about her whereabouts and activities reaching the "wrong" people back in Chechnya, a concern also reported in other studies of refugees in the UK (Williams 2006). Others I spoke with simply did not feel they had enough in common with migrants from their countries of origin; those who felt this way were often among the very first ones from their region of origin, class or educational background to arrive and did not see themselves as part of a larger migration movement.

Maria Paula from Colombia, for example, came to London as a student in 2007 in her twenties and had one initial contact, the son of a friend of her mother's. He formed part of the Colombian elite who had come to the UK to study at Oxbridge and worked in sectors such as banking. He turned out not to be a crucial contact in Maria Paula's settlement process, because his interests and lifestyle differed so much from hers. Nor did she feel she had much in common with those in the other part of the Colombian community in London, consisting of people primarily working as cleaners and with relatively low levels of education. Maria Paula noted that when the Colombian embassy organized events for Colombians in London, it was not "for people like her", i.e. educated middle-class people who did not form part of the elite but also were not working class. Her friends were mainly of non-Colombian backgrounds and people she had met at university when she first arrived in London.

Similarly, Gabriela from Brazil (aged 37) could not relate to fellow Brazilians when she came to London, explaining this in terms of regional differences within Brazil, as well as a lack of shared interests. Francisca from Chile (aged 35) told me that yes, there were quite a few other Chileans in London, but most came to study and planned to return. They formed a tight social milieu to which she couldn't relate, partly because she had more permanent plans to stay in the UK and also because she wanted to distance herself from the educated Santiago middle-class social circles which she had been part of back home.

Another important reason for limiting contacts with co-ethnics mentioned by my informants is social control. Their migration was partly motivated by the desire to get away from tight-knit communities of origin, as well as wanting to explore new ways of life and find a place where they felt less constrained in how they identified and led their lives. de Haas points to the danger of "automatically conceiving migration as an act of group solidarity or as part of household livelihood strategies" (2010, 1606). My research participants' statements attest to the attempt to build a new life away from tight social structures experienced in the home community, which, many feared, might be reproduced by becoming too involved with co-ethnics in London. This is especially true for women, who often felt that home country norms and customs were stultifying. Aika emphasized that one reason she did not want to live with Kyrgyz people in London or return to Kyrgyzstan was that she enjoyed her new freedoms gained in the UK as a woman:

> It was kind of "ah, actually I don't have to do this if I don't want to", and there was a, I don't know [in Kyrgyzstan] you're kind of a waitress you're kind of a slave in a way you know. If you're the youngest you have to do this, if you're a woman you have to do this, or if you are a sister-in-law you have to ... you know it's always this kind of rigid some sort of regulation within the society you have to follow and it was really tiring. And once you've been exposed that things can be different you realize, do you really want to be back in that society?

Likewise, a twenty-five-year-old refugee woman from Yemen preferred staying in a youth hostel while looking for work and establishing herself financially, rather than living with one of the Yemeni families she knew in London.

I'm trying my best to be, to have space, not to be in contact with them, because, for me I want to start a new life, and I don't want someone to be like, controlling me from above. And they don't understand the space and the privacy and this stuff. So I'm trying to stay away from them.

These attempts to "start a new life away from tight-knit communities could also be related to the life-stage of these relatively young pioneer migrants.

On a more practical level, research participants also said that spending time with co-ethnics would simply limit their ability to improve their English and expand their knowledge about the place where they settled, an issue also observed by Ryan (2011).

And there is another critical point that is interlaced with many of the examples presented here. Those who arrive with a secure legal status and are fairly highly educated typically do not feel the same need to seek economic and social support from co-ethnics as those with less education or precarious legal status. As Bakewell, de Haas, and Kubal (2012, 431) note,

> ... the more highly skilled and wealthier pioneers are likely to be less dependent on family and kin to migrate, as well as to settle and feel good in the destination, because of their financial and human as well as cultural capital, which allow them to migrate more independently. As they are less dependent on family networks and ethnic business clusters and more likely to be attracted by job opportunities, they are also less likely to cluster at destinations, thereby lowering the chances for migration system formation.

Although none of my research participants arrived with much financial capital, they made up for this as well as their limited social capital with high cultural capital. A study of professional Brazilian migrants in the UK found that they saw their migration as an individual project whose success did not depend on family or co-ethnic acquaintances, but rather on their professional establishment in Britain (Kubal, Bakewell, and de Haas 2011a). Among my research participants with high cultural capital, including refugees whose initial motivation to move to the UK was political rather than to enhance their career, the goal of professional establishment and ultimately social upward mobility in the UK was at the centre of their settlement strategies Wessendorf (2017). What is noteworthy is that the research participants who had very little cultural capital relied more heavily on co-ethnic and religious social networks which, as mentioned earlier, might be due to limited knowledge of English and, over time, might well change. For my research participants, cultural capital thus clearly enabled and shaped relations that extended beyond co-ethnics.

Conclusion

An important part of the demographic condition of today's super-diversity in certain urban areas is the presence of pioneer migrants who lack social capital and do not follow established migration movements, and who are differentiated by such characteristics as legal status, religion, country of origin and educational background. This article is an attempt to describe patterns of settlement among these pioneer migrants, with a particular focus on social network formation. As described in earlier literature on pioneer migration, many of the first people to move to a new country have higher financial and cultural capital than those who follow established migration routes (Browning and Feindt 1969; de Haas 2010; MacDonald and MacDonald 1964; Petersen 1958). They are among the innovators who individually and often independently chose to attempt a new life in an unknown place. Many of my research participants arrived in the UK with high cultural capital, but little to no social capital and limited financial means. Their pathways of settlement extremely varied, but some similarities could be identified. Only a small minority arrived without even one connection. Most migrants had one contact, often indirect, for example in the form of an address on a piece of paper, a package to pass on to a friend of a friend from back home or a telephone number. While these initial contacts were usually with co-ethnics, most migrants soon expanded their networks to people with whom they had things in common beyond national or ethnic backgrounds. Such new relations were sometimes along linguistic lines, with people who spoke the same language and with whom they shared common interests; other times, new relations were formed on the basis of shared educational backgrounds. Many research participants distanced themselves from co-ethnics. Reasons for this ranged from wanting to improve their English, to issues around social control and gender relations, or political factors related to conflicts in their country of origin, as exemplified by the Chechen refugee. However, distancing from co-ethnics was also related to high cultural capital in terms of educational background and knowledge of English, which enabled them to form social relations with people of similar educational backgrounds. The social networks of migrants with little cultural capital in terms of knowledge of English, educational background and embodied cultural capital, it is critical to emphasize, were more constrained and limited to co-ethnics or people with the same language or religion. As I have pointed out, this might be due to the limited period of time they had resided in London at the time of the research; with longer residence in London and greater proficiency in English, their networks might well expand and diversify. Indeed, other studies have shown not only that co-ethnic networks are crucial for working-class migrants (Cheung and Phillimore 2013) but that these migrants also have a range of social relations and interactions beyond co-ethnics (Hudson, Phillips, and Ray 2009; Moroşanu 2013; Werbner 1999).

Much of the literature on migration and migrant settlement has looked at migrants who form part of larger and longer-established migration movements, assuming that social relations upon settlement are primarily defined by ethnicity and nationality. With the example of pioneer migrants, and, it should be said, mostly highly educated pioneers, this article has shed light on the variegated pathways of settlement which result from diversified immigration into super-diverse contexts. These pioneer migrants do not follow the pathways of settlement previously assumed to be common by way of settling into ethnic enclaves or communities. Rather, they innovatively and actively build networks across categories such as ethnicity, language and nationality. Moroşanu (2013) describes such social network formation as patchworking, which sums up well the ways in which pioneer migrants meet people through places like work, house shares and civil society organizations and form relations with people of different backgrounds.

It is difficult to describe these types of relationships in the way that categories such as bridging or bonding social capital have been used, assuming that the categories across which migrants bridge or bond are defined by ethnicity and nationality. Like Ryan's (2011) Polish research participants, the pioneer migrants who participated in this study formed bridging relations across ethnicity and country of origin, although they bonded with people of similar educational backgrounds.

Looking at pioneer migrants' pathways of settlement helps us to refocus our attention on other-than-ethnic factors of super-diversity such as legal status, class, religion and educational background when analysing migrant settlement (Wessendorf 2017). Furthermore, examining pioneer migrants' settlement in places which are super-diverse raises questions about notions of integration and cohesion which emphasize the need for migrants to build bridging relations beyond their (ethnic) "group". The fact is that many pioneers already have established these kinds of bridging relations. While some pioneer migrants find comfort in meeting co-ethnics, almost all of the participants in this research also formed social relations beyond co-ethnics, people who are not necessarily British born, but who form part of the super-diverse social fabric of London. The example of pioneer migrants demonstrates the importance of moving away from "groupist" (Brubaker 2004) approaches towards analysing migration and migrant settlement and showing the variegated backgrounds represented in patterns of immigration in the twenty-first century.

Note

1. For a critical evaluation of migration systems theory, see Bakewell, de Haas, and Kubal (2012).

Acknowledgements

I would like to thank all the research participants for taking their time to talk to me. This research took place while based at the Institute for Research into Superdiversity (IRiS) at the University of Birmingham, and I would like to thank my colleagues for inspiring discussions. I would also like to thank Jenny Phillimore for continuing feedback and support.

Disclosure statement

No potential conflict of interest was reported by the author.

Funding

This research was funded by the FP7 European Commission FP7 Marie Skłodowska-Curie Research Fellowship Programme [Grant number 621945].

References

Bakewell, O., H. de Haas, and A. Kubal. 2012. "Migration Systems, Pioneer Migrants, and the Role of Agency." *Journal of Critical Realism* 11: 413–437.
Berg, M. L. 2011. *Diasporic Generations: Memory, Politics, and Nation Among Cubans in Spain*. New York: Berghahn.
Blokland, T. 2003. *Urban Bonds*. Cambridge: Polity.
Bourdieu, P. 1986. "The Forms of Capital." In *Handbook of Theory and Research for the Sociology of Education*, edited by J. G. Richardson, 241–259. New York: Greenwordpress.
Bourdieu, P. 1990. *The Logic of Practice*. Stanford, CA: Stanford University Press.
Boyd, M. 1989. "Family and Personal Networks in International Migration: Recent Developments and New Agendas." *International Migration Review* 23: 638–670.
Browning, H. L., and W. Feindt. 1969. "Selectivity of Migrants to a Metropolis in a Developing Country: A Mexican Case Study." *Demography* 6: 347–357.
Brubaker, R. 2004. *Ethnicity Without Groups*. Cambridge, MA: Harvard University Press.
Butcher, M. 2017. "Re-working Encounter: The Role of Reflexivity in Managing Difference." *Social & Cultural Geography*, 1–20. doi:10.1080/14649365.2017.1346198.
Butler, T., and C. Hamnett. 2011. *Ethnicity, Class and Aspiration: Understanding London's New East End*. Bristol: Policy.
Cheong, P. H., R. Edwards, H. Goulbourne, and J. Solomos. 2007. "Immigration, Social Cohesion and Social Capital: A Critical Review." *Critical Social Policy* 27: 24–49.
Cheung, S., and J. Phillimore. 2013. *Social Networks, Social Capital and Refugee Integration*. London: Nuffield Foundation.
CIC (Commission on Integration and Cohesion). 2007. *Our Shared Future*. London: Communities and Local Government.
de Haas, H. 2010. "The Internal Dynamics of Migration Processes: A Theoretical Inquiry." *Journal of Ethnic and Migration Studies* 36: 1587–1617.
Dekker, R., and G. Engbersen. 2012. *How Social Media Transform Migrant Networks and Facilitate Migration. IMI Working Paper 64*. Oxford: International Migration Institute, University of Oxford.
Fox, J. E., and D. Jones. 2013. "Migration, Everyday Life and the Ethnicity Bias." *Ethnicities* 13: 385–400.
Glick Schiller, N., and A. Çağlar. 2013. "Locating Migrant Pathways of Economic Emplacement: Thinking Beyond the Ethnic Lens." *Ethnicities* 13: 494–514.

Glick Schiller, N., A. Çağlar, and T. C. Guldbrandsen. 2006. "Beyond the Ethnic Lens: Locality, Globality, and Born-Again Incorporation." *American Ethnologist* 33: 612–633.

Goodson, L. J., and J. Phillimore. 2008. "Social Capital and Integration: The Importance of Social Relationships and Social Space to Refugee Women." *The International Journal of Diversity in Organisations, Communities and Nations* 7: 181–193.

Granovetter, M. 1973. "The Strength of Weak Ties." *American Journal of Sociology* 78: 1360–1380.

Hickman, M. J., N. Mai, and H. Crowley. 2012. *Migration and Social Cohesion in the UK*. Basingstoke: Palgrave Macmillan.

Hudson, M., J. Phillips, and K. Ray. 2009. "'Rubbing Along with the Neighbours' – Everyday Interactions in a Diverse Neighbourhood in the North of England." In *Everyday Multiculturalism*, edited by A. Wise, and S. Velayutham, 199–215. Basingstoke: Palgrave Macmillan.

Hynes, P., and R. Sales. 2010. "New Communities: Asylum Seekers and Dispersal." In *Race and Ethnicity in the 21st Century*, edited by A. Bloch, and J. Solomos, 39–61. Basingstoke: Palgrave Macmillan.

Jones, R. C. 1998. "Remittances and Inequality: A Question of Migration Stage and Geographic Scale." *Economic Geography* 74: 8–25.

Kubal, A., O. Bakewell, and H. de Haas. 2011a. *The Evolution of Brazilian Migration to the UK: Scoping Study Report*. Oxford: International Migration Institute, University of Oxford.

Kubal, A., O. Bakewell, and H. de Haas. 2011b. *The Evolution of Ukrainian Migration to the UK: Scoping Study Report*. Oxford: International Migration Institute, University of Oxford.

Lamont, M., and S. Aksartova. 2002. "Ordinary Cosmopolitanisms. Strategies for Bridging Racial Boundaries among Working-Class Men." *Theory, Culture & Society* 19 (4): 1–25.

Lindstrom, D. P., and A. López Ramírez. 2010. "Pioneers and Followers: Migrant Selectivity and the Development of U.S. Migration Streams in Latin America." *Annual American Academy of Political and Social Sciences* 630: 53–77.

Mabogunje, A. 1970. "Systems Approach to a Theory of Rural–Urban Migration." *Geographical Analysis* 2: 1–18. doi:10.1111/j.1538-4632.1970.tb00140.x.

MacDonald, J. S., and L. D. MacDonald. 1964. "Chain Migration, Ethnic Neighborhood Formation, and Social Networks." *Millbank Memorial Fund Quarterly* 42: 82–97.

Massey, D. S., J. Arango, G. Hugo, A. Kouaouci, A. Pellegrino, and J. E. Taylor. 1998. *Worlds in Motion: Understanding International Migration at the End of the Millennium*. Oxford: Clarendon Press.

Meissner, F. 2016. *Socialising with Diversity: Relational Diversity Though a Superdiversity Lens*. Basingstoke: Palgrave Macmillan.

Meissner, F., and S. Vertovec. 2015. "Comparing Super-Diversity." *Ethnic and Racial Studies* 38: 541–555.

Moroşanu, L. 2010. "Mixed Migrant Ties. Social Networks and Social Capital in Migration Research." In *Best Participant Essays Series 2010/43. CARIM – V Summer School on Euro-Mediterranean Migration and Development*.

Moroşanu, L. 2013. "'We All Eat the Same Bread': The Roots and Limits of Cosmopolitan Bridging Ties Developed by Romanians in London." *Ethnic and Racial Studies* 36: 2160–2181.

Neal, S., K. Bennett, H. Jones, A. Cochrane, and G. Mohan. 2015. "Multiculture and Public Parks: Researching Super-diversity and Attachment in Public Green Space." *Population, Space and Place* 21 (5): 463–475.

Petersen, W. 1958. "A General Typology of Migration." *American Sociological Review* 23: 256–266.
Phillimore, J., R. Humphris, and K. Khan. 2014. *Migration, Networks and Resources: The Relationship Between Migrants' Social Networks and Their Access to Integration Resources*: KING Project – Applied Social Studies Unit.
Portes, A. 1998. "Social Capital: Its Origins and Applications in Modern Sociology." *Annual Review of Sociology* 24: 1–24.
Portes, A., and E. Vickstrom. 2011. "Diversity, Social Capital, and Cohesion." *Annual Review of Sociology* 37: 461–479.
Putnam, R. D. 2000. *Bowling Alone: The Collapse and Revival of American Community*. New York: Simon & Schuster.
Ryan, L. 2011. "Migrants' Social Networks and Weak Ties: Accessing Resources and Constructing Relationships Post-migration." *Sociological Review* 59: 707–724.
Vertovec, S. 2007. "Super-diversity and Its Implications." *Ethnic and Racial Studies* 30: 1024–1054.
Visram, R. 2002. *Asians in Britain: 400 Years of History*. London: Pluto.
Wellman, B. 1999. "The Network Community: An Introduction." In *Networks in the Global Village: Life in Contemporary Communities*, edited by B. Wellman, 1–48. Boulder; Oxford: Westview Press.
Werbner, P. 1999. "Global Pathways: Working Class Cosmopolitans and the Creation of Transnational Ethnic Worlds." *Social Anthropology/ Anthropologie Sociale* 7 (1): 17–35.
Wessendorf, S. 2013. *Second-Generation Transnationalism and Roots Migration. Cross-Border Lives*. Aldershot: Ashgate.
Wessendorf, S. 2014. *Commonplace Diversity. Social Relations in a Super-diverse Context*. Basingstoke: Palgrave Macmillan.
Wessendorf, S. 2017. "Pathways of Settlement Among Pioneer Migrants in Super-diverse London." *Journal of Ethnic and Migration Studies*. doi:10.1080/1369183x.2017.1341719.
Wessendorf, S. forthcoming. "'All the People Speak Bad English.' Communicating Across Differences in a Super-diverse Context." In *The Routledge Handbook on Language and Superdiversity*, edited by A. Creese, and A. Blackledge. London: Routledge.
Williams, L. 2006. "Social Networks of Refugees in the United Kingdom: Tradition, Tactics and New Community Spaces." *Journal of Ethnic and Migration Studies* 32: 865–879.
Wimmer, A. 2004. "Does Ethnicity Matter? Everyday Group Formation in Three Swiss Immigrant Neighbourhoods." *Ethnic and Racial Studies* 27 (1): 1–36.
Wimmer, A., and N. Glick Schiller. 2002. "Methodological Nationalism and Beyond. Nation State Formation, Migration and the Social Sciences." *Global Networks* 2: 301–334.

Coming of age in multi-ethnic America: young adults' experiences with diversity

Van C. Tran

ABSTRACT
How do young adults experience diversity? How does the transition into adulthood shape these experiences? How do these experiences differ across contexts with varying levels of diversity? Comparing data gathered in four US communities, this article suggests three findings. First, children of immigrants are more comfortable with diversity because diversity is the norm in the communities in which they grew up. In contrast, their native counterparts from homogeneous settings encounter diversity as an exception that increasingly becomes the norm as they transition into adulthood. Second, the transition into adulthood structures these experiences, which are grounded in daily interactions at schools, neighbourhoods and workplaces, leading to diverse friendships and relationships. Third, local context shapes young adults' experiences with intergroup relations. This is especially true in super-diverse New York City where immigration history, ethnic diversity and multiculturalism create a welcoming and inclusive context. The article ends with implications for research on super-diversity.

Since the end of the Second World War, large-scale immigration has resulted in unprecedented ethnoracial diversity in both the US and Western Europe. From debates on affirmative action and racial inclusion on college campuses to cultural competency and diversity training in the workplace, the benefits and challenges of diversity are highly contested on both sides of the Atlantic (Pettigrew and Tropp 2006; Wessendorf 2014; Alba and Foner 2015; Zukin, Kasinitz, and Chen 2015; Warikoo 2016). Today most young adults in these societies grew up in a social milieu that was significantly more multi-ethnic and diverse than that in which their parents came of age (Kasinitz et al. 2008; Waters et al. 2011). How do they experience this diversity? How does the transition into adulthood shape these experiences? How do these experiences differ across local contexts with varying levels of diversity?

This article takes a grounded approach to these questions by using qualitative data from a national study of young adults which combines four regional studies conducted in Iowa, Minnesota, New York City and San Diego. The study is an interdisciplinary collaboration from the MacArthur Foundation's Research Network on Transitions to Adulthood and Public Policy. It includes 422 in-depth, semi-structured interviews with young adults from diverse backgrounds in 2002–03. Its sample includes three native-born groups (native white, native black and Puerto Rican) and ten second-generation groups.

The young adults in this study came of age during a period when racial and ethnic diversity was rapidly increasing. From 1970 to 2010, the white population of the US declined from eighty-three to sixty-four per cent whereas the minority population doubled (US Census Bureau 2017). This ethnoracial diversity is unevenly distributed across local communities in the US. In traditional gateways such as New York and San Diego, diversity and super-diversity have been the norm for the last half century as a result of ongoing immigration (Foner 2017). In other places such as the Iowa research site, ethnic diversity is rare and communities have been mostly insulated from the process of ethnic change unfolding across the country.

This *multi-group* and *cross-site* analysis makes three key contributions. First, it compares how the second generation (those born in the US with immigrant parents) and their counterparts of native parentage experience diversity. Because the post-1965 second generation is predominantly from a minority background, they are often more comfortable with ethnic differences. In contrast, those from a majority background are more likely to report being surprised by the cultural and social practices among their friends from a minority background. Second, it highlights how the transition into adulthood shapes how diversity is experienced. Specifically, key turning points in life such as going to college, getting a job, making friends, choosing a partner, and raising children are all opportunities that invite the respondents to grapple with the role of cultural and social differences. Third, it examines diversity and intergroup relations in four varying contexts: two extremely heterogeneous and two relatively homogeneous settings.

This analysis has implications for the debate on super-diversity which captures the multi-dimensionality of diversity in contemporary Europe (Vertovec 2007; Foner 2017). Although the respondents in the study did not use the term "super-diversity", their experiences with diversity are multidimensional. They understand diversity in terms of ethnoracial origin, language, culture, religion, socioeconomic background, and life perspectives. And yet, they are also quick to relate these multiple dimensions of differences to ethnoracial origin, which is often both more visible and central to processes of inequality (Kasinitz et al. 2008; Wimmer 2015). While super-diversity is a useful framework in understanding these experiences, this paper also underscores the continuing centrality of race in shaping these experiences in the American context.

Diversity and the transition into young adulthood

A robust literature has documented how young adults are transitioning into adulthood, focusing on key turning points in life such as leaving for college, entering the workplace, getting married, having children and establishing independent households. The consensus is that young adults today are taking longer than their parents' generation to complete these transitions (Furstenberg, Settersten, and Rumbaut 2005). Whereas this transition was smooth and uniform for the baby boomer generation, young adults who grew up in the post-1965 period have often taken a more circuitous, complicated and convoluted path into adulthood (Waters et al. 2011). Many macro-level factors account for this major shift, including prolonged periods of advanced education, women's increased labour force participation, rising cohabitation and delayed marriage, changing norms on gender and family life, as well as the high cost of living in many major cities that makes it harder for young adults to achieve financial independence.

Although this literature has focused on experiences of transitioning into young adulthood, it has yet to examine how this transition shapes young adults' encounter with everyday diversity. This gap is striking because this transition often intensifies social interactions with individuals from a wide range of social backgrounds as young adults leave the comfort of their parental home and their ethnic community. Specifically, young adults encounter social differences in their residential neighbourhoods (i.e. past and current neighbourhoods), their educational institutions (i.e. high schools and colleges) and their workplaces. More importantly, entry into adulthood plays a major role in structuring attitudes towards diversity in consequential ways. A positive experience with diversity can encourage further interactions in the future whereas a negative experience can solidify prior prejudices against a particular group (Pettigrew and Tropp 2006). Furthermore, experiences with others can impact the second generation and their native counterparts differently. Because the second generation have largely grown up in multiethnic, arguably super-diverse communities, they may be more inclined to see ethnic diversity as the norm, not the exception (Kasinitz et al. 2008; Lee and Zhou 2015). For native white respondents who grew up in mostly white neighbourhoods, diversity is more often something they begin to encounter only as they enter adulthood (Carr and Kefalas 2009).

The focus on young adults is important for three reasons. First, this generation of young adults grew up in an America which was far more demographically diverse and in which there was a stronger social norm favouring the acceptance of diversity than did previous generations (Lee and Bean 2010;

Warikoo 2016). In contrast to their parents' generation, these young adults generally have more positive attitudes towards intergroup relations. Second, young adulthood is a period of significant developmental, intellectual and psychological growth, which is embedded in a series of important personal and professional choices that map onto the key turning points in life (Mortimer 2003; Furstenberg, Settersten, and Rumbaut 2005). Third, young adults present a strategic research site for examining experiences with diversity and intergroup relations. In particular, the contrast between the second generation and their native counterparts of the same age reveals how early experiences with diversity shape subsequent intergroup relations in the context of an increasingly diverse American society (Jiménez 2017).

How local context matters for intergroup relations

A robust theoretical research agenda has highlighted the importance of local context in shaping intergroup relations and processes of immigrant integration. The three major studies of the second generation have been context-specific, focusing on immigrant gateways such as Los Angeles, New York and San Diego (Portes and Rumbaut 2001; Kasinitz et al. 2008; Lee and Zhou 2015). Recent research has adopted an explicitly comparative approach across cities, countries and continents (Crul and Mollenkopf 2012; Foner and Waldinger 2013; Alba and Foner 2015). Within the US, the "city as context" framework highlights the key features of particular cities in shaping the integration of immigrants and promoting cultural diversity (Foner 2007). Beyond the US, the "integration context theory" similarly argues that differences in institutional arrangements across local and national contexts shape immigrant assimilation by providing immigrants and their children with unequal opportunities for mobility (Crul and Schneider 2010).

In majority-minority settings such as New York and San Diego, a "culture of civility" generally governs most public interactions (Alba and Foner 2017, 239). One key reason for this prevailing positive attitude towards intergroup relations may be the selective out-migration of native whites from these areas, especially those in socioeconomic positions that make them vulnerable to job competition from new immigrants (Domina 2006). Another factor is these areas' history and experiences with immigration. This is particularly the case in New York where the combination of immigration history, ethnic diversity and multiculturalism creates a welcoming and inclusive context of integration that Foner (2007, 1000) colloquially calls a "particular New York way". In contrast, new immigrant destinations not only lack this positive history and attitude, but also have few existing institutional infrastructures to integrate new immigrants (Marrow 2011). These new destinations encompass a variety of contexts, ranging from rural and small towns to inner-ring suburbs and new exurbs across the country (Waters and Jimenez 2005).

Latinos are increasingly settling in these destinations, where they face significant prejudice from both non-Hispanic blacks and non-Hispanic whites (Marrow 2011). Because these destinations often lack prior familiarity with immigration, immigrants often face more negative social and political reception from natives (Marrow 2011).

Super-diversity in cross-atlantic perspectives

As a concept, super-diversity captures the "multi-dimensional perspective on diversity" where ethnoracial origin is not the only defining dimension of difference (Vertovec 2007, 1026). By shifting from an "ethnic lens" to a "multidimensional lens", the concept draws attention to other key variables such as gender, education, age and immigrant generations (Crul 2016, 54). Although super-diversity research highlights the inadequacy of ethnicity as the sole marker of social differences in Europe, most research in the US remains entrenched in ethnoracial differences (Wimmer 2015). To be sure, US scholars have noted that differences *within* ethnoracial groups by social class, legal status, immigrant generation and age cohorts can be as large as inequalities *across* ethnoracial groups (Kasinitz et al. 2008; Alba, Jiménez, and Marrow 2014). This US trend towards noting more complexity in migration channels, compositions and streams is similar in its spirit, if not in its form and its terminologies, to the super-diversity debate in Europe (Vertovec 2007).

How useful is super-diversity in the US context? While super-diversity as a concept has been widely influential in Europe, the concept has not been adopted by scholars in the US. This is puzzling. Demographically, the immigrant population in the US, which stood at around forty-one million in 2013, exceeds that of any European country in terms of its size, and it is extraordinarily diverse. The US is also a classic settler society with a long history of immigration from a wide range of countries and regions (Alba and Foner 2015). In New York City, super-diversity would aptly describe the immigrant communities at the turn of the twentieth century, although scholars often homogenize that diversity in the recounting of that history (Foner 2017). Analytically, this paper engages with the utility of the super-diversity framework empirically by examining how young adults encounter cultural and social differences in the US context. In so doing, this paper responds to Vertovec's (2007, 1045) call for "better qualitative studies of super-diversity" by combining the descriptive (i.e. the lived experiences) and the methodological (i.e. the grounded approach) aspects of this conceptual framework. Despite increasing diversity, this analysis also clearly points to the centrality of race and ethnicity in shaping young adults' lives.

Data and methods

This analysis draws on the MacArthur Foundation's Research Network on the Transition to Adulthood's study of US young adults, which collected 422 in-depth, semi-structured interviews with young adults aged 21–38 years old. From 2002 to 2003, four research teams conducted in-depth interviews with an ethnoracially and socioeconomically diverse group of young adults in Iowa, Minnesota, New York and San Diego. The study's goal was to understand how young adults transition into adulthood. This national study combined four regional studies that began separately, but were brought together and harmonized to collect compatible data across sites. This accounts for the unique sampling of specific ethnic groups as well as other differences in the sampling methods across the four sites (for more details on the data set and its relationship to the original surveys, see Waters et al. 2011). The network was led by Frank Furstenberg Jr. and the study was led by Mary Waters. The regional research teams included Linda Borgen, Patrick Carr, Douglas Hartmann, Jennifer Holdaway, Philip Kasinitz, Maria Kefalas, John Mollenkopf, Jeylan Mortimer, Ruben Rumbaut and Teresa Swartz.

In Iowa, the sample includes 104 interviews with freshmen at Ellis High School in the years 1986–88 and 1991–93. This sampling strategy yielded a sample of young adults that might have dropped out of high school at any point (Carr and Kefalas 2011). The Iowa sample includes three subgroups whom the original investigators termed: "stayers", "leavers" and "returners". Stayers and returners were still living in Iowa when interviewed, whereas the leavers had moved away and were interviewed wherever they were living at the time of the interview (Carr and Kefalas 2009). In Minnesota, the sample includes fifty-four interviews with participants from the longitudinal Youth Development Study who were initially sampled when they were in ninth grade in 1988 (Swartz, Hartmann, and Mortimer 2011). In New York, the sample includes 103 participants from the Immigrant Second Generation in Metropolitan New York study (Waters et al. 2011). In San Diego, the interview sample includes 134 participants from the Children of the Immigrant Longitudinal Study (Borgen and Rumbaut 2011). Whereas the Iowa sample is predominantly white, the samples from New York and San Diego contained significant numbers of the immigrant second generation from various ethnoracial backgrounds. Taken together, this large *multi-group, multi-site* sample is the first of its kind to capture a spectrum of young adult experiences. The top panel in Table 1 presents selected demographic characteristics of the sample.

The interviews were between two and four hours long. All interviews were tape-recorded and professionally transcribed. Ervin Kosta at the Center for Urban Research at the CUNY-Graduate Center managed all the coding activities by a team of graduate students. All interviews were systematically coded and analysed in *Atlas.ti* using a list of family and theme codes. The *family codes* capture the respondents' characteristics (e.g. age, gender, ethnic background, etc.) whereas the *theme codes* focus on the key themes from the interviews. Specifically, the analysis starts with a set of theme codes related to diversity, intergroup relations, and racial attitudes. It identifies the most salient themes

Table 1. Demographic characteristics of qualitative sample and research sites.

Sample characteristics	Iowa (N = 104)	Minnesota (N = 54)	New York (N = 130)	San Diego (N = 134)
Age (%)				
18–25	47.1		33.9	88.0
26–28	16.7	16.6	22.3	11.9
29–38	36.3	83.3	43.8	
Gender (%)				
Male	51.0	24.0	55.0	46.0
Race/ethnicity (%)				
White	98.0	66.7	10.8	
African-American		7.4	9.2	
Hmong		18.5		
Puerto Rican			12.3	
Dominican			7.7	
CEP			9.2	
West Indian			8.5	
Russian Jewish			13.1	
Chinese			28.5	9.7
Mexican				29.9
Filipino				26.1
Cambodian, Laos				14.2
Vietnamese				12.7
Other	2.0	9.4	0.8	7.5
Education (%)				
High school graduate or less	23.0	13.0	14.6	20.5
Some college education	35.5	44.4	35.4	56.1
College graduate or more	41.3	42.6	50.0	23.5
Site characteristics	Iowa State	Minnesota/St Paul Metro	New York City	San Diego County
Population				
Total population	2,909,839	2,707,701	8,091,428	2,863,859
Ages 18–34 (%)	22.9	25.4	25.8	24.4
Race/ethnicity (%)				
Hispanic	7.4	6.3	27.9	27.6
White	85.2	76.8	33.2	50.6
Black	2.6	6.9	24.2	5.4
Asian	2.9	8.0	12.6	10.9
Nativity/generation (%)				
First generation	10.9	16.2	42.1	25.4
Second generation	2.1	4.7	25.1	19.6
Third-plus generation	87.0	79.0	32.8	55.0

Source: Adapted from Table A.1 and Table I.4 in Waters et al. (2011).

at each site while paying attention to cross-site comparisons. While the national study includes individuals aged 21–38, this analysis is limited to those aged 21–35 in the sample because this is the age traditionally associated with young adulthood.

The dataset has a number of unique *strengths*. It is the only national study of young adults with a broad sample of the second generation and their native counterparts. It includes respondents from a wide range of ethnic groups and the inclusion of four research sites provides an opportunity to examine the contextual variations on young adults' experiences. At the same time, the dataset has several *limitations*. Most notably the research at each of the four sites was led by a different team of researchers and the data were only partially harmonized. Though the research teams adopted the same interview schedule, the sampling procedures vary based on existing priorities for each research team. I should note that I did not collect and code the interviews myself. However, I did have access to all transcripts and field notes by the research teams which helped contextualize the interviews and the findings. This distance from the data collected is both a disadvantage and an advantage. On the one hand, I did not have intimate knowledge of each research site (with the exception of New York City). On the other hand, approaching the dataset with this sense of distance allows broad comparative analyses. Even though secondary analyses of survey data are common, if not ubiquitous, in quantitative research, secondary analyses of qualitative data such as those in this article are indeed rare because few qualitative datasets are made available with such level of precision and details. Yet today large teams of qualitative researchers are increasingly able to collect and to share their interviews with researchers interested in similar topics (Deterding and Waters forthcoming), making secondary analysis and comparative work more feasible. To be sure, researchers need to be sensitive about data quality, coding, ethics, replication and generalizability, but these concerns are universal to both qualitative and quantitative datasets.

The bottom panel in Table 1 provides the demographic composition by research site. Ellis, Iowa epitomizes small-town, rural America with a homogenous population. Ellis is located in northern Iowa with a population of only 2,000. Its population reflects the general composition of Iowa where eighty-five per cent are white and only eleven per cent is foreign-born. In addition to a more diverse population, Minneapolis/St Paul, Minnesota has a strong and diversified economy, excellent public schools and a relatively generous social welfare system. The city is also home to significant refugee communities: Hmong refugees first arrived in the 1970s, followed by Somali refugees in the 1990s. Yet the area of 2.7 million remains seventy-seven per cent white, with only seven per cent black, eight per cent Asian and six per cent Hispanic. New York City boasts one of the most diverse populations in the country. This diversity, coupled with the city's historical role in receiving and integrating immigrants, creates an arguably "super diverse" context in which diverse talents are recruited by global and local companies, cultural practices and ethnic holidays are celebrated, and a vibrant and socially mixed urban youth culture has thrived (Foner 2007; Kasinitz et al. 2008). Further, while the idea of diversity is most often thought of in terms of ethnicity, the size of the city and the variety of its population helps to create a setting in which social bonds can be formed on the basis of class, gender, religion, sexuality and other identities which cut across ethnic and racial divisions. San Diego is the second largest city in California and the eighth largest in the US. The city has a long history of immigration from Mexico, with a sizable influx of Southeast Asian refugees arriving in the 1980s and 1990s. While San Diego has a slim white majority, a quarter of the city is Hispanic. It also boasts a diverse Asian population that includes Filipinos, Vietnamese and Chinese.

Encountering diversity in the transition into young adulthood

Background and upbringing

Reflecting upon their experience growing up in Ellis, Iowa, most respondents recall a predominantly white setting with little diversity along ethnoracial, cultural and religious lines. The respondents' high school experience includes white classmates from very similar background. For Iowan leavers who have lived in more diverse places, the stark contrast between their homogenous small town and other communities is striking. In retrospect, they describe their town as one characterized by a high level of ignorance of social differences.

> Q What would make you leave? Push you out?
> A The mentality. The social mentality of the community. From my perception, a lot of the people that participate in this community were born and raised here and have very few life experiences outside of northeast Iowa and some don't even have a lot of experiences outside of maybe the surrounding counties. Their perceptions of other people typically fall in that bigoted category or if you're not like them then maybe the value of your life or your existence isn't significant to them. (23-year-old white female, Iowa)

In contrast, young adults in the other sites are quick to mention the benefits associated with diversity. They recount experiences growing up in diverse neighbourhoods and attending high schools where most people from different backgrounds got along well with each other. When asked, this respondent immediately lists the many types of social diversity in her neighbourhood.

> Our immediate neighbors, yes, to our left and to our right are [yuppies]. However, we do have a diverse group. We have working class, we have retired, we have immigrants, we have, we are literally on a melting pot block. We have Asians, we have Mexicans, we have whites, we have blacks, we have Latins, we have Vietnamese, we have Chinese. (29-year-old white female, Minnesota)

In college settings

For Iowan respondents, the decision to leave for college reflects a major turning point in life. For the majority of young adults from Iowa, the college environment puts them into contact with people from other races for the first time. Having no prior experience interacting with people from different backgrounds, many young adults remember these initial encounters with diversity as quite "scary":

> Q Did college change you? Did it open you up to things?
> A Maybe a little. Because like in this small town I had never had to be around like anybody, you know, anybody of a different color, race or anything and when I got there I was petrified. Like the first week I was bawling "cause I was like I am scared to death.
> Q What was scary about it?
> A Yeah. I mean you just kind of are put in there with a lot of strangers. And you have to, you know, I live in this little tiny room, you know, with somebody that you have no clue who they are or how they you know, do things. (28-year-old white female, Iowa)

In fact, many wish their high school experiences had better prepared them for the diversity they encountered:

> Q How could high school have better prepared you?
> A How to relate, how to express myself, how to um you know just relate with different people with different backgrounds um different cultural backgrounds. You know we"re all white, all white. And uh you know it was a big deal going to college and having um African American teammates. (31-year-old white male, Iowa)

By contrast, respondents in New York and San Diego are quick to relate that their high school experiences increased their awareness of and comfort with diversity.

> Q How helpful was your high school experience in terms of all that you've done since?
> A Well, it just helped me to be aware of like other people instead of just focusing on people from my own background. You know I realized that other people have a lot to offer. Even if they're different, I learn a lot from them. (25-year-old Mexican male, San Diego)

However, many respondents from all four sites report that they did not even realize that they grew up in homogenous neighbourhoods until they had left for college – where there was more diversity of all forms – and returned.

> Q So, tell me about that neighborhood that you grew up in.
> A Well, I really liked it "cause I had a lot of friends, I was in high school. I never really, one thing I never really noticed until I came back from Berkeley was, it's predominantly white. And old. Like elderly. And when I was going to high school, most of my classmates and friends were all white as well. Like Jewish. And I never even really thought about it. I mean, I definitely noticed it, but I never really thought about it too much. And then when I went to Berkeley and there's such diversity. You know, all sorts of people. Like as soon as I came back, it really hit me. Like wow, the neighborhood I grew up in was really like homogenous. (23-year-old Chinese/Filipino female, San Diego)

In the workplace

The next transition into adulthood involves work. For those who never went to college, this often represents their first encounter with diversity. The workplace brings further exposure and provides a social context to work with and to learn from others with diverse backgrounds. This respondent describes a workplace where there was an "open and honest" discussion on diversity.

> A   Growing up in a white community, never having any relationship with any different nationality, blacks, Hispanics, whatever and then you are twenty-some years old and you go to a city and oh my gosh you are with all these different people, and I'"m glad the people I was working with were so open on that, cause I don't know, somehow you can just tell, and my boss, she was black, a lady I worked with was black, and then I had a Korean and something else, I don't remember what it was. All these other people and they were so open and honest, and they had questions, you know and, sometimes, I just felt you don't talk about people's race, religion, and stuff like that because you might step on toes, these guys were so open and honest. (30-year-old white female, Iowa)

> For the second generation, exposure to the American mainstream is an experience with diversity. This respondent describes college as crucial in preparing him for future encounters with whites in the workplace, especially those in positions of authority. Because there are few minorities in charge, learning how to deal with "white people" in these positions is a skillset that is important.

> Q   Did [college] help you get prepared for work itself?
> A   I think so. It allowed me to get more experience. I mean, I hate to say it but I had more experience with white people and dealing with them. It helped me to deal with them on a somewhat of a peer level. I learned how to deal with them as professors, someone in an authoritative figure. That's why college helped because it made me see that they are a little different than us. They have different ways of dealing with things. [...] That was one of the problems in the firm on Wall Street. The guy that brought me in was white. I come in, I'm Spanish. I'm pretty dark at that. (28-year-old Dominican male, New York)

Young adults' friendship networks reflect the diverse workplaces they find themselves in. With higher levels of educational achievement, most members of the second generation have left behind the co-ethnic economy that often defines their parents' labour market experience. The majority work in settings where they frequently interact with people from other backgrounds. In fact, many companies find it is in their best interest to promote diversity within the organization to better serve their increasingly diverse clienteles. In return, many respondents appreciate the range of diversity among their coworkers and rarely see it as a problem. This is especially true in New York City.

> Q At your current workplace, what are your co-workers like?
> A It's mixed. I mean, they're not, again, it's diverse. The ages are diverse. The youngest, probably, I don't know, twenty-three, twenty-four, to the oldest, like fifty. It's very mixed. Different cultures, different talents. Very diverse.
> Q It's equal in background between the supervisors and the employees. Are they white?
> A It's extremely diverse, and I think the firm actually promotes diversity. (33-year-old Colombian male, New York)

In residential neighbourhoods

Residential choice is another key moment. In contrast to the respondents in Iowa and Minnesota, the second generation in New York and San Diego speak about the importance of living in a diverse community. Having spent most of their lives in diverse settings, they observe that people in diverse places are less prejudiced and more tolerant. This respondent and his family live in Bayside, Queens, which he describes as "a very nice community" with "a great deal of ethnic diversity".

> Q Is [diversity] something that is important to you?
> A (Sigh) I would say yes. To my wife also. We feel that a neighborhood that is more ethnically diverse would be ethnically more tolerant and there would be less discrimination involved. My wife has a friend who has a house in Douglaston and she feels that she constantly is having problems with the neighbors. People are driving their cars over her lawn and she feels this is partly due to the racism. (29-year-old Chinese male, New York)

Yet even in New York or San Diego, the second generation mostly interact with others like themselves. Many of the second generation have little, if any, exposure to native whites (Kasinitz et al. 2008). As a result, many feel awkward and out-of-place when they find themselves in predominantly white settings. Many did not realize how much they have taken diversity for granted until they are in a social context where they were among one of the few non-white individuals. For example, this respondent feels that diverse settings allow him to blend in more easily:

> A And, when I grew up, I lived in a predominantly white community back in Kansas and there were some times when I was being ridiculed by other kids, and um ... for the way I looked. I was different. Coming to California and living in the community, East San Diego, there's just a melting pot. You fit in. You felt comfortable, because everybody looks different. You really learn from all these different types of cultures and you don't really judge people for who they are. (25-year-old Vietnamese male, San Diego)

In friendship networks

The social realms of school, work and residential life provide opportunities for befriending others from diverse backgrounds. In contrast to Iowa and Minnesota, respondents from New York and San Diego generally grew up with a more diverse circle of friends. This San Diegan respondent explains how open and accepting her friends are of her mixed Chinese-Filipino heritage.

> Oh yeah, most of my friends were multi-racial-internationally. Everybody was from everywhere. My best friend is black, African-American and white mixed. But growing up I mean had a lot of Asian friends, a lot of Mexican friends, and a lot of Black friends and White friends and everybody. I never really would notice anybody's race as a part of that. Like if they were my friend – they were my friend. (25-year-old Chinese/Filipino female, San Diego)

When asked if most of their friends are from the same ethnic group, the typical response from a New York respondent tends to be "they are from all over the world", followed by a detailed listing of most major ethnic or racial groups. This respondent illustrates this point:

> No. All over. Different ethnicities, Caucasian, Latin American and I had very good friends that were Jamaican American I had very good friends that were Asian Black American, you know it was pretty much those people that are around me, my probably my, some of my best friends, the ones in grade school, are Puerto Rican Spanish the same, a lot of them were Jewish. My best friend now is a Jewish guy, you know, so all over the gamut. (32-year-old West Indian male, New York)

In fact, a diverse friendship circle is the norm for the second generation in New York and San Diego. This is generally seen as positive. This respondent illustrates this when stating that her background and those of her friends were never an "issue".

> No, not at all. You don't want to be in a circle of friends where everyone has the same experience, everyone has the same type of stories to tell. That's boring. I have, you know once in a while I go out to dinner with a group of friends who all are Chinese. And I'm just sitting there like, "oh gosh", I mean, they're my friends, but they're boring, you know? They don't add any flavor to the conversation. You want a mix- a group, variety. Everyone has different input and perspective on an issue. (26-year-old Chinese female, New York)

Dating, relationships and marriage

When thinking about dating or marriage, Iowan stayers find that their choices are quite limited. Their potential partners tend to be someone who comes from a similar social background. As one of our respondents put it, in small town Iowa, "there is nobody to date other than you know ... the white". Social norms and parental expectations structure young people's choices in terms of whom they perceive as suitable partners. One female respondent related that her father would disown her if she were to ever bring a black man home. In contrast, Iowan leavers are much more open to the possibility of dating and marrying someone of a different group. Even though their personal experiences allow them to put interracial relationships into perspective, the majority choose not to engage in such a relationship to conform to the strong social norms of their towns.

> Well, I'm not prejudiced but I don't like it. I don't like blacks and whites getting married and Mexicans and whites getting married. I don't know why because if you are happy, you're happy but I don't know why I don't like it. I just don't like it. But when I got to college, there were a lot of black people and I was scared of them and I didn't want nothing to do with them. But then I got to know them and I gave them a chance and I was really best friends with one black guy but I would never date a black guy, never and uh, because my dad's very prejudiced, very, very, very and he said if we ever brought a black guy home he would shoot us and all that. I would not marry a black guy and maybe that's because of my dad's thinking. (31-year-old white female, Iowa)

In contrast, San Diegans and New Yorkers are generally open to interracial dating and marriage. In fact, many report dating across ethnoracial lines, reflecting the general acceptance of diversity. Most answer without any hesitation that they would enter into these relationships whereas many others are currently in various stages along the continuum of dating, cohabitation and marriage.

> Q Did your mother or father expect you to marry or date a certain type of person?
> A I guess they really don't just because of the fact that my sister, my older sister, she's really opened the door to other cultures. I mean, her first boyfriend was African American. Actually, two of them were African American. She's never had a Filipino boyfriend. She married a gentleman that was half Mexican and half Korean. Which was very interesting to me because she broke away from dating African Americans and I guess their marriage is pretty cool. My father gets along. My mother gets along with him pretty well. And, for them I guess it doesn't really matter what culture I get married in just as long as I'm happy. (26-year-old Filipino female, San Diego)

Intergenerational differences

In all four sites, the majority of young adults feel that their parents are too narrow-minded, and their grandparents even more so. Most express that they are more open-minded than their parents when it comes to interracial friendships and intergroup relationships. This respondent represents this intergenerational shift in attitudes towards diversity.

> Q What would you change about how you were raised?

A   Um, I guess well my parents grew up in the Midwest as well, and they're pretty, my parents are better about it than some, but they are pretty narrow minded and not necessarily accepting of a lot of things, you know diversity and you know different races, different sexual inclinations and things like that. [And] then I hear my grandparents who are even worse, um and so I think that's where they got it from, so I guess that would be the one thing that I would change. A little more, how do I want to say, a little more accepting of people of difference. (30-year-old white female, Iowa)

While young adults feel strongly about their parents' old-fashioned attitudes towards race relations, they also express optimism that their generation is more tolerant. They note that this lack of acceptance comes from both white and non-white individuals of their parental generation.

Cause older people when they get to a certain age, they have their own set ways. "I've never liked this, so I'm not gonna like it now." I think younger generations is gonna have more of that diversity. More of a way of acting around different people. Not just "Oh, you're this color. We shouldn't be friends." You know, older people, I'm not saying all older people, but some of them are like "You know, I've never got along with white people, I'm never gonna like white people." (22-year-old Puerto Rican/ West Indian female, New York)

From diversity to super-diversity in everyday life

In sum, this generation of young adults speak positively about the diversity that they encounter in their lives. And yet, encountering social differences can also be a challenging experience, mostly due to young adults' lack of prior exposure and negative stereotypes. Here, social context matters, as young adults in New York and San Diego are more at ease with diversity than those in Iowa and Minnesota. Lack of prior exposure to other groups is cited as the single most important reason why young adults may find diversity initially challenging and intimidating. During their entry into adulthood, most young adults have come into contact with people from various social backgrounds. As a result of these often-positive encounters, young adults become much more appreciative of different life perspectives, cultural and religious practices, cuisines and ways of life. These experiences, in turn, lead them to be less judgmental of others, to modify pre-existing negative stereotypes, and to embrace diversity. Most of the respondents describe this iterative process as one through which their intellectual horizons are broadened. However, there are also important exceptions. Specific negative incidents with members of another group – being a victim of a crime or of discrimination when growing up – can have a long-lasting effect on young adults' perception of certain groups.

Race, class and immigrant status intersect in shaping young adults' experience of diversity. Native whites who grew up in homogenous neighbourhoods benefit the most from exposure to diversity at college or in the workplace, as they often have the least prior exposure to people from other backgrounds. This pattern is most robust and evident in interviews with whites in Iowa and Minnesota. For the second generation, diversity is part of their experience bridging two worlds – American society and the world of their parents (Kasinitz et al. 2008; Borgen and Rumbaut 2011). Since many grew up mostly around co-ethnics or other minorities, they are often exposed to whites for the first time at college or workplace settings. Class also matters. Those who grew up in poor neighbourhoods often experienced diversity and intergroup relations as a challenge and they recount vivid stories of gangs, drugs, and violent fights between blacks and Hispanic groups or between Hispanic and Asian groups. In contrast, respondents from less poor communities, particularly in New York City, generally argue that highly diverse settings render social differences less salient and allow New Yorkers to blend in more easily. Consistent with much of the super-diversity literature, in settings where "everybody is from everywhere" group boundaries are less sharply drawn and ultimately less important (see Crul 2016).

Respondents generally report that their experiences with diversity are multidimensional. Building on the super-diversity framework, this article does not presume that ethnoracial origin is the primary axis of differentiation. Instead, it documents the multiple dimensions of diversity in young adults' experiences. And yet, this analysis also highlights the centrality of race and ethnicity in shaping their experiences because these categories remain highly salient in structuring their daily lives, from their segregated neighbourhoods to their integrated workplaces. For many young Americans, embracing diversity opens up new understandings and deepens existing relationships, especially when these encounters occur in an inclusive context in which cultural differences are meaningfully engaged and groups interact with each other on an equal basis (Pettigrew and Tropp 2006). For some, these experiences are initially challenging, but ultimately rewarding.

Given the recent rise of anti-immigrant sentiments both in the US and in Europe (Alba and Foner 2017), the benefits and challenges of diversity and super-diversity are once again highly contested. Nevertheless, it is notable that among this generation of young adults encounters with super-diversity in everyday life have indeed led many see cultural diversity in a more positive light. Whether this openness and acceptance of differences will endure as this generation ages is an open question, one that will remain at the forefront of future debates on diversity, inclusion and equality.

Acknowledgements

I would like to thank Mary Waters for providing me access to the qualitative interviews from this national study of transition into young adulthood. I am also grateful to all the PIs involved with the data collection at all four research sites for their contributions to this project and for sharing their qualitative interviews with me, which made this secondary analysis possible. Participants of the Workshop on "Super-Diversity: A Transatlantic Conversation" at The Graduate Center of City University of New York and of the Race, Ethnicity and Migration Workshop at Columbia University provided helpful feedback and suggestions. Nancy Foner, Phil Kasinitz, Jan Willem Duyvendak, Harris Beider, David Goodwin, along with four anonymous reviewers and the ERS editors, provided critical comments that significantly improved the final version.

Disclosure statement

No potential conflict of interest was reported by the author.

ORCID

Van C. Tran http://orcid.org/0000-0002-2532-6811

References

Alba, Richard, and Nancy Foner. 2015. *Strangers No More: Immigration and the Challenges of Integration in North America and Western Europe*. Princeton, NJ: Princeton University Press.
Alba, Richard, and Nancy Foner. 2017. "Immigration and the Geography of Polarization." *City & Community* 16 (3): 239–244.
Alba, Richard D., Tomás R. Jiménez, and Helen B. Marrow. 2014. "Mexican Americans as a Paradigm for Contemporary Intra-Group Heterogeneity." *Ethnic and Racial Studies* 37 (3): 446–466.
Borgen, Linda, and Ruben G. Rumbaut. 2011. "Coming of Age in 'America's Finest City.' Transitions to Adulthood among Children of Immigrants in San Diego." In *Coming of Age in America*, edited by Mary C. Waters, Patrick J. Carr, Maria J. Kefalas, and Jennifer Holdaway, 103–127. Berkeley: University of California Press.
Carr, Patrick J., and Maria J. Kefalas. 2009. *Hollowing Out the Middle: The Rural Brian Drain and What It Means for America*. Boston: Beacon.
Carr, Patrick J., and Maria J. Kefalas. 2011. "Straight from the Heartland: Coming of Age in Ellis, Iowa." In *Coming of Age in America*, edited by Mary C. Waters, Patrick J. Carr, Maria J. Kefalas, and Jennifer Holdaway, 28–49. Berkeley: University of California Press.
Crul, Maurice. 2016. "Super-Diversity vs. Assimilation: How Complex Diversity in Majority-Minority Cities Challenges the Assumptions of Assimilation." *Journal of Ethnic and Migration Studies* 42 (1): 54–68.
Crul, Maurice, and J. Mollenkopf. 2012. *The Changing Face of World Cities*. New York: Russell Sage Foundation.
Crul, Maurice, and Jens, Schneider. 2010. "Comparative Context Integration Theory: Participation and Belonging in New, Diverse European Cities." *Ethnic and Racial Studies* 34 (4): 1249–1268.
Deterding, Nicole, and Mary C. Waters. Forthcoming. "Qualitative Coding: A 21st Century Approach." *Sociological Methods and Research*.
Domina, Thurston. 2006. "Brain Drain and Brain Gain: Rising Educational Segregation in the United States, 1940–2000." *City & Community* 5 (4): 387–407.
Foner, Nancy. 2007. "How Exceptional Is New York? Migration and Multiculturalism in the Empire City." *Ethnic and Racial Studies* 30: 999–1023.

Foner, Nancy. 2017. "A Research Comment: What's New about Super-Diversity?" *Journal of American Ethnic History* 36 (4): 49–57.

Foner, Nancy, and Roger Waldinger. 2013. "New York and Los Angeles as Immigrant Destinations: Contrasts and Convergence." In *New York and Los Angeles: The Uncertain Future*, edited by Andrew Beveridge and David Halle, 343–358. New York: Oxford.

Furstenberg, Frank, Richard A. Settersten Jr., and Rubén G. Rumbaut. 2005. *On the Frontiers of Adulthood: Theory, Research, and Public Policy*. Chicago: University of Chicago Press.

Jiménez, Tomás R. 2017. *The Other Side of Assimilation: How Immigrants are Changing American Life*. Oakland: University of California Press.

Kasinitz, Philip, John H. Mollenkopf, Mary C. Waters, and Jennifer Holdaway. 2008. *Inheriting the City: The Children of Immigrants Come of Age*. New York: Russell Sage Foundation.

Lee, Jennifer, and Frank Bean. 2010. *The Diversity Paradox: Immigration and the Color Line in Twenty-First Century America*. New York: Russell Sage Foundation.

Lee, Jennifer, and Min Zhou. 2015. *The Asian American Achievement Paradox*. New York: Russell Sage Foundation.

Marrow, Helen B. 2011. *New Destination Dreaming: Immigration, Race and Legal Status in the Rural American South*. Stanford, CA: Stanford University Press.

Mortimer, Jeylan T. 2003. *Working and Growing Up in America*. Cambridge, MA: Harvard University Press.

Pettigrew, Thomas F., and Linda R Tropp. 2006. "A Meta-Analytic Test of Intergroup Contact Theory." *Journal of Personality and Social Psychology* 90: 751–783.

Portes, Alejandro, and Ruben G. Rumbaut. 2001. *Legacies: The Story of the Immigrant Second Generation*. Berkeley: University of California Press.

Swartz, Teresa, Douglas Hartmann, and Jeylan Mortimer. 2011. "Transitions to Adulthood in the Land of Lake Wobegon." In *Coming of Age in America*, edited by Mary C. Waters, Patrick J. Carr, Maria J. Kefalas, and Jennifer Holdaway, 50–83. Berkeley: University of California Press.

US Census Bureau. 2017. "Percent Minority: 1970–2042." https://www.census.gov/newsroom/cspan/1940census/CSPAN_194011.pdf.

Vertovec, Steven. 2007. "Super-Diversity and Its Implications." *Ethnic and Racial Studies* 29 (6): 1024–1054.

Warikoo, Natasha. 2016. *The Diversity Bargain: And Other Dilemmas of Race, Admissions, and Meritocracy at Elite Universities*. Chicago, IL: University of Chicago Press.

Waters, Mary C., Patrick J. Carr, Maria J. Kefalas, and Jennifer Holdaway. 2011. *Coming of Age in America: The Transition to Adulthood in the Twenty-First Century*. Berkeley: University of California Press.

Waters, Mary C, and Tomas Jimenez. 2005. "Assessing Immigrant Assimilation: New Empirical and Theoretical Challenges." *Annual Review of Sociology* 31: 105–125.

Wessendorf, Susanne. 2014. *Commonplace Diversity. Social Relations in a Super-Diverse Context*. London: Palgrave Macmillan.

Wimmer, Andreas. 2015. "Race-Centrism: A Critique and a Research Agenda." *Ethnic and Racial Studies* 38 (13): 2186–2205.

Zukin, Sharon, Philip Kasinitz, and Xiangming Chen. 2015. *Global Cities, Local Streets: Everyday Diversity from New York to Shanghai*. New York: Routledge.

Super-diversity as a methodological lens: re-centring power and inequality

Sofya Aptekar

ABSTRACT
Super-diversity as a methodological lens calls for a study of dynamics of new and diversified social groups that moves away from more traditional approaches focused on ethnicity. In examining the potential of super-diversity as a methodological lens, I identify a risk of downplaying the effect of "old" categories of difference that are likely to continue to shape social structures as well as space. I propose a re-centring of power and inequality in the study of super-diversity by situating its study within an urban culturalist approach, with sociological tools borrowed from ethnomethodology and symbolic interactionism. This proposal is illustrated through the analysis of two public spaces in a super-diverse New York neighbourhood. I conclude by raising questions about the use of super-diversity discourse in the public and policy spheres.

Socrates Sculpture Park, New York City. It is a warm Saturday, and I am spending time in this park as a researcher of public space in Astoria, a diverse neighbourhood in Queens. I stroll past the stalls of the farmers market, watching the mostly white vendors and customers, many of the latter wearing expensive casual clothing and toting yoga mats. A guest chef is demonstrating how to prepare sauces to go with a duck breast. There is a group of Latina women pushing strollers laden with shopping bags. They walk past the tent that processes low-income food credits accepted at the market, and join other Latina women who are shopping at the stand of a Mexican immigrant pepper farmer. A lesbian couple in their forties, one white, one African American, wear matching bike helmets as they shop.

Elsewhere in the park, there is a scattering of people, many of whom are looking at or taking pictures of the sculpture installations. Others are enjoying the waterfront views of Manhattan. A group of young East Asian women make their away around the perimeter of the park, chatting and taking pictures. A

Middle Eastern group of four children, a man, and a woman wearing a hijab, move leisurely past the installations, the two younger children frolicking in the grass. An elderly white couple sit in foldable lawn chairs, observing the action. A Latina woman looks over the water, holding the hand of a young girl. In a shady corner, a South Asian man and a young boy are casting fishing rods, a huge grin on the boy's face. Two young African American men are sitting on the railing, sharing tinny music on their phones. By the hedges on the other side of the park are three bedraggled looking white men, nursing concealed drinks.

As I walk around, I hear English and Spanish, and several languages I cannot definitively identify. There are people of various ages, race, ethnicity, immigration status, socio-economic status, sexual orientation, people with disabilities and without, locals and visitors from elsewhere in the city and beyond. This one small urban park seems to encapsulate not just local diversity, but super-diversity, with its implication of multi-dimensional complexity and the challenges it poses to researchers and policy-makers (Meissner 2015; Vertovec 2007). The concept of super-diversity calls on social scientists to recognize the new immigration-driven reality in cities like London and New York, where there is differentiation of not just ethnicity, but a myriad of other variables that intersect in ways that lead to unequal opportunities within ethnic groups as well as between them, including along dimensions of religion, age, gender, legal status, and class (Vertovec 2007). In public spaces like Socrates Sculpture Park and in the surrounding immigrant-rich neighbourhood, the lens of super-diversity allows us to move beyond ethnicity, the traditional preoccupation of urban and migration scholars. By conceptualizing these spaces as super-diverse, scholars are able to free themselves from assumptions about what type of difference matters, providing a fresh way to approach old questions of integration, transnationalism, and tolerance (Meissner and Vertovec 2015). Vertovec (2007) argues that using super-diversity helps scholars study new patterns of inequality and prejudice. Responding to a context of heightened urban conflict, particularly the 2001 riots in several UK cities, he explains that the super-diversity approach can illuminate the conditions under which diverse populations engage meaningfully with each other.

In this paper, I raise questions about super-diversity as a methodological lens. Vertovec (2007, 1047) proposes a qualitative approach that focuses on interactions between actors, analysing both the meanings of these interactions and the structural forces and social categories that shape understandings and behaviour. In elaborating the approach, Meissner (2015) highlights the multi-dimensional nature of diversity and the imperative to investigate "social patterns that are not necessarily marked by perceived inequalities, but where the simultaneity of multiple axes of differentiation results in positively or ambivalently perceived social relations" (557). Thus, the concept of super-diversity rightly draws attention to the complexity of different dimensions of difference. But while foregrounding it, and improving on ethnocentric foci of much of migration research, it risks downplaying the differences among differences. In other words, while researchers orient themselves to new emergent patterns of complexity, particularly while looking for "key forms of space and contact that might yield positive benefits" (Vertovec 2007, 1046), they should not assume that the rise of super-diversity necessarily brings a decline in the role of the "old" categories of race, class, and gender. These categories may seem less reliable as signifiers of commonalities or differences in everyday encounters. However, they can continue to wield influence by shaping social organization of institutions, spaces, and communities.

This paper seeks to contribute to the body of critical responses to super-diversity (e.g. Boccagni 2015; Hall 2017; Makoni 2012; Ndhlovu 2016). Makoni (2012) noted the tendency to romanticize the diversification of diversity, leading to "a careful concealment of power differences" and "an illusion of equality in a highly asymmetrical world" (192). Everyday interactions, which may take place without much apparent conflict across difference occur within a macro structure of systemic oppressions that remains powerfully salient. These systems of oppression are grounded in long histories of unequal distribution of power and resources by race, class, and gender – the very categories the strength of which may appear to be fading in everyday encounters taking place amidst a dazzling super-diversity. Moreover, as Hall (2017) points out, super-diversity is inextricable from the violent and discriminatory border regimes that produce it. How do we incorporate an analysis of power, structural inequality, and hegemony into the ethnographic study of everyday super-diversity?

In what follows, I explore these questions, arguing that much can be gained in the study of immigration, cities, and public space by adding an ethnomethodological and symbolic interactionist lens to the super-diversity approach. By treating difference as an ongoing accomplishment rather than a set of interrelated variables, and social actors as actively interpreting their social contexts in interactions, the study of super-diversity can avoid overemphasizing the patina of positive or neutral sociality and remain sufficiently sensitive to exclusions, interplays of power, and reproduction of inequality unfolding in everyday interactions. In addition, I argue for an urban culturalist approach (Borer 2006) to super-diversity, focused on the role of urban space in meaning-making, place identities, and reactions and interactions with place and in place. I provide two ethnographic examples from Astoria, New York, to illustrate the ways in which these methodological approaches can help illuminate the everyday accomplishment of difference and reproduction of inequality without reifying social categories. Situated in a setting marked by immigration-driven super-diversity, these examples focus on public space as a research site for studying interactions with place and between social actors. I also find that public space actors use diversity as a cultural construct to promote particular interests.

Super-diversity as a methodological lens

Meissner and Vertovec (2015) identify three aspects of super-diversity: descriptive, methodological, and practical. The methodological leverage of super-diversity comes from casting off the straitjacket of ethnicity, and, instead, analysing the dynamics of new and diversified social groups and cross-cutting categories. Super-diversity as a methodological lens calls for approaches that promise progress in "rethinking patterns of inequality, prejudice and segregation; gaining a more nuanced understanding of social interactions, cosmopolitanism and creolization; elaborating theories of mobility; and obfuscating the spurious dualism of transnationalism versus integration" (Meissner and Vertovec 2015, 543). I argue that super-diversity might hold such potential, but that it can also obscure enduring structures of inequality by over-focusing on emergent social categories, and that it can benefit from being interpolated with other methodological approaches.

A new literature engaging with super-diversity has emerged in the past decade. Berg and Sigona (2013) praise the "diversity turn" and super-diversity as an approach to the study of urban space, challenging ethnographers to move away from essentializing ethnicity. Padilla, Azevedo, and Olmos-Alcaraz (2015) even contend that research with a super-diversity lens can help break the cycle of reification of ethnic Otherness. Drawing on their multi-sited ethnography of two Southern European cities, they argue that everyday difference comes to be viewed positively by locals, and that analysis of conflict moves beyond race and ethnicity. Similarly, Acosta-García and Martínez-Ortiz (2015) use a super-diversity lens by focusing on "collective intermingling" (641) rather than discrete migration streams in Mexico, and Biehl (2015) argues that this lens helps her understand access to housing in Istanbul that is shaped by more than gender and race.

Several recent studies analyse the dynamics and implications of super-diversity specifically in urban public spaces. For instance, Wilson (2011) argues that ordinary encounters on a diverse Birmingham bus can have lasting effects on the way people understand difference. Although she shows how these encounters could reinforce prejudice and exclusion, there is also a strong potential for an affective disruption of dominant categorizations and norms that can lead to recognition and even tolerance. Neal et al. (2015) draw on interviews in which they brought together strangers using city parks to show that people become oriented towards mixing and tolerance through enjoyment of these public spaces. Other recent ethnographic studies show that diversity can become an unremarkable fact of everyday life in super-diverse settings (Jones et al. 2015; Wessendorf 2014), and that people in such settings often negotiate differences in everyday encounters with ease and a cosmopolitan orientation (Neal et al. 2013).

Some of the recent research on lived and routine super-diversity incorporates Gilroy's (2004) arguments for illuminating social dispositions that lead to convivial patterns of coexistence in diverse neighbourhoods. Although attention to everyday conviviality in super-diverse settings can be seen a corrective to reified, colonial categories of race and ethnicity (Gilroy 2004), Ndhlovu (2016) argues that it replicates a Western, elite, and neoliberal conceptualization of identity. Relatedly, in an analysis of multiculture in the UK that could be extended to super-diversity, Fortier (2008) points out that it serves to obscure histories of racist domination with visual spectacle of seemingly inclusive mixing of diverse people. Hall (2017) argues that super-diversity's connection to "structures of economic and political power and the inequalities they secure is not explicitly advanced" (1565, see also Boccagni 2015).

Thus, the relationship between fleeting civil, or even convivial, interactions among people of different racial and ethnic categories and durable structures of inequality is not always apparent in research utilizing the super-diversity framework. Moreover, we are cautioned by Valentine (2008) to remain cognizant of the gap between superficial everyday practices of urban dwellers and their deeply held values and beliefs. Gidley (2013) points out that observation in public space alone as an ethnographic approach does not reveal key differences in private lives. Public behaviour and everyday routine interactions should certainly not be dismissed, yet how do we analyse and understand the significance of these interactions? Several recent US-based studies have focused on neighbourhoods that are diverse, have a reputation for tolerance, and celebrate their diversity. However, deeper analysis reveals that even there, socio-economic and racial inequality is reproduced through daily encounters and durable social structures (Mayorga-Gallo 2014; Tissot 2015; Zelner 2015). What do everyday interactions then say, if anything, about who has more access to power? Whose options in life are limited by structural inequality and discrimination, and whose are enhanced? Moreover, how do we answer these questions with ethnographic methodologies? I propose that the strengths of the super-diversity framework are maximized when it is situated within an urban culturalist approach (Borer 2006), with tools borrowed from ethnomethodology (West and Fenstermaker 1995) and symbolic interactionism (Anderson and Snow 2001).

First developed by Garfinkel (1988), ethnomethodology is a subfield of sociology focused on how people make meaning and produce social life in everyday settings. Since it rejects reifying social categories, it is an excellent fit for super-diversity as a methodological lens. At the same time, ethnomethodologists are interested in empirically studying how hierarchies and inequalities are maintained through using an ethnographic approach focused on everyday encounters. They investigate and compare the salience of social categories to see how seemingly objective social properties achieve their taken-for-grantedness (Zimmerman 1978). Particularly useful here is West and Fenstermaker's (1995) call to conceptualize "difference as an ongoing interactional accomplishment" (8). By looking at how people *do difference*, scholars can study how social categories take on their meaning in social interactions, and understand how these categories variably constrain people. Ultimately, these social categories are both an outcome of inequality and are used to rationalize inequality. This focus on the accomplishment of difference, rather than plotting the many simultaneous axes of super-diversity, promises to illuminate the mechanisms through which power hierarchies are produced and reproduced.

Symbolic interactionism, a related and at times overlapping micro-sociological tradition, situates the study of social interactions within social contexts. Goffman's (1959, 1971) theoretical and methodological approaches, for example, treat people as social actors who make decisions as they interpret social situations, interact, and "perform" their roles, rather than simply react to stimuli or be passive receptacles of dominant cultural categories. Ethnographic approaches that adopt this perspective can uncover the interplay of power in social interactions, trace patterns of inclusion and exclusion that directly affect material outcomes, and bring to light struggles over the very definitions of categories that structure interaction *and* access to resources (Anderson and Snow 2001).

Urban culturalism (Borer 2006, 2010) brings the interactionist approach to the study of the city and highlights the spatial dimension. Borer (2006) identifies six areas for urban culturalist research, three of which are useful here. The first is urban community and civic culture, exemplified by Mario Small's (2004) analysis of changing cultural frames that characterize the relationship of people to their neighbourhoods. The second is urban identities and lifestyles: how urban residents use place to construct their identities. The third area of urban culturalist research is attuned to how people cope with the complexity of urban life by making urban places meaningful through interactions and place design. Researchers who want to make sense of these meanings should observe reactions to places and interactions among actors (Borer 2006; Lofland 1998).

Altogether, these three sociological approaches promise to enrich the study of super-diversity by providing tools to analyse power hierarchies, stratification, and inequality without abandoning an ethnographic focus on the everyday in urban spaces.

Tracing power in a super-diverse community garden

Examples from my research help to illustrate these points. A community garden in Astoria, Queens, epitomized super-diversity: there were more than forty languages spoken by recent and long-term immigrants who gardened there, and the variation in socio-economic status, race, ethnicity, gender, sexuality, religion, and disability was remarkable. Whether or not this super-diversity is new in New York is arguable, and it is important not to overstate its influence (Foner 2017). By starting with an urban culturalist perspective that centres place, and using an ethnomethodological lens and an interactionist approach, I was able to move my analysis beyond description of the dizzying super-diversity to tracing local power inequalities. I did find that differences other than race and ethnicity mattered in the community garden context. At the same time, dominant societal hierarchies also found their way into what on the surface appeared to be a multicultural haven. In the process, I came to see the role of diversity as an ideology that served particular interests in the garden.

The community garden is located in a super-diverse Queens neighbourhood. Astoria's population is fifty-five per cent white, ten per cent black, sixteen per cent Asian, eighteen per cent other or multiple races, and thirty per cent Hispanic of all races (US Census Bureau 2016). Native Americans living in Queens were decimated by smallpox in the seventeenth century, and the area that became known as Astoria was settled by waves of European immigrants. Contemporary Astoria still bears the marks of immigration from Italy, and then Greece, which dominated in the early and mid-twentieth century, respectively (Alexiou 2013). No single immigrant group comes close to demographic dominance among more recent newcomers. Forty-six per cent of Astoria residents were born outside of the US, with the largest groups coming from Greece, Mexico, Ecuador, Colombia, Italy, and Bangladesh as well as North Africa (US Census Bureau 2016). Astoria is also home to a spatially segregated African American population, many of whom are migrants from the US South and their descendants. The last decade has seen an influx of affluent, largely non-Hispanic white residents who are attracted to Astoria's proximity to Manhattan. Developers turn old factories into upscale apartments and build brand new luxury developments. Local political leaders talk of Astoria's immigration-driven diversity as a laudable quality that distinguishes the neighbourhood, focusing on European-origin groups and rarely acknowledging the presence of African Americans.

At the time of my research, the community garden contained about 120 plots, used by individuals and groups, as well as several common spaces and a shared community plot. It was surrounded by a tall chain-link fence with a locked gate. As part of the New York City-regulated community garden system, the garden had to be open to the public at least twenty hours per week, allowing people who were not garden members to spend time there. The garden was run by an elected steering committee and overseen by a city-affiliated non-profit organization. I spent around 220 hours there as a participant observer from 2011 to 2013. I began my fieldwork as a volunteer in the shared community plot, eventually becoming a garden member and sharing a plot with another gardener. I am a white middle-class immigrant woman in my thirties who grew up in New York City. Different aspects of my identity shaped how respondents related to me and interpreted my presence in the field (Mayorga-Gallo and Hordge-Freeman 2017). I was variably seen as a fellow immigrant, a fellow "real" New Yorker (vis-à-vis gentrifiers), and a privileged white woman to either identify with or suspect. In addition to participant observation, I conducted seventeen semi-structured interviews with locals involved in various ways with the garden.

The visual and aural spectacle of the community garden communicates super-diversity. Visitors marvel at the many languages, ethnicities, ages, and the number of people with various physical and mental disabilities. Even long-time members of the garden sometimes remarked that this was a unique place for forming relationships with people very different from them. These sentiments were expressed, for instance, by members of a group that worked together to develop a new technology for converting compost into fuel: a working-class Chinese immigrant woman suffering the effects of a devastating accident, an African American man eking out a precarious living as an organizer in local public housing, and a second-generation child of European immigrants, an artist who had moved to Astoria before the full-fledged onset of gentrification. The parochial nature of the garden provided an opportunity to engage in a meaningful way across lines of difference, something that is usually more difficult in other public spaces like parks, sidewalks, and buses.

Taking an urban culturalist perspective focused my ethnographic research on people's meaning-making around place itself. By observing how people worked with the material space, how they talked about it to me and to each other, and by uncovering assumptions about what the space meant to them, I came to the conclusion that there were distinct and clashing ways of imagining the garden (Aptekar 2015). Some gardeners treated the garden primarily as a place to grow food. Others were concerned with aesthetics of green urbanism. I became sensitive to the varying ways that gardeners viewed the garden through observing everyday interactions, which revealed small and large tensions and shared norms that developed around this space. I tried to examine how people *did* super-diversity in everyday encounters, and, in the process, analysed which of the many differences among them mattered more than others, in what contexts, and how. I found that there were opportunities to disrupt dominant hierarchies, and gardeners with less power were sometimes able to draw on their localness and protected social status as elderly and/or disabled to defend and promote their interests. These instances of disruption were partly facilitated by alliances with more privileged gardeners who could use various forms of capital to lend legitimacy to their claims. Nevertheless, in interacting with each other and with the materiality of the space, gardeners tended to recreate entrenched hierarchies that structured the world outside the garden gates. Spoken and unspoken rules governing the space controlled the people in that space. These rules were ostensibly race-, gender-, and class-blind, yet were deeply influenced by these axes of inequality.

For example, one chilly November day, I was with three gardeners in the communal plot, planting garlic that would come up the following spring. Two of the three, both middle-aged Asian immigrant women, Mika (middle class and Japanese) and Tai (working class and Chinese), started to mark the small area that we had already planted. They placed a small tree branch in the ground and put an empty water bottle on top. The third woman, Becky, a white attorney in her early forties, rushed over and said: "No, you can't stick that up here. Take it down". Mika said: "We need to mark the area". To which Becky replied: "There are many ways to mark it better, like with markers in the cabinet". Mika and Tai did not respond, and although their facial expressions and body language betrayed irritation, they removed the recycled water bottle and found small popsicle sticks and twine. Becky did not object to these. This exchange was a clash of two garden visions. Primarily concerned with enhancing food production, Mika and Tai had tried to use immediately available materials to facilitate their planting task. For Becky, orderly and "natural" appearance of the garden was more important than functionality, even if it slowed down a repetitive task undertaken with fingers cramped with cold. The largely implicit rules about the way the garden should look privileged the aesthetic sensibilities of more affluent gardeners (Zukin 1998), who tended to be native-born whites originally from outside of New York. In this interaction, as in many others, there was a grudging deference to these seemingly neutral rules, which regulated people by regulating the space. Becky was one of the garden leaders and was periodically involved in censoring the appearance of Tai's plot, who was an avid recycler of "ugly" plastic materials. Becky's dominance in this encounter came both from her access to multiple forms of capital and the spatial regulation of the garden. Distinct power dynamics structured super-diverse encounters in ways that reproduced systems of domination shaped by race and class inequalities.[1]

In multiple everyday encounters, mostly without any overt conflict, these actors and many others negotiated difference among multiple dimensions. On the surface, it seemed that diverse people interacted with each other civilly, and the differences that mattered were not those so often privileged by social scientists. For instance, claims to localness or being known as a skilful gardener could be effectively used to leverage influence. But what was also clear is that larger societal inequalities, especially race and class, continued to be important in the garden and pointed to the dynamics of power in social interactions. In looking at how hierarchies and inequalities were maintained in everyday encounters, I came to understand the social categories that structured interactions, as well as access to valued outcomes.

The gardeners who had more power in the garden due to their class and race often employed their social, cultural, economic, and human capital to their advantage. They were able to get what they wanted: for the garden to look a certain way, for nonconforming gardeners to toe the aesthetic line, to control access to the garden, and even influence what plants would be cultivated. Not surprisingly, as recent research on the discourse of diversity suggests (Ahmed 2012; Bell and Hartmann 2007; Berrey 2015; Mayorga-Gallo 2014), perceptions and claims of diversity can help buttress inequitable realities. The city government-affiliated non-profit organization that oversaw this community garden encouraged gardens that reflected the diversity of the city, even intervening in those that appeared to be controlled by one ethnic group. As Martinez (2010) documents in a study of the Lower East Side, some gardens function as a restorative and resistive spaces for one ethnic community (e.g. Puerto Rican *casita* gardens), rather than formally regulated and open gardens favoured by non-profit organizations. Leaders of the Astoria garden could point to its racial and linguistic diversity to deflect criticism. One member of the steering committee – likely confiding in me as a perceived in-group member – explained to me that they did not have to worry about the city closing the garden down because city officials had their hands full with more problematic gardens. This garden, she said, had "its diversity going for it".

While technically public in the sense of providing open access, a space like the Astoria community garden, with semi-permeable physical, symbolic, and social boundaries fosters more deeply engaged relations than the fleeting encounters characteristic of many other public spaces. The garden is a clearly bounded space, where place-specific friendships developed and, in some cases, extended beyond the boundaries of the garden itself. Moreover, users actively worked with the design and material elements of the garden through such activities as weeding, pruning, and planting, presenting multiple opportunities to understand place-specific meaning-making and the ongoing accomplishment of difference that reproduced power inequalities. In the following section, I return to a very different site in Astoria, described in the opening section. Unlike the community garden, Socrates Sculpture Park is characterized by fleeting interaction or even non-interaction, which poses methodological difficulties.

Moving beyond fleeting interactions

Socrates Sculpture Park is a public park with open access, run by a private–public partnership that manages it as an exhibition space for new sculpture. A typical experience at the park opened this paper, illustrating the apparent super-diversity of park visitors and the non-conflictual tenor of the space. However, these impressions belied the ways in which the park replicated race and class inequalities through practices of exclusion, as well as through a context of class-specific consumption of cultural products. To uncover these dynamics below the surface of peaceful super-diversity, I again employed insights from ethnomethodology and symbolic interactionism, with a focus on meaning-making in and through space, everyday accomplishment of difference, and reproduction of inequality. It was also necessary to situate the park in its neighbourhood context and learn from people who avoided the park as well as those who visited it. I found that the diversity discourse itself was used to legitimate the park as an inclusive space that was attractive to the more affluent visitors.

Like the community garden, the park seemed, at first sight, to embody a setting where an inclusive super-diversity had become normalized and accepted. Park visitors appeared diverse in terms of race, ethnicity, class, gender, sexuality, if a bit less so by age and disability than people in the garden. There did not seem to be obvious conflicts among those who used the park. This strong impression of a convivial super-diverse space was illustrated by my disagreement with a film crew making a documentary about the neighbourhood's diversity. When reacting to my presentation of preliminary findings, which highlighted practices of direct and indirect exclusion, the filmmakers contested my assessment of the park. They argued that their, admittedly few, visits to the park revealed a remarkably inclusive diversity of humanity. They pointed, as an example, to the footage showing a white belly dancer, a group of young African American children, a middle-aged man with "Puerto Rico" embroidered on his hat, girls in hijabs, and a young white couple with a dog on a leash. However, my research, attuned to the ongoing accomplishment of difference and the interplay of power in interaction, revealed that this impression of super-diversity hid practices of exclusion.

While conducting the study, I spent approximately 100 hours of ethnographic fieldwork in the park between 2011 and 2013. I visited the park at different times of day and week, participating in organized activities, such as film screenings and classes, as well as unstructured activities, such as looking at the sculptures and waterfront views or eating lunch there. I conducted unstructured interviews with park users, and drew on semi-structured interviews with neighbourhood residents who did not use, but spoke to me about, the park. I also interviewed one staff member. As a white middle-class woman, my presence in this park was unremarkable, although it may have appeared less purposeful than that of other white middle-class women because I was not jogging, walking a dog, or caring for children.

Getting at the structures of power when studying a place with few enduring relationships was an ongoing challenge. Tracing the contours of inequality was difficult because so much of the interaction was fleeting. In understanding how people accomplished difference and reproduced inequalities in interaction, it was essential to understand the larger neighbourhood context around the park, its institutional history, and what the park meant to people who rarely or never went there, as well as those for whom it was a regular destination. As in my research in the community garden, I focused on how various kinds of differences operated as a way of getting at mechanisms through which inequality was reproduced. I found that more affluent, mostly white visitors (living locally or visiting) used the park more openly and freely than working-class immigrants and African Americans living nearby.

Locating and talking to those who did not use the park deviates from the approach taken by many parks researchers (e.g. Neal et al. 2015), but it proved crucial for identifying less obvious processes of exclusion. I came to realize that the occasional presence of groups of African American children, noted by the film crew as evidence of inclusion, signalled a youth programme on an organized visit, different from the more casual use of the park by white children and their caretakers. The presence of African American children without their parents actually highlighted how rare it was to see African American *families* in this park, even though it was only a short walk from a heavily African American area. Meanwhile, many white parents with young children who lived in the nearby new luxury housing routinely visited the park. Some working-class locals thought the park was like a museum with an entry fee, due to features such as a staffed tent at the entry, as well as a dearth of benches and the presence of strikingly modern sculptures (rather than the more traditional statues found in local parks). They thought it was normal for children to go to the park on an organized trip with a school group, but they did not feel comfortable going on their own. Many others did go to the park, but stayed at its literal margins, either on the prohibited side of the waterfront fence, or semi-hidden in the dense hedges that marked the boundary (Aptekar 2017).

Another example illustrates how urban culturalist analysis of interactions with material culture and between people helps illuminate inequalities in what might seem a convivial super-diverse space. I walked into the park with someone I met through the community garden. Alexis was a middle aged, Asian immigrant woman who worked assorted odd jobs like dog-sitting. She had grown up in an English-speaking Caribbean country and had lived in New York for many decades. At this time, one of the showcased artists had put up a large tent with Thai food given out to visitors without charge. There was no sign indicating this, and I only learned that the food was free when looking up the exhibit online later. Among other things, this exhibit was billed as celebrating local diversity, although it was referred to as the diversity of the larger borough of Queens, rather than the neighbourhood, and the selected restaurant was not Astoria-based.

Passing by the side of the tent, Alexis yelled out: "Any samples?" and was ignored by the uniformed workers inside. As we approached, she yelled her question again, and one of the women workers stared at Alexis. Smoothing over the awkwardness in a classic manner described by Goffman (1959), Alexis shrugged and said: "Oh well, I guess they don't hear me". A few moments later, we walked through an exhibit featuring miniature versions of local smokestacks. It was crowded with predominantly white visitors, who appeared middle class. Alexis became frustrated by the signage, which was not obviously connected to the smokestacks: "Why do they write stuff like this? How are we supposed to know what they mean?". Right after that, two young Latino people staffing the tent at the main entrance asked us if we wanted a t-shirt with the exhibit logo on it. Alexis asked whether it was free, and they said no. Alexis's frustrated attempts to make sense of the park point to indirect practices of exclusion stemming from class-specific cultural consumption norms. The material content and social norms of public spaces contribute to spaces that satisfy cultural preferences patterned by class (Zukin 1995). No one bars Alexis from entering and enjoying the park, but her expectations and understandings, at least in this case, do not mesh well with the unspoken norms and rules governing this space, which articulate far more comfortably with the expectations of more affluent visitors.

The delivery of diversity, often through food, for cultural consumption was part of the strategy of putting the park on New York's competitive cultural map. This diversity tended to be conceptualized as diversity of the iconically diverse larger borough of Queens, rather than the immediate neighbourhood. The emphasis was on immigration-driven diversity with only a rare mention of African Americans, thereby having the effect of reinforcing racial divisions. Demonstrable engagement with the local community, such as through programming for local minority children – while undoubtedly enriching the cultural experiences of these children – was also part of crafting an image of the park as a diverse and authentic attraction. Research shows that ethnic and racial diversity is attractive as a neighbourhood amenity to new affluent residents (Brown-Saracino 2010; Zukin 1995).

Digging beyond the appearance of convivial super-diversity in this site necessitated expanding beyond the urban space under study. Walking through the neighbourhood with an informant (Low 2015; Neal et al. 2015), and observing her interact with physical elements of the park and actively interpret situations as they arose, allowed me to parse the ways in which inequality is reproduced in everyday encounters. More specifically, I was able to see how the sometimes subtle practices of exclusion shaped meaning-making practices of marginalized urban residents. Situating the park within the residential patterns of the surrounding neighbourhood and comparison with other local public places enabled me to note the differences in use of the park by different groups. Goals and strategies of the park leadership, gathered through interviews and secondary material, such as the park website, pamphlets, and media articles, were also useful for understanding how diversity as a concept was used to frame the park as an attractive and authentic space.

Super-diversity: a few cautions

I used the examples of the community garden and the sculpture park to show some of the ways the super-diversity lens can be used methodologically without losing sight of inequality. There are benefits to employing the concept of super-diversity, including its focus on emergent differences and social categories, as well as attention to how they may actually matter to people in contexts of complex and dynamic interplay among multiple variables (Vertovec 2007). This focus meshes well with sociological approaches grounded in traditions of ethnomethodology and symbolic interactionism, particularly when centred in urban space. Ethnographic study of everyday interactions in highly diverse spaces can tell us about inequalities in access to power and life chances, provided that scholars consider and contextualize meaning-making practices of social actors. In contrast to Meissner's (2015) call to investigate "social patterns that are not necessarily marked by perceived inequalities" (557), it is critical to emphasize that super-diversity goes hand in hand with inequality.

This means that being open to a wide range of social categories in super-diverse urban spaces must be combined with a clear-eyed focus on and understanding of macro patterns of stratification. Super-diversity is a descriptive concept that draws attention to the multiplicity of intersecting social categories in global cities. It helps scholars move away from traditional analyses of race, class, and gender inequalities towards investigations of emergent categories and the lived everyday complexity on the scale of urban places. This can be valuable and innovative, particularly as a corrective to the reification of ethnicity in traditional migration studies. At the same time, traditional migration studies are criticized by critical race theorists for turning a blind eye on the processes of racialization and structural racism (e.g. Treitler 2015). If scholars of super-diversity turn away from persistent inequalities that continue to structure super-diverse contexts and dismiss research that analyses race, class, and gender inequalities as outdated, they will rightly face the same criticism. For instance, instead of critiquing intersectionality for focusing too much on traditional categories, as Meissner and Vertovec (2015) do, scholars of super-diversity should embrace an emphasis on matrices of oppression highlighted by intersectional approaches (Crenshaw 1989).

In both research sites described in this paper, it became clear that diversity as a concept was used to reproduce dominant power hierarchies. In the community garden, gardeners with more access to various forms of capital used diversity discourse as a signal to the authorities that the status quo in the management of the garden need not be scrutinized for fairness. In the sculpture park, diversity discourse was used by park staff to promote the park as a site of cultural consumption with marketable authenticity. Notably, Vertovec (2007) writes that the city of London used its diversity to make a successful bid for the 2012 Olympic Games. This use of diversity to sell the city as attractive was a new development, even as the detrimental effects of Olympic Games on the more powerless members of hosting communities are well documented (Kennelly and Watt 2011; Minnaert 2012). On a much smaller scale, Socrates Sculpture Park and the community garden are also using the discourse of diversity in ways that support a vision of public space that benefits more powerful members of society.

Although super-diversity is a term born of scholarly pursuits, it has now crossed over into policy and public arenas, particularly in the European context (Meissner and Vertovec 2015). Future work should investigate the use of super-diversity beyond academia, such as Boccagni's (2015) critique of its use in social work. Existing research indicates that the flexible and multivalent concept of diversity can obscure practices of oppression and exclusion. Berrey (2015) shows that commitment to diversity in a Chicago housing redevelopment actually works to undermine demands for racial justice and does little to remedy enduring structures of inequality. Mayorga-Gallo's (2014) research in a diverse neighbourhood in North Carolina demonstrates that discourses of diversity support white homeowners' privilege. Diversity language is used to exacerbate inequalities in higher education, both in the US, where Warikoo (2016) shows how elite universities turn diversity into a commodity, undermining policies that seek to redress social injustice, and in the UK and Australia, where Ahmed (2012) reveals how the language of diversity is used to reproduce structural racism. In what ways and through which configurations of policies can super-diversity operate in a similar way, especially in light of Ndhlovu's (2016) criticism of super-diversity as marked by "colonial matrices of power" (33)? Further, what work can super-diversity do, as a scholarly tool and discursive formation, to illuminate or obfuscate processes of inequality inherent in capitalist regimes where borders are porous to wealth and the wealthy but sometimes deadly to the poor? In this article, I have argued for the merits of super-diversity as a methodological lens, provided it is combined with a set of methodological tools that sharpen its ability to examine the role of enduring inequalities and ensure a vigilance against lapsing into uncritical celebrations of conviviality.

Note

1. Gender, too, is key to understanding power dynamics in the community garden and beyond, but I limit my discussion to race and class here.

Acknowledgements

The author thanks the four anonymous reviewers and the participants of the Workshop on Superdiversity: A Transatlantic Conversation, where an earlier version of this paper was presented.

Disclosure statement

No potential conflict of interest was reported by the author.

Funding

Research for this article was undertaken within the GlobaldiverCities Project (http://www.mmg.mpg.de/subsites/globaldivercities/about/) funded by the European Research Council Advanced Grant [269784], awarded to Prof. Steven Vertovec and based at the Max Planck Institute for the Study of Religious and Ethnic Diversity, Göttingen, Germany (www.mmg.mpg.de).

References

Acosta-García, Raúl, and Esperanza Martínez-Ortiz. 2015. "Mexico Through a Superdiversity Lens: Already-Existing Diversity Meets New Immigration." *Ethnic and Racial Studies* 38 (4): 636–649.
Ahmed, Sarah. 2012. *On Being Included: Racism and Diversity in Institutional Life.* Durham, NC: Duke University Press.
Alexiou, Nicholas. 2013. "Greek Immigration in the United States: A Historical Overview." Hellenic-American Oral History Project: Greek Americans, Queens College, City University of New York. http://www.qc.cuny.edu/Academics/Degrees/DSS/Sociology/GreekOralHistory/Pages/Research.aspx.
Anderson, Leon, and David Snow. 2001. "Inequality and the Self: Exploring Connections from an Interactionist Perspective." *Symbolic Interaction* 24 (4): 395–406.
Aptekar, Sofya. 2015. "Visions of Public Space: Reproducing and Resisting Social Hierarchies in a Community Garden." *Sociological Forum* 30 (1): 209–227.
Aptekar, Sofya. 2017. "Looking Forward, Looking Back: Collective Memory and Neighborhood Identity in Two Urban Parks." *Symbolic Interaction* 40 (1): 101–121.
Bell, Joyce, and Douglas Hartmann. 2007. "Diversity in Everyday Discourse: The Cultural Ambiguities and Consequences of 'Happy Talk'." *American Sociological Review* 72 (6): 895–914.
Berg, Mette Louise, and Nando Sigona. 2013. "Ethnography, Diversity and Urban Space." *Identities* 20 (4): 347–360.
Berrey, Ellen. 2015. *The Enigma of Diversity: The Language of Race and the Limits of Racial Justice.* Chicago, IL: University of Chicago Press.
Biehl, Kristen Sarah. 2015. "Spatializing Diversities, Diversifying Spaces: Housing Experiences and Home Space Perceptions in a Migrant Hub of Istanbul." *Ethnic and Racial Studies* 38 (4): 596–607.
Boccagni, Paolo. 2015. "(Super)Diversity and the Migration–Social Work Nexus: A New Lens on the Field of Access and Inclusion?" *Ethnic and Racial Studies* 38 (4): 608–620.
Borer, Michael. 2006. "The Location of Culture: The Urban Culturalist Perspective." *City and Community* 5 (2): 173–197.

Borer, Michael. 2010. "From Collective Memory to Collective Imagination: Time, Place, and Urban Redevelopment." *Symbolic Interaction* 33 (1): 96–114.

Brown-Saracino, Japonica. 2010. *A Neighborhood That Never Changes: Gentrification, Social Preservation, and the Search for Authenticity*. Chicago, IL: University of Chicago Press.

Crenshaw, Kimberly. 1989. "Demarginalizing the Intersection of Race and Sex: A Black Feminist Critique of Antidiscrimination Doctrine, Feminist Theory and Antiracist Politics." *The University of Chicago Legal Forum* 1989: 139–167.

Foner, Nancy. 2017. "A Research Comment: What's New About Super-diversity?" *Journal of American Ethnic History* 36 (4): 49–57.

Fortier, Anne-Marie. 2008. *Multicultural Horizons: Diversity and the Limits of the Civil Nation*. London: Routledge.

Garfinkel, Harold. 1988. "Evidence for Locally Produced, Naturally Accountable Phenomena of Order, Logic, Reason, Meaning, Method, Etc. in and as of the Essential Quiddity of Immortal Ordinary Society, (I of IV): An Announcement of Studies." *Sociological Theory* 6 (1): 103–109.

Gidley, Ben. 2013. "Landscapes of Belonging, Portraits of Life: Researching Everyday Multiculture in an Inner City Estate." *Identities* 20 (4): 361–376.

Gilroy, Paul. 2004. *After Empire: Melancholia or Convivial Culture?* London: Routledge.

Goffman, Erving. 1959. *The Presentation of Self in Everyday Life*. New York: Doubleday.

Goffman, Erving. 1971. *Relations in Public: Microstudies of the Public Order*. New York: Basic Books.

Hall, Suzanne M. 2017. "Mooring 'Super-Diversity' to a Brutal Migration Milieu." *Ethnic and Racial Studies* 40 (9): 1562–1573.

Jones, Hannah, Sarah Neal, Giles Mohan, Kieran Connell, Allan Cochrane, and Katy Bennett. 2015. "Urban Multiculture and Everyday Encounters in Semi-public, Franchised Cafe Spaces." *The Sociological Review* 63 (3): 644–661.

Kennelly, Jacqueline, and Paul Watt. 2011. "Sanitizing Public Space in Olympic Host Cities: The Spatial Experiences of Marginalized Youth in 2010 Vancouver and 2012 London." *Sociology* 45 (5): 765–781.

Lofland, Lyn. 1998. *The Public Realm: Exploring the City's Quintessential Social Territory*. Hawthorne, NY: Aldine de Gruyter.

Low, Kelvin. 2015. "The Sensuous City: Sensory Methodologies in Urban Ethnographic Research." *Ethnography* 16 (3): 295–312.

Makoni, Sinfree. 2012. "A Critique of Language, Languaging and Supervernacular." *Muitas Vozes, Ponta Grossa* 1 (2): 189–199.

Martinez, Miranda. 2010. *Power at the Roots: Gentrification, Community Gardens, and the Puerto Ricans of the Lower East Side*. Lanham, MD: Lexington Books.

Mayorga-Gallo, Sarah. 2014. *Behind the White Picket Fence: Power and Privilege in a Multiethnic Neighborhood*. Chapel Hill: University of North Carolina Press.

Mayorga-Gallo, Sarah, and Elizabeth Hordge-Freeman. 2017. "Between Marginality and Privilege: Gaining Access and Navigating the Field in Multiethnic Settings." *Qualitative Research* 17 (4): 377–394.

Meissner, Fran. 2015. "Migration in Migration-Related Diversity? The Nexus between Superdiversity and Migration Studies." *Ethnic and Racial Studies* 38 (4): 556–567.

Meissner, Fran, and Steven Vertovec. 2015. "Comparing Super-diversity." *Ethnic and Racial Studies* 38 (4): 541–555.

Minnaert, Lynn. 2012. "An Olympic Legacy for All? The Non-infrastructural Outcomes of the Olympic Games for Socially Excluded Groups (Atlanta 1996–Beijing 2008)." *Tourism Management* 33 (2): 361–370.

Ndhlovu, Finex. 2016. "A Decolonial Critique of Diaspora Identity Theories and the Notion of Superdiversity." *Diaspora Studies* 9 (1): 28–40.

Neal, Sarah, Katy Bennett, Allan Cochrane, and Giles Mohan. 2013. "Living Multiculture: Understanding the New Spatial and Social Relations of Ethnicity and Multiculture in England." *Environment and Planning C: Government and Policy* 31: 308–323.

Neal, Sarah, Katy Bennett, Hannah Jones, Allan Cochrane, and Giles Mohan. 2015. "Multiculture and Public Parks: Researching Super-Diversity and Attachment in Public Green Space." *Population, Space and Place* 21 (5): 463–475.

Padilla, Beatriz, Joana Azevedo, and Antonia Olmos-Alcaraz. 2015. "Superdiversity and Conviviality: Exploring Frameworks for Doing Ethnography in Southern European Intercultural Cities." *Ethnic and Racial Studies* 38 (4): 621–635.

Small, Mario Luis. 2004. *Villa Victoria: The Transformation of Social Capital in a Boston Barrio.* Chicago, IL: University of Chicago Press.

Tissot, Sylvie. 2015. *Good Neighbors: Gentrifying Diversity in Boston's South End.* New York: Verso Books.

Treitler, Vilna Bashi. 2015. "Social Agency and White Supremacy in Immigration Studies." *Sociology of Race and Ethnicity* 1 (1): 153–165.

US Census Bureau. 2016. "2008–2012 American Community Survey." Summary File. US Census Bureau's American Community Survey Office.

Valentine, Gill. 2008. "Living with Difference: Reflections on Geographies of Encounter." *Progress in Human Geography* 32 (3): 323–337.

Vertovec, Steven. 2007. "Super-Diversity and Its Implications." *Ethnic and Racial Studies* 30 (6): 1024–1054.

Warikoo, Natasha. 2016. *The Diversity Bargain: And Other Dilemmas of Race, Admissions, and Meritocracy at Elite Universities.* Chicago, IL: University of Chicago Press.

Wessendorf, Susanne. 2014. *Commonplace Diversity: Social Relations in a Super-Diverse Context.* Basingstoke: Palgrave Macmillan.

West, Candace, and Sarah Fenstermaker. 1995. "Doing Difference." *Gender & Society* 9 (1): 8–37.

Wilson, Helen. 2011. "Passing Propinquities in the Multicultural City: The Everyday Encounters of Bus Passengering." *Environment and Planning A* 43: 634–649.

Zelner, Sarah. 2015. "The Perpetuation of Neighborhood Reputation: An Interactionist Approach." *Symbolic Interaction* 38 (4): 575–593.

Zimmerman, Don. 1978. "Ethnomethodology." *The American Sociologist* 13 (1): 6–15.

Zukin, Sharon. 1995. *The Culture of Cities.* Cambridge, MA: Blackwell.

Zukin, Sharon. 1998. "Urban Lifestyles: Diversity and Standardisation in Spaces of Consumption." *Urban Studies* 35 (5–6): 825–839.

◌ OPEN ACCESS

A discourse of displacement: super-diversity, urban citizenship, and the politics of autochthony in Amsterdam

Paul Mepschen

ABSTRACT
The notion of super-diversity has been employed to describe the urban condition in cities across the world. By focusing on the politics of culturalization in the Netherlands, I engage with scholars who claim that super-diversity may lead to a normalcy of difference. I argue that in the Netherlands a culturalist common sense has emerged which divides Dutch society into distinct and internally homogeneous cultures and which represents Dutch culture as a threatened entity that must be protected against the mores and moralities of minoritized, racialized outsiders. Focusing on working-class whites in a neighbourhood in Amsterdam, I show how plans to demolish and restructure their neighbourhood fuelled a discourse of displacement in antagonistic relation to "Others". Rather than normalizing differences, this culturalist common sense has brought into being a field of knowledge and both reflected and supported views that produce and reinforce boundaries between "ordinary" neighbours and cultural and social others.

Following local elections in March 2011, Dutch Prime Minister Mark Rutte bore witness to the far-reaching transformation of political discourse in the Netherlands over the past few decades. In response to the electoral victory of his free-market, conservative-liberal party, VVD, Rutte stated: "We are going to give this beautiful country back to the Dutch, because that is our project." His words echoed an earlier promise he had made when presenting his first cabinet back in October 2010 to "give the country back to hard-working Dutchmen". Rutte's statement exemplified the normalization of exclusionary politics built on an image of "the people" – in this case, the rhetorical figure

---

This is an Open Access article distributed under the terms of the Creative Commons Attribution-NonCommercial-NoDerivatives License (http://creativecommons.org/licenses/by-nc-nd/4.0/), which permits non-commercial re-use, distribution, and reproduction in any medium, provided the original work is properly cited, and is not altered, transformed, or built upon in any way.

of the hardworking Dutchman. The people referred to in this political discourse, it must be emphasized, do not form "a shapeless demos, but a specific *ethnos*, or *natio*" (Farris 2017, 66). They are autochthonous, that is, "born from the soil" (Geschiere 2009).

The figure of the hardworking ordinary Dutchman also plays a central role in the rhetoric of the rightwing populist Freedom Party (*Partij voor de Vrijheid*, PVV). Its leader and single member, Geert Wilders, has for many years claimed to represent "hardworking Dutch people" like "Henk and Ingrid" (sometimes "Henk and Anja"). Wilders argues: "We choose for the people who don't have it easy [*die het niet cadeau krijgen*]. Not for the elite, but for Henk and Ingrid." Wilders' discourse draws boundaries between "ordinary people" and pluralist elites as well as between "white autochthones" and people of migrant background. "Henk and Ingrid", Wilders once famously said, "have to pay for Ahmed and Fatima. They have a right to a safer Netherlands that is more Dutch". Class and cultural boundaries thus merge in a discourse that gives rise to rightwing populism and its social persona: the ordinary everyman, "originally Dutch", and assumed to be white. This representation raises important questions for the social-scientific study of difference and diversity.

In this article, I will discuss the complex relationship between super-diversity – which seems to hold the promise of a *normalization* of difference as diversity becomes a fact of life while the very notion of a majoritarian culture loses significance – and the re-emergence of nativist and culturalist perspectives that impose meaning in everyday, local settings.

Super-diversity and the culturalization of citizenship

The rise of nativist and culturalist populisms to political prominence demands analysis of the politics and discourses that inform the reconstruction and politicization of majoritarian identities in Europe (Mepschen 2016a, 2016b). The study of the condition of super-diversity (e.g. Vertovec 2007; Wessendorf 2014; Meissner and Vertovec 2015; Crul 2016) should therefore not overlook new articulations of cultural essentialism (Hall 1992) or ethnic absolutism (Gilroy 1987) – which are made visible in the growing political strength of rightist and populist movements and parties all over Europe (e.g. Shoshan 2016). I thus begin by discussing the relationship between different but related bodies of literature concerning these questions: the literature focusing on super-diversity and the work on the culturalization of citizenship in contemporary Europe (Duyvendak, Geschiere, and Tonkens 2016).

The concept of super-diversity must, in the first place, be seen as descriptive (Wessendorf 2014). As Meissner and Vertovec argue, the notion describes the "new multicultural condition of the twenty-first century" (2015, 542). One of the most influential concepts that has emerged in recent years to describe the urban condition in the era of late-capitalist globalization and mass-immigration, the concept holds the promise of making sense of the heterogeneity of urban experience today. It points to a diversification of diversity, characterizing the lived reality of an increasing number of people in urban areas across the world. The concept, it is argued, provides "a lens to describe an exceptional demographic situation characterized by the multiplication of social categories within specific localities" (Wessendorf 2014, 1). One of its strengths, therefore, is that it is enables scholars to move beyond the ethno-focal lens that has long been dominant in the study of migrant politics and identities. From this perspective, the term is not simply descriptive, but can also be read as critical: if taken seriously it has important methodological and epistemological consequences for the study of multiculturalism, ethnic diversity, and cultural essentialism (cf. Back and Samsher 2016). It forces scholars to move beyond ethno-focal assumptions, to take seriously the various differentiations within communities and groups, and necessitates an unfreezing of the "static, substantialist categories that deny the fluidity – hence, the mutability, of figurational patternings" (Emirbayer 1997, 308).

There is resonance here with the critical work that has been done on the culturalization of citizenship (e.g. Beekers 2015; Balkenhol, Mepschen, and Duyvendak 2016; Duyvendak, Geschiere, and Tonkens 2016; Mepschen, 2016a; Modest and Koning 2016; Van Reekum 2016; Vollebergh 2016). The latter concept gives name to the ascent of a discursive genre, an interpretive frame, that carves up societies in distinct, internally homogeneous and delimited cultures, and that represents native cultures as threatened entities that must be protected against the allegedly deviant mores and moralities of minoritized and racialized outsiders. Central to the process of culturalization is the mobilization of a notion of culture as an integral whole – a static totality – and the equation of social groups with a particular ethnos and a reified culture. Such reified cultural frameworks ignore the relational, processual, and conflictual character of community and identity formation. They simplify reality by creating an illusion of cultural unity, reducing cultural others to a knowable and perceivable essence.

Gerd Baumann's critique of essentialist and totalizing conceptions of culture, and the alternative he formulates, shares some of the perspectives developed within the super-diversity framework. Baumann advocates an understanding of culture as a "triple helix in perpetual motion" (2007). Cultures, he argues, always have to "strike new balances among three factors: changing material circumstances ('survival'), changing motivations and cognitive structures ('sense-making'), and changing patterns of action and behaviour ('agency')" (Baumann 2007, 112). The three elements of this helix constantly act upon each other: change is the key-word here and culture is always in motion. It is not an essence but a process. This understanding of culture as a "perpetuum mobile" (Baumann 2007), as dynamic, processual, and historical, is at odds with the substantialist and nativist use of culture in culturalist, ethno-focal discourses used by both politicians and scholars alike. In the Netherlands, social research in the fields of ethnicity and integration has sometimes suffered from a lack of reflexive analysis and therefore from a form of analytic naturalization. One of the consequences has been that whiteness has long been ignored as an object of study and analysis. Whiteness has not been understood as a social construct but as "the standard against which all other categories are (implicitly) compared" (Emirbayer and Desmond 2012, 6).

This assessment is highly relevant for the research on the culturalization of citizenship and autochthony in the Netherlands. Like whiteness, autochthony has implicitly (and sometimes explicitly) functioned as the un-reflexive norm, a neutral category, a natural fact without a history or relational context. Thus, it functions, like whiteness, as a reference category (Emirbayer and Desmond 2012; Wekker 2016) against which "othered" cultures can be measured, or a cultural whole into which minoritized and racialized "others" can be reasonably expected to integrate. Willem Schinkel has pointed out that, unlike the supposed cultures and ethnicities of Others, autochthony is not understood as an ethnos; it denotes the sense that everything that is not autochthonous is automatically "ethnic", while autochthony itself is exempt from ethnicity and as a result from social-scientific scrutiny (Schinkel 2007, 172–174). As Schinkel points out, much research on migrant integration has a tendency to reproduce this differentiation mechanism, in which society is divided into allochthonous (ethnic/cultural, outside) and autochthonous (neutral/inside) parts (cf. Geschiere 2009, 130–168).

As Richard Alba and Jan Willem Duyvendak suggest (2018), scholars working with the concept of super-diversity tend to ignore majoritarian discourses and groups in the study of ethnicity and diversity. As Alba and Duyvendak point out, the super-diversity lens focuses mostly on horizontal processes of living together. From that perspective, it might be true that increasingly – in super-diverse European cities – there is no such thing as a mainstream culture or a dominant ethnic group. Certainly, this is increasingly true in a demographic sense. But this approach does not take into full account the question of symbolic and institutional power – including racism. Rather than a situation in which "everybody will adapt to everyone" (Crul 2016), we see ever stricter discursive and institutional reinforcements of particular conceptions of majoritarian national cultures – in the form of stringent immigration and integration policies for instance. These transformations at the level of public discourse and policy have important effects at the level of people's everyday lives (Mepschen 2016c).

Susanne Wessendorf, in her study of diversity in Hackney, argues that in that part of London – where she lives and works – diversity has become commonplace (2014): "Diversity has become habitual and part of the everyday human landscape" (Wessendorf 2014, 3). By focusing on what I call the culturalization of everyday life in an Amsterdam neighbourhood in New West,

I stress a different aspect, one that Wessendorf also alludes to when she argues that, even in Hackney, in the private realm, cultural particularity and boundary construction remain the dominant modes of negotiating diversity. One aspect of Amsterdam New West that struck me was that so few people that I spoke with exhibited any indifference to difference. The powerful emergence of autochthony in the Netherlands stands in contrast, it seems to me, with Wessendorf's notion that in Hackney 'almost everybody comes from elsewhere' (2014, 2). Autochthony precisely denotes a clear and powerful boundary between those who come from elsewhere and those who can claim to have been "born from the soil" and thus to be home in the nation (cf. Geschiere 2009; Duyvendak 2011). This boundary between so-called autochthonous and allochthonous residents plays a key role in everyday discourse, especially among people ethnicized as autochthonous in New West. That is to say, the way people negotiate self-understanding and alterity in everyday life is intimately entwined with political and public discourse, which imposes meaning upon everyday life.

In what follows, I focus on the perspectives of the autochthonous residents of Amsterdam New West and show how plans to demolish and restructure their neighbourhood fuelled a discourse of displacement in antagonistic relation to "Others", that is, native elites as well as post-migrant neighbours. Rather than normalizing differences, this culturalist common sense brings into being a field of knowledge and emphasizes particular views that enable people to distinguish between "ordinary" neighbours and cultural others. This furthermore structures how people perceive and interpret the social and political problems they encounter in everyday life in the neighbourhood, while mobilizing particular attitudes vis-a-vis Others.

A discourse of displacement

My analysis of Amsterdam New West builds on eighteen months of ethnographic fieldwork in 2009–2011 in this super-diverse area also known as the Western Garden Cities, which was built after 1950 under an urban expansion plan based on the garden city model (Mepschen 2016a). I lived in the district for five months, although data collection took place in a period of mostly fulltime, day-to-day research during the entire eighteen months in the field. Participant observation was a central part of the research. For instance, I worked as a volunteer in the neighbourhood museum, leading neighbourhood tours and helping out in the museum. I was also involved in numerous neighbourhood meetings and got to know a large number of residents in the neighbourhood personally. I interviewed over eighty local residents, officials, and neighbourhood activists – many of them more than once. I also "hung out" and chatted with people in coffee bars, during events, and in their homes, which gave me access to tacit and everyday forms of experience and knowledge. While starting out with "grand tour" observations, after four months I chose a number of case studies to focus on. The case I zoom in on below draws on one of these case studies. The ethnographic data I discuss are based on "close-up observation in real time and space" (Wacquant 2004, 388) and "sustained immersion into the everyday realities" of the neighbourhood (Wacquant 2004, 389).

In the late summer of 2009, I visited a festival on Plein 40–45, a central square in Slotermeer, the oldest neighbourhood of Amsterdam New West. Organized by the local municipality to celebrate urban renewal, banners and flyers proclaimed "*Slotermeer verandert*" (Slotermeer is changing). Colourful pamphlets, images, and videos depicted the planned future of the neighbourhood. A local folk dance group performed; children had their faces painted and climbed and jumped on a bouncy castle. Neighbourhood organizations presented themselves and local administrators explained how their policies would make things better, safer, and more beautiful. But on the margins of the festival, I encountered a group of residents who felt the less festive side of the politics of urban regeneration, residents who were attached to the neighbourhood but would be forced to leave their homes and community should the renewal plans be ratified. This group – mostly "white" residents of three quarters Slotermeer, the Louis Couperusbuurt, and two neighbouring sections – used the occasion of the festival to show their resistance to the plans for urban renewal.

The Louis Couperusbuurt at the time consisted of 670 homes: almost all basic, low-rent apartments owned by semi-public housing corporations. The plans to renew the quarter designated most of these homes for demolition. In their place, a completely new neighbourhood would emerge – higher, more spacious, more beautiful, and for the most part, more expensive. Much of the low-rent public housing would be replaced by owner-occupied and high-rent apartments.

A central figure in the resistance was Rick, whom I first met at the festival. Rick[1] was a born Amsterdammer, 50 years old, sharing a low-rent apartment in the quarter with his partner and three cats. The two-room apartment of 32 square metres was small, as Rick put it, but he appreciated his little garden, the green surroundings, and the hassle-free parking. Like other parts of New West, the Louis Couperusbuurt was green and spacious, reflecting the priority given to green spaces in the original planning (cf. Feddes 2011). Rick was a foreman at a company that constructed public gardens and courtyards in urban renewal areas; he knew from personal experience that urban restructuring was on the Amsterdam agenda. Rick had known many people who had been "demolished away" (*weggesloopt*) or "deported" (*gedeporteerd*) – as he and other critics of urban renewal often termed it. Nevertheless, he had not expected "renewal mania" (*sloopwaanzin*) to come his way. Rick saw his neighbourhood as quiet, respectable, and ordinary: *"netjes en gewoon*". The fact that almost half of the residents of the Couperusbuurt were of (post-)migrant origin notwithstanding, he told me several times that he perceived the quarter to be predominantly "white". "The neighborhood here is for the greatest part white people." I will return to this use of the notion of whiteness below.

Rick emphasized that he saw most of his neighbours as hard-working people who had a job to go to in the morning. "Sixty per cent of the people here have a job. The other forty per cent are either too old to work or are jobless. And it's the jobless people who are causing trouble!" Rick felt that he and his "hardworking", "ordinary" neighbours were being punished for the unruly behaviour of a small group of residents. He emphasized that the neighbourhood was a quarter of ordinary Amsterdammers (*gewone Amsterdammers*). He impressed upon me, several times, that most of his neighbours did not cause trouble. I asked Rick about Mohammed Bouyeri, the Dutch-Moroccan, self-proclaimed Islamist who was living in the Louis Couperusbuurt in 2004 when he murdered the filmmaker Theo van Gogh (cf. Buruma 2006; Stengs 2009). That had caused an uproar in the neighbourhood, with journalists and television crews suddenly roaming the quarter looking for "the ghetto". Rick asked:

> Because one lunatic Moroccan lived here it is supposed to be a bad neighborhood? [...] I cannot understand the position that indeed Mohammed B. lived here and we are blamed for that ... What does it prove? What does it prove?

Rick defended the respectability of the Louis Couperusbuurt and spoke of the demolition plans in terms of disrespect and displacement: "What in my eyes is happening is that the people who live here are being evicted and pushed back into deprived neighborhoods." In contrast to the discursive construction of New West as disadvantaged and troubled, Rick saw the deprived neighbourhoods as located elsewhere. The Louis Couperusbuurt, in his eyes, was a respectable place.

Super-diverse, working-class neighbourhoods in the Netherlands such as the Louis Couperusbuurt are seen to reflect a society in crisis (cf. De Koning 2013). They figure in public discourse and the popular imagination as the stages on which a "multicultural drama" is being played out, revealing that Dutch society does not have its house in order (Duyvendak 2011) and that the body social is sick (Schinkel 2007). Indeed, these neighbourhoods figure in public representation as sites of social disintegration and a developing culture of poverty (Blokland-Potters 1998). Many forms of social anxiety, insecurity, and fear are projected onto these polyethnic, "disadvantaged" spaces: the alleged crumbling of social cohesion, insecurity about national identity, the rise of Islam in the public sphere, and problems with migration, segregation, and integration (see Van Eijk 2010; Mepschen 2016a). It is in this context that Rick's remarks that his neighbours were mostly "white" must be understood. It points to the close relationship that in the Netherlands is suggested between the respectability of a neighbourhood and the number of racialized individuals living in it. As Justus Uitermark has pointed out, indexes that calculate the "livability" of neighbourhoods consider the high concentration of "non-western allochthones" as a factor for a lower score (see Uitermark 2011). Rick's strategy to defend the respectability and "livability" of his neighbourhood by denying the multiethnic character of the quarter resonates with an increasingly dominant discourse that associates super-diversity with social problems, disintegration, and a lack of livability.

Urban regeneration and renewal, the buzzwords of the large-scale urban restructuring that aimed to generate greater class and cultural heterogeneity and set in motion a process of gentrification are considered vital - in the eyes of the city government and urban planners – to improving livability in these Amsterdam New West quarters (e.g. Blokland-Potters 1998; Oudenampsen 2010; Van Eijk 2010; Uitermark 2011). Until the 1990s, New West had comparatively low levels of unemployment, social marginalization, and petty crime (Hellinga 2005). But beginning in 1990, the Amsterdam municipal services, local district boards, and city advisors began drawing "doomsday scenarios" (Hellinga 2005, 8) for the future of New West. A new narrative emerged portraying the postwar areas of Amsterdam, where it was feared that physical decline of the housing stock and accumulating social problems would lead to a downward spiral and ghettoization. The concentration of low-rent public housing and the projected growth of the share of ethnic minorities were deemed perilous to stability in what came to be called "concentration neighborhoods" (see Uitermark 2003).

To facilitate the social management of such areas – and to improve their position within the urban housing market – the city government embraced the large-scale socio-spatial restructuring of these neighbourhoods. In the so-called development areas – the parts of the city, including New West, that were considered weakest – restructuring entailed the demolition of social housing and the construction of owner-occupied and high-rent homes. This change in policy orientation can be seen as a shift from "social to spatial make-ability" (Oudenampsen 2010). Whereas the former combined the wish to regulate the city with efforts to emancipate and regulate its inhabitants, the latter focused on the gentrification of specific areas to attract more desirable residents. Urban renewal in working-class and culturally diverse neighbourhoods thus no longer focused primarily on the population currently residing there, but on envisioned future residents. It is in this context that the case of the Louis Couperusbuurt (one quarter in the New West district called Slotermeer) and the resistance of its residents must be understood.

Active resistance to the demolition plans was concentrated among working- and middle-class whites over the age of fifty who were not only emotionally attached to the neighbourhood, but also had much to lose in terms of their financial well-being and lifestyles. As I have detailed elsewhere (2012, 2016a), their lack of voice in the planning was a lightning rod for resistance – leading to a discourse of displacement grounded in a deep sense of distrust towards political institutions and housing corporations, anger over the lack of democratic participation, and the emergence of a powerful trope among white working-class residents of the Couperusbuurt that construed "ordinary" people as the victims of displacement and forces beyond their control. I understand this discourse – reluctantly – as one of resistance (Goetz 2013) in and through which residents asserted their "right to stay put" (Hartman 2002). The discourse of displacement not only challenged the lack of transparency and real democratic participation in decision-making, but the very narrative used to justify their displacement.

At the heart of the resistance was the defence of respectability and the claim that housing corporations had deliberately "created the argument" for demolition through intentional neglect and disinvestment. Indeed, the corporation's slackness in maintenance and its housing allocation policy were interpreted as deliberate, as a strategy to legitimize the future demolition of the quarter. This notion – that the corporation was engaged in a deliberate metaphoric demolition of the neighbourhood – was well captured by one of my interlocutors: "They care about only one thing – breaking up the neighbourhood. They do everything to create the arguments for demolition. They are deliberately downgrading the neighborhood!" When the Slotermeer Labor Party leader Van Rijssel, who supported the demolition plans, named the Couperusbuurt "the worst neighborhood of Slotermeer", this was interpreted as part and parcel of the symbolic demolition of the quarter and provoked outrage among residents. As I argue below, however, the discourse of displacement did not *only* refer to political elites and housing corporations, but also articulated autochthonic and racist perspectives on the world.

Residents implicitly challenged the received notion that high concentrations of public housing produce neighbourhoods with social problems. Whereas it has now become common sense that specific features of poor neighbourhoods cause deprivation – the dynamic referred to as neighbourhood effects in the social science literature – white working-class residents of the Couperusbuurt blamed policies of neglect and disinvestment (Mepschen 2012, 2016a). They complained, for instance, about a lack of maintenance of the housing stock. In their struggle for the "right to stay put", they drew boundaries between ordinary, respectable citizens and neglectful, incompetent, and undemocratic establishments. Within this boundary work emerged the figure of the "ordinary person" whose right to the city must be defended. As I elaborate below, the discourse of displacement that circulated in New West not only drew boundaries between ordinary people and local urban elites or political establishments, but also sometimes between "respectable" autochthones and racialized Others, who were construed as agents in the metaphoric demolition of the neighbourhood. As one resident told me: "The problem is [...] with the ... especially with the foreign people, or let's say, yes, with the, the non-Dutch people, all the windows are closed, all ... a blanket in front of the window [as opposed to a 'respectable' curtain]." What is at stake here is the emergence of a particular representation in which cultural others are seen through the lens of socially shared beliefs surrounding alterity. Such beliefs are essential, of course, to the constitution of a peculiar autochthonous sense of entitlement and ownership (Mepschen 2016a, 111–156).

Whose right to the city?

The discourse of displacement was entwined – sometimes – with a nativist narrative that assumes that certain people are "naturally" entitled, or more entitled, to certain spaces. As argued, nativist discourse not only informs some white residents' sense of belonging and home, it also informs their sense of entitlement. In the struggle over public housing, a form of welfare chauvinism has emerged that pits ordinary Amsterdam citizens – racialized as white – against those of migrant origin.

One of my interlocutors was Marian. She had grown up in Amsterdam New West in a middle-class, social-democratic family, only a six-minute bicycle ride away from her current home in the Louis Couperusbuurt. A single woman with a job as an educator in a school for special-care children, she had just turned fifty when I first spoke to her in 2010. She had lived in the neighbourhood since the early 1980s – her first apartment since leaving her family home. When in March 2009 Marian learned of the plans to demolish the Couperusbuurt, she worried that her whole life would be turned upside down. Like Rick, she exemplified a category of residents who feared that the demolition of the neighbourhood would have enormous personal and financial consequences. Both rented in the low-rent, social housing sector, in which they arrived respectively 16 and 30 years ago when they had had much lower incomes. Protected by the remnants of a once-robust welfare state, they enjoyed a non-commercial rent. Both Rick and Marian had been socially mobile but had not moved (up) in terms of their housing arrangements. The percentage of their monthly income devoted to rent had in fact declined considerably since they first moved into the Couperusbuurt.

People like Marian and Rick were referred to by policy makers and housing corporation officials as *scheefwoners*, a term used for those whose occupation of a home in public housing was no longer seen as appropriate. These are people with relatively high incomes who nevertheless remain in state-sponsored housing – and they are "the number 1 target group for current policies" (Uitermark 2011). *Scheefwoners* are thus seen as people who no longer belong in public housing and should be seduced – or forced – to find a home outside the public housing sector, on the open market. Like many other residents of the Couperusbuurt, Rick and Marian, who had average incomes, had built their lives around their low rents. Marian travelled. When I visited her home, the first thing I saw was a huge map of the world with hundreds of pins in it, indicating all the locations she had visited. She told me:

> Ten years ago I thought of moving house. I had met a guy; we thought of living together. And we did for a while, in this house, but it is small, too small for two people. So I looked around for a bigger apartment, thought of buying something in that new flat building they had just built five minutes from here. But the costs! The transition would be extreme. And I thought: but I want to keep driving a car, and I want to keep traveling. I was happy with the way I lived. And ever since, the housing prices have just exploded. The transition would be even bigger now.

Rick and his partner had a "Japanese garden" outside Amsterdam where they resided during weekends and the summer. They also donated a lot of money to charities for animals. I once asked Rick if he would consider buying an apartment if the demolition could not be stopped:

> No! That would mean I would have to change my whole life and I don't want to do that. It is as simple as that. We want to keep going to the theater. […] And we have the speedboat, a big one, which costs a lot of money. And I can do these things because I have a low rent, because I am satisfied with this small home. They call us *scheefwoners*, but why? We pay 240 euro rent every month, which is not much, but look at what we get for it: 32 square meters and a little garden, that's all. It is the choice we make.

Both Rick and Marian were faced with the prospect that not only their homes, but their whole ways of life, would be "demolished". As their incomes were now too high, neither would be able to find a new home in the low-rent sector. Forced to search for much more expensive housing in the overheated Amsterdam housing market, they would have to give up many of the things they valued in their lives. Marian's words capture this sense of frustration and displacement:

> Am I allowed to have a home at all? Do I have rights, as a single person? Do I have to make room for all those families? […] It is other people's opinion that my home is too small for me. That I don't belong here. Yes, it's a difficult question. Yes, I simply do not agree. I do not want to leave. I could have left if I wanted to, but I do not want to pinch and scrape only to be able to live in a large and expensive apartment.

Rick responded to questions about the discourse of *scheefwonen* with a quite different interpretation:

> You can call this *scheefwonen*, but look at what some people pay who have housing benefits. People who live in a house of almost one hundred square meters, which should be much more expensive compared with what I have. Perhaps 800, 900 euro. And they have benefits! Everything. They pay 300 euro

only. [And they have] a nice place. So what is *scheefwonen*? That people live in a home they can only afford because they get benefits, or what I do? It is because I work and pay taxes that I make that possible. So people who can't afford it are put in those houses and I pay 240 euro for a very small apartment, but I also pay for the home of those other people. Do you understand?

Rick's ideas about whiteness re-emerged in his understanding of *scheefwonen*, where he opposed the common, hard-working Dutchman to the allochthonous Other of migrant origin. This trope in local discourse – the "common Dutchman" who falls victim to displacement by migrants and their descendants – became entangled in Rick's personal narrative of displacement. Rick told me how years ago he had a florist's business in a white neighbourhood that had become populated by immigrants. His regular customers moved out and the shop could not be sustained because, he argued, "allochtones didn't buy flowers and stuff like that". Rick thus lost his business, which he blamed on the demographic transformation of his neighbourhood. As he said:

> Now I am being driven out of my home again. And why? Because they want larger apartments! And why do they want larger apartments? For *allochtonen*! Because Dutch people (*Hollandse mensen*) have a maximum of four in a family. So I am again being driven out of my apartment. The houses that will be built here are for large families.

This perception of the neighbourhood restructuring plans – as if they were deliberately targeting white, Dutch, "ordinary" residents – had wide support in Slotermeer. Rick himself insisted that most of his friends shared the view that "ordinary Amsterdammers" were being pushed out of town. "That is not a feeling I have, it is the truth!" Among many people I talked with in Slotermeer, urban renewal had reinforced their conviction that immigrants were being favoured and that "ordinary people" were being displaced. Rick's narrative pit *Hollandse mensen* against those of migrant origin – autochthonous against allochthonous residents – by superimposing issues of (welfare) entitlement and the distribution of services and rights atop the debate on the sociospatial restructuring of New West.

Rick: Look, I understand, those people with big families also have to live somewhere. But, well, sorry, I have other ideas about the issue, but that is my own personal ...
PM: What is your idea about it, then?
Rick: They should just make sure they [the allochthones] have fewer children. Why do they have four children, even five? Yes. Look, I will tell you again, they came to the Netherlands as guest workers back then. Yes – and at one point that changed very quickly to allochtoon. Yes, you know? Look, if people have to be helped, that's fine with me, but not when it's only for economic reasons. And that is how it happened with them. Look, most of the problems we have are with all those people.
PM: But, one second, which people?

Rick: Allochtonen! [...] The neighborhood here is mostly white people. A couple of them live here. They got a house here in the past. Because they came alone. But now they let their wife (*hun vrouwtje*) come over. And, well, then kids will follow soon; and, well, these homes are too small for that. And those are the people who are in favor of the demolition. That's the hard reality; that's the truth.

The discourse of displacement that emerged around ordinary people asserting their "right to stay put" thus not only reflected a symbolic dichotomy between "the people" and "the establishment", but also between autochthonous citizens and racialized others. In this dynamic, we can discern the idea of autochthonous voicelessness that is omnipresent in Dutch rightwing populist discourse: the notion that "ordinary people", racialized as white, lack political representation and voice, while post-migrants are heard and even favoured when it comes to the distribution of homes and the redistribution of income through subsidized rents. People with a migration background, construed as cultural outsiders, have come to be seen as the agents of social change – foreign bodies that are seen to threaten people's everyday lifeworlds.

To give an example: the idea that "strangers" are pushing out "ordinary people" became tangible when residents discussed their views on the rationale behind the renewal plans. Many residents did not tire of emphasizing that autochthonous, ordinary people were forced out of their small homes to make room for immigrants with larger families. One resident, Mary, told me she had moved to Slotermeer in the early 1980s from Amsterdam Old West to get away from "all the immigrants". Like Rick, she interpreted the restructuring plans as an effort to displace white residents.

> I have been on the run from those Moroccans all my life – at least that's how I feel. I know I am not supposed to say it, but, well, it's the truth. Now they want to build a beautiful new neighborhood for Muslims and Moroccans and what have you here.[2] A Muslim neighborhood! And why? Look at the politicians here! Do you think they are there for the common good? They don't care about ordinary Dutch people anymore. They want to make this into a multicultural ghetto. They are pushing us out.

The sense of displacement due to immigration and the feeling that those of migrant origin were being favoured was also evident in everyday discourse surrounding the district's still dominant Labor Party (PvdA), which was often called *de Partij van de Allochtonen* – the party of allochthones. People told me, for instance, that they no longer felt represented by Labor now that most of its representatives in the municipality had migrant backgrounds. It was not just that post-migrants were somehow thought to have intimate ties to a political or civil society elite; it was also the sense that autochthonous Dutch residents had been abandoned, had lost these ties and intimacies.

In this trope, the right to stay put was redefined in a very particular way: a sense of displacement had become interwoven with issues of cultural and social entitlement and income redistribution in a shrinking welfare state. In Marian's perspective, these questions were not fully connected to the issue of immigration. In our conversations, Marian took considerable pains to distance herself from the anti-immigrant rhetoric of some of her white neighbours, including Rick. But for Rick, his sense of displacement was clearly tied to the question of immigration and welfare redistribution in the now ethnically heterogenous city. He asserted his right to stay put in the Couperusbuurt through a discourse in which "ordinary" whites became victims of "allochthonous [welfare] spongers" (cf. Ceuppens 2006) and their elite sponsors. The right to the city was tied to a culturalist discourse that framed certain citizens – being autochthonous – as more entitled than Others.

Conclusion

The transformative diversification of Slotermeer, the Louis Couperusbuurt, and other urban multiethnic neighbourhoods in the Netherlands is often misunderstood and misrepresented as a shift from homogeneity to heterogeneity. While this sense of rupture is politically mobilized in contemporary struggles over the future of the "multicultural" Netherlands, it is not accurate. From its beginnings in the early 1950s, New West has been a religiously and socially diverse area (Hellinga 2005; Heijdra 2010). Moreover, a relatively high level of socio-economic heterogeneity, owing to the influx of postcolonial migrants from Indonesia and people from the rural north, further increased the district's cultural and social diversity in the 1950s. Indeed, the sociologist Van Doorn called for an aggressive integration policy targeting rural migrants in the district as early as 1955 (Heijdra 2010).

This is not to say that real transformations have not taken place since then: the feel, aesthetic, and phenomenology of the neighbourhoods I studied in Amsterdam New West have all changed since the 1980s. Turkish-Dutch residents, for instance, have taken over large parts of the Slotermeer's retail trade, affecting the range of shops on the streets (Nio, Reijndorp, and Veldhuis 2009). The central market in Slotermeer increasingly caters to the quarter's poorest, mostly migrant origin residents, fuelling a sense of alienation and discontent among more affluent working-class whites who now often shop elsewhere. Indeed, one of my respondents/interviewees told me he always looked forward to his weekly shopping trip to Amstelveen – a relatively white suburb on the outskirts of Amsterdam. It felt like "coming home", he said. The point is, however, that the demographic transformations of recent decades cannot simply be understood as a shift from homogeneity to heterogeneity.

These transformations have increasingly influenced how those of immigrant origin have been delineated in culturalist terms. Many of the people whom Nio, Reijndorp, and Veldhuis (2009) refer to as the original city dwellers in Amsterdam (*oorspronkelijke stedelingen*) – working- and middle-class whites aged over fifty – speak of these transformations in terms of decline, loss, discomfort, the shrinking of their life-worlds, and a lack of recognition and voice. Urban regeneration and changing housing policies indeed signal a wider practice and public culture of neoliberal reform and gentrification that renders working-class spaces like the Louis Couperushuurt and Slotermeer anachronistic, as spatially and temporally out of place. Many residents in New West engaged with the notion – voiced widely in debates about the future of Amsterdam New West – that the Western Garden Cities, developed in the 1950s, were a thing of the past. Whereas some residents protested by reaffirming the modernist ideology that informed the original vision of New West, others developed a more defensive and emotional response. "What they mean", I heard several residents say, "is that we are no longer of this time". Remarks like this denote an affective sense of temporal displacement and an ongoing attachment to a time now past – a passing exemplified by the withering of the Amsterdam public housing tradition. As Andrea Muehlebach and Nitzan Shoshan observe: "Housing [...] appeared as an index of a peculiar affective relationship that citizens cultivated with the nation-state that often took on an elaborate and extensive caregiver role" (Muehlebach and Shoshan 2012, 329). In this perspective, the current, post-Fordist transformation of housing policies points to a more fundamental transformation of the relationship between citizens, the nation-state, and government, in which certain groups of citizens feel abandoned and bereft.

It is this reality that provides the political and cultural foundations upon which rightwing ethno-political entrepreneurs can build their political narratives. The politics of ethno-political nationalism in the Netherlands indeed structures how white residents in New West negotiate and discuss conflicts over their neighbourhood's future. The everyday idioms that I encountered resonate – unevenly and hence not in a totalizing manner – with the discourses circulated by rightwing populists in the political sphere which rest on culturalized and racialized constructions of "ordinary people" as white and autochthonous. In other words, rightwing populism in the Netherlands is grounded not only in the construction of an antagonistic relation between the people and institutional elites, but in the exclusion of racialized Others. While many autochthonous residents feel they have been rendered anachronistic – temporally and spatially displaced – rightwing populism holds the promise of re-centering and de-marginalizing precisely those white, working- and middle-class residents who feel they have become peripheral. The rise and normalization of culturalist, rightwing populist political discourses produce what I have called a culturalist common sense, which – rather than normalizing difference and leading to a dissolution of majoritarian culture – leads to a reinforcement of Dutch cultural nationalism and racism.

Notes

1. Rick, like all other names in this article, is a pseudonym.
2. This remark was in response to an earlier statement by the chairman of one of the districts that would later make up New West, Ahmed Marcouch, who had proposed creating a "Muslim district" in Amsterdam.

Disclosure statement

No potential conflict of interest was reported by the author.

References

Alba, Richard, and Jan Willem Duyvendak. 2018. "What about the Mainstream? Assimilation in Super-Diverse Times." *Ethnic and Racial Studies*. Special issue on Superdiversity.
Back, Les, and Sinha Samsher. 2016. "Multicultural Conviviality in the Midst of Racism's Ruins." *Journal of Intercultural Studies* 37 (5): 517–532.
Balkenhol, Markus, Paul Mepschen, and Jan Willem Duyvendak. 2016. "The Nativist Triangle: Sexuality, Race and Religion in the Netherlands." In *The Culturalization of Citizenship. Autochthony and Belonging in a Globalizing World*, edited by J. Duyvendak, P. Geschiere, and E. Tonkens, 97–112. Basingstoke: Palgrave Macmillan.
Baumann, Gerd. 2007. "Why Integration Is a Dirty Word. Critique of a Duplicitous Concept in Times of Globalization." In *Wildness and Sensation. Anthropology of Sinister and Sensuous Realms*, edited by Rob van Ginkel and Alex Strating, 110–121. Apeldoorn: Het Spinhuis.
Beekers, Daan. 2015. "Precarious Piety. Pursuits of Faith Among Young Muslims and Christians in the Netherlands." *PhD thesis*, VU Amsterdam.
Blokland-Potters, Talja. 1998. *Wat stadsbewoners bindt. Sociale relaties in een achterstandswijk*. Kampen: Kok Agora.
Buruma, Ian. 2006. *Murder in Amsterdam*. New York: Penguin Press.
Ceuppens, Bambi. 2006. "Allochthons, Colonizers and Scroungers. Exclusionary Populism in Belgium." *African Studies Review* 49 (2): 147–186.
Crul, Maurice. 2016. "Super-Diversity Vs. Assimilation: How Complex Diversity in Majority – Minority Cities Challenges the Assumptions of Assimilation." *Journal of Ethnic and Migration Studies* 42: 54–68.
De Koning, A. 2013. "Creating an Exceptional Problem Neighbourhood. Media, Policy and Amsterdam's 'Notorious' Diamantbuurt." *Etnofoor* 25 (2): 13–30.
Duyvendak, Jan Willem. 2011. *The Politics of Home: Belonging and Nostalgia in Europe and the United States*. New York: Palgrave Macmillan.
Duyvendak, Jan Willem, Peter Geschiere, and Evelien H. Tonkens, eds. 2016. *The Culturalization of Citizenship: Belonging and Globalisation in a Globalising World*. London: Palgrave.
Emirbayer, Mustafa. 1997. "Manifesto for a Relational Sociology." *American Journal of Sociology* 103 (2): 281–317.
Emirbayer, Mustafa, and Matthew Desmond. 2012. "Race and Reflexivity." *Ethnic and Racial Studies* 35 (4): 574–599.
Farris, Sara. 2017. *In the Name of Women's Rights: The Rise of Femonationalism*. Durham, NC: Duke University Press.

Feddes, Yttje. 2011. *De groene kracht. De transformatie van de Westelijke Tuinsteden.* Amsterdam: SUN Trancity.
Geschiere, Peter. 2009. *The Perils of Belonging: Autochthony, Citizenship and Exclusion in Africa and Europe.* Chicago, IL: University of Chicago Press.
Gilroy, Paul. 1987. *There Ain't No Black in the Union Jack: The Politics of Race and Nation.* London: Hutchinson.
Goetz, Edward G. 2013. "The Audacity of HOPE VI. Discourse and the Dismantling of Public Housing." *Cities (London, England)* 35: 342–348.
Hall, Stuart. 1992. "The Question of Cultural Identity." In *Modernity and Its Futures*, edited by S. Hall, D. Held, and A. McGrew, 274–316. Cambridge: Polity Press.
Hartman, Chris. 2002. *Between Eminence and Notoriety. Four Decades of Radical Urban Planning.* New Brunswick, NJ: CUPR Press.
Heijdra, Ton. 2010. *Amsterdam Nieuw West. De geschiedenis van de Westelijke Tuinsteden.* Amsterdam: Uitgeverij René de Milliano.
Hellinga, Helma. 2005. *Onrust in park en stad. Stedelijke vernieuwing in de Amsterdamse Westelijke Tuinsteden.* Amsterdam: Het Spinhuis.
Meissner, Fran, and Steven Vertovec. 2015. "Comparing Super-Diversity." *Ethnic and Racial Studies* 38: 541–555.
Mepschen, Paul. 2012. "Gewone mensen. Populisme en het discours van verdringing in Amsterdam Nieuw West." *Sociologie* 8 (1): 66–83.
Mepschen, Paul. 2016a. "Everyday Autochthony. Difference, Discontent and the Politics of Home in Amsterdam." PhD-diss., University of Amsterdam.
Mepschen, Paul. 2016b. "Sexual Democracy, Cultural Alterity and the Politics of Everyday Life in Amsterdam." *Patterns of Prejudice* 50 (2): 150–167.
Mepschen, Paul. 2016c. "The Culturalization of Everyday Life. Autochthony in Amsterdam New West." In *The Culturalization of Citizenship. Autochthony and Belonging in a Globalizing World*, edited by Jan Willem Duyvendak, Peter Geschiere, and Evelien Tonkens, 73–96. Basingstoke: Palgrave Macmillan.
Modest, Wayne, and Anouk de Koning. 2016. "Anxious Politics in the European City: An Introduction." *Patterns of Prejudice* 50 (2): 97–108.
Muehlebach, Andrea, and Nitzan Shoshan. 2012. "Introduction." *Anthropological Quarterly* 85 (2): 317–343.
Nio, Ivan, Anton Reijndorp, and Wouter Veldhuis. 2009. *Atlas Westelijke Tuinsteden. De geplande en de geleefde stad.* Amsterdam: SUN-Trancity.
Oudenampsen, Merijn. 2010. "Amsterdam Noord. Van sociale naar ruimtelijke maakbaarheid." *Justitiële Verkenningen* 5 (10): 27–40.
Schinkel, Willem. 2007. *Denken in een tijd van sociale hypochondrie: aanzet tot een theorie voorbij de maatschappij.* Kampen: Klement.
Shoshan, Nitzan. 2016. *The Management of Hate: Nation, Affect, and the Governance of Right-wing Extremism in Germany.* Princeton, NJ: Princeton University Press.
Stengs, Irene. 2009. "Dutch Mourning Politics: The Theo Van Gogh Memorial Space." *Quotidian: Journal for the Study of Everyday Life* 1 (1). http://www.quotidian.nl/ www.quotidian.nl/vol01/nr01/a02.html.
Uitermark, Justus. 2003. "'Social Mixing' and the Management of Disadvantaged Neighborhoods: The Dutch Policy of Urban Restructuring Revisited." *Urban Studies* 40 (3): 531–549.
Uitermark, Justus. 2011. "An Actually Existing Just City? The Fight for the Right to the City in Amsterdam." In *Cities for People, Not for Profit: Theory/Practice*, edited by N. Brenner, P. Marcuse, and M. Mayer, 194–214. Oxford: Blackwell.

Van Eijk, Gwen. 2010. "Exclusionary Policies Are Not Just About the 'Neoliberal City'. A Critique of Theories of Urban Revanchism and the Case of Rotterdam." *International Journal of Urban and Regional Research* 34 (4): 820–834.

Van Reekum, Rogieri. 2016. "Raising the Question: Articulating the Dutch Identity Crisis Through Public Debate." *Nations and Nationalism* 22 (3): 561–580.

Vertovec, Steven. 2007. "Super-diversity and Its Implications." *Ethnic and Racial Studies* 30 (6): 1024–1054.

Vollebergh, Anick. 2016. "The Other Neighbor Paradox: Fantasies and Frustrations of "Living Together" in Antwerp." *Patterns of Prejudice* 50 (2): 129–149.

Wacquant, Loïc. 2004. "Following Pierre Bourdieu into the Field." *Ethnography* 5: 387–414.

Wekker, Gloria. 2016. *White Innocence: Paradoxes of Colonialism and Race.* Durham, NC: Duke University Press.

Wessendorf, Susanne. 2014. *Commonplace Diversity: Social Relations in a Super-Diverse Context.* London: Palgrave Macmillan.

∂ OPEN ACCESS

"We have to teach them diversity": on demographic transformations and lived reality in an Amsterdam working-class neighbourhood

Fenneke Wekker

ABSTRACT
This article aims to contribute to the ongoing debate on what the notion of super-diversity means in the practice of everyday life. Whereas the founder of the super-diversity concept, Steven Vertovec, primarily uses the term to point to specific demographic transformations, other scholars have deployed it in more ideological or theoretical terms. Based on ethnographic research in a working-class area of Amsterdam, this study analyses how and to what extent a new demographic super-diverse reality is lived on the ground. Whereas some studies show that super-diverse demographics can result in a super-diverse lived reality in which ethnic and racial diversity becomes the "new normal", this article reveals a different situation. The findings of this study suggest that demographic transformations leading to increased migration-driven diversity can reinforce boundaries between groups of neighbourhood residents based on dominant class, racial and ethnic distinctions.

Introduction

The concept of super-diversity, since it was coined by Vertovec (2007), has taken on a life of its own. Vertovec's aim to "encapsulate a range of ... changing variables surrounding migration patterns" (Meissner and Vertovec 2015, 542), resonated well with the difficulties and "newness and novelty" (Phillimore 2015) often confronting policymakers, welfare organizations and scholars in the context of the diversification of migrant populations and rapidly changing demographics in urban settings. Whereas Vertovec introduced the term as a descriptive tool to interrogate the "complexities ... of migration-driven diversity" (Meissner and Vertovec 2015, 542), recently the term also has been deployed by a variety of scholars in theoretical and ideological ways (for an overview and criticism of the multiple uses of the super-diversity notion, see Meissner 2015).

In initiating the concept of super-diversity, Vertovec intended to highlight three interconnected aspects: the description of transformed demographics arising from new global migration flows, the need for a new methodology to address complex and new social formations and more practical or policy-oriented aspects arising from the diversification of migrant statuses, migrations flows and channels (Meissner and Vertovec 2015). As Meissner and Vertovec (2015, 543) note, in contrast to the original meaning of the super-diversity term, it is often used "simply to mean the increasing presence of 'more ethnic groups'". Whereas Vertovec aimed to address "patterns of diversification among ethnic groups themselves" (Vertovec 2007, 1026), the focus in subsequent scholarly work on super-diversity has often been on the impact of growing ethnic, religious and racial diversity in urban settings, on – how residents perceive others and interact in the context of this new diversity. This article responds to the latter strand of scholarly literature, focusing on the implications of super-diverse demographics for everyday social life in urban settings.

In general, social scientists who use the term super-diversity refer to an urban setting where more people than before originate from a wider variety of different countries and speak a wider range of languages, and where many different religious, cultural and ethnic minorities live together (e.g. Creese and Blackledge 2010; Blommaert and Varis 2011; Sepulveda, Syrett, and Lyon 2011; Duarte and Gogolin 2013; Ram et al. 2013; Padilla, Azevedo, and Olmos-Alcaraz 2015). In addition, some scholars have employed super-diversity to emphasize the changing power balance in urban settings which have a growing and internally diversified migrant population. Numerous authors (Phillips 2008; Spoonley 2015; Crul 2016) argue that super-diverse demographics may create majority–minority cities where no single ethnic group dominates the public or semi-public sphere through sheer numbers. In such a super-diverse context, diversity, it has been contended, comes to be seen as the new normal (Wessendorf 2014). In a similar vein, Crul (2016, 57) argues in his discussion of super-diversity and assimilation that:

> The idea of assimilation or integration becomes at any rate more complex in a situation where there is no longer a clear majority group into which one is to assimilate or integrate.... The group into which one assimilates in the concrete situation of a neighbourhood or a school is, as a result, more and more unlikely to be the old majority group but rather an amalgam of people of different ethnic backgrounds, migration cohorts, migration statuses and socio-economic positions.

Thus, a theme in some of the literature on super-diversity emphasizes that demographic super-diverse settings engender new power balances, including reduced cultural dominance of an "old ethno-racial majority" as well as less pressure on newer ethno-racial minorities to assimilate to the former dominant group. Sometimes, this development is accompanied by expressly optimistic and sometimes even ideological phrases. Social life in super-diverse urban communities, for example, has sometimes been presented as becoming more morally progressive, a "scenario of empowerment and hope" (Crul, Schneider, and Lelie 2013, 11) marked by "a general appreciation of diversity" (Wessendorf 2010, 20). The twenty-first century, in one view, is even perceived as morally requiring "the normalization of superdiversity in our rapidly changing modern world" (Geldof 2015).

The study presented here provides a contrasting view. Whereas several scholars show that "commonplace diversity" and mutual assimilation can be a result of changing demographics in super-diverse settings, this article reveals that a super-diverse demographic reality can reinforce distinctions and create boundaries between residents, based on class, ethnicity, skin colour and lifestyle. As Wessendorf (2014, 176) has also highlighted in her book on commonplace diversity, considerations of race and class can continue to dominate everyday social interactions and impede conviviality even in urban settings where ethnic, cultural and religious diversity has become "surprisingly banal" (Wessendorf 2014).

Based on ethnographic research on social interventions in a demographically super-diverse working-class neighbourhood in Amsterdam, this article shows how social relations and power dynamics continue to reflect long-institutionalized class, ethnic and racial distinctions despite the declining number of residents from the old, native white majority. Existing boundaries between the white, native Dutch and those labelled foreigners (seen as "originally not from this soil"[1] due to their colour or ethnic background, even if born in the Netherlands) are emphasized and indeed have been strengthened in the context of increased ethnic and racial diversity.

The area where I conducted my fieldwork can be considered a demographically super-diverse area. Over the last forty years, large numbers of old immigrant-groups from the former Dutch colonies – mainly in the Caribbean – and from Morocco and Turkey – who arrived as guest workers during the 1950s and 1960s – have settled in the neighbourhood, in large part because of its cheap housing. In addition, in the past two decades new immigrants (cf. Vertovec 2007, 1042–1043) from Eastern Europe, the Middle-East, as well as from different African countries have arrived in the area. Both the older and newer waves of immigration are internally diverse in terms of legal statuses, migration channels, class, gender, sexuality and age, contributing to the contemporary demographic situation of super-diversity (Vertovec 2007, 1043). Given the concentration of immigrants and their offspring, as well as increasing levels of poverty, unemployment, crime, domestic violence, school-drop outs and feelings of insecurity among residents (VROM 2007, 2009; Wittebrood and Permentier 2011), this neighbourhood has raised concerns among and attracted the attention of policymakers and social welfare organizations.

The social interventions at the core of my research aim to enhance mutual integration and social cohesion among residents who differ along the lines of ethnicity, country of origin, race and religion. I was especially interested in how social workers, with financial support from the government, sought to integrate and indeed help individuals from the former majority group – white "natives" of Dutch descent – adjust to the new super-diverse reality in their neighbourhood. To what extent did these social worker initiatives help to establish mutual adaptation and integration within this majority–minority setting? And how were these top-down attempts at social engineering experienced by white native Dutch residents?

In what follows, I set the stage by explaining the Dutch tradition of state-sponsored social interventions in working-class neighbourhoods to situate my fieldwork. I then draw on my ethnographic findings to document how the manager and social workers at the community centre tried to "open up the world views" of elderly white working-class residents and help them acclimatize to the super-diverse era in which their old majority group has declined in numbers. I go on to discuss how the white working-class visitors at the centre responded to these top-down initiatives. Doing so entails an analysis of the intersections of class, race and ethnicity. As we will see, class distinctions, based on the middle-class norms of conduct underpinning the centre's activities, encouraged a process of ethnic leveraging. Using this strategy, working-class visitors to the community centre resisted the implicit charges of the social workers of being "narrow-minded", "immoral" and "pathological" by comparing themselves favourably to ethnic, racial and religious "others". A strong sense of "we" arose among the white working-class visitors, who erected barriers to distinguish themselves from ethnic and racial outsiders. The article ends with some reflections on the implications of the findings for the concept of super-diversity.

Doing ethnography of Dutch social engineering

The Netherlands has a long history of social engineering, dating back at least to the 1920s. Whereas national and local governments initially sought to uplift members of the working class and to mould them as receptacles of middle-class norms and values, interventions today mostly target the economic and cultural integration of immigrants and their descendants into Dutch society (Duyvendak and Wekker 2016a). From the perspective of social workers and service providers, social integration is a two-way process demanding efforts from both immigrants and the "native" population (e.g. Minkler 2012; Simpelaar 2016). Current interventions, therefore, encompass instructing white working-class residents on how to live with the diversity of ethnic, racial and religious "others" in their communities and wider society. The underlying assumption is that heterogeneous urban settings will become better places to live as local networks are strengthened through mutual integration and adaptation, and by all residents learning to live with diversity. The notion of super-diversity in which no ethnic majority is (or should be) dominant resonates with Dutch policy discourse as well as with the practices of local social workers and service providers.

The working-class area in which I pursued ethnographic research is generally considered disadvantaged. It is home to a large concentration of less well-educated immigrants and their descendants, and its residents report high rates of poverty, unemployment, criminality, domestic violence and youth delinquency (VROM 2007, 2009; Wittebrood and Permentier 2011). At the same time, members of the "native", white working-class population, whose proportion has shrunk in recent decades, complain of feeling more and more out of place in their increasingly diverse surroundings (Duyvendak and Wekker 2016b). Current policies and social interventions focus on community-building and the creation of empowered local networks encompassing a wide range of residents. Heterogeneous networks in terms of class and ethnicity, it is believed, can help overcome integration problems (Veldboer, Kleinhans, and Duyvendak 2002). Activities such as neighbourhood gardening, computer lessons, street barbecues and neighbourhood dinners are encouraged by the national and local government through subsidies to local social organizations.

The local community centre in which my research took place provided inexpensive dinners to neighbourhood residents three times a week. By organizing these dinners, social workers were seeking to counter loneliness and isolation among residents. Above all, they sought to facilitate encounters between people of different cultural backgrounds and generations "to reduce mutual fear and incomprehension", according to the manager of the community centre. By building local community, social workers believed that the neighbourhood would become a better place to live, that social control and conviviality would increase and that residents would know where and how to find help when needed. Current state-supported attempts to reach out to residents "of all kinds" and help them "bridge their differences" thus fit well within the Dutch tradition of top-down social interventions in working-class and immigrant areas.

Over the course of four months, I conducted 14 in-depth interviews of 2 hours each with regular visitors, 3 lengthy interviews with the restaurant manager, and intensive participant observation with a regular group of about 40 visitors who came to dine at the community centre three nights each week. I had dinner with them, witnessed ongoing conversations and numerous discussions and participated in all kinds of activities organized by the restaurant's management and social workers to improve the lifestyles of the working-class visitors. This included activities that sought to open up their world views and bridge differences with ethnic and racial others. The group consisted mostly of elderly native Dutch residents; only three persons of non-Dutch descent were regularly present at the community dinners during my fieldwork. This struck me as odd, given the proportion of non-Dutch ethnic minorities living in the neighbourhood (Wittebrood and Permentier 2011). The question then arose as to how this predominantly white, native Dutch community restaurant had come into being in a demographically super-diverse neighbourhood – and what this revealed about how the area's demographic changes affected the level of experience and everyday social interaction.

Dealing with "strangers" in a community centre

As this section shows, the activities designed by social workers to encourage white working-class residents to "open up to strangers" had unforeseen and unintended outcomes. Based on their outcomes, I distinguish between two types of community-building practices: those that encouraged a sense of togetherness among smaller groups of self-chosen restaurant friends and those that encouraged a sense of solidarity and collective resistance among all visitors – turning them into a white working-class group sharing similar interests, experiences and an identity (cf. Brubaker 2004).

The first type of activity is illustrated by the practice of changing tables. While most visitors wished to remain at familiar tables and sit with their restaurant friends, the manager at times made them mix with others. This meant that all visitors had to sit with different people and converse on some predetermined topic such as "how to manage your budget". The restaurant manager explained:

> Participation is important to me. So, if you don't want to participate, don't come for dinner. (...) The moment we say: "Today we're going to change tables", everyone is going to sit down at a different table with people they don't regularly sit down with (...). When someone responds by saying "I don't want to sit here or there", just don't come; because you're obstructing things then. In this restaurant, you make a reservation for a meal, not for a particular place to sit. So, one time you can join your regular group, and the other time we do things differently. That's how we mix people, that's how the restaurant gets its added value. (Interview with the restaurant manager)

The practice of mixing was unpopular; visitors at the centre were at times openly reluctant, especially as they felt forced to mix. In fact, complaints about the mixing strategy and the manager's high-handedness created a bond among the tablemates. As one of my respondents stated: "He [the manager] tries to tear us apart. But that won't happen. We'll become a bit angry then". Instead of encouraging visitors to open up to strangers, the mixing strategy made the regulars more aware of the importance of their "own little club", leading to efforts to distinguish themselves from other groups of visitors at the restaurant. Another respondent explained: "We simply don't know them. We do know them by their faces, but not by their names, so they cannot sit with us".

Whereas the mixing strategy created a sense of togetherness among small groups of restaurant friends, other activities aroused an overarching sense of solidarity among the centre's white native Dutch working-class visitors. Activities in this category explicitly addressed these visitors *as a group* of people in need of educating on certain societal, cultural, health and financial issues. A young social worker explained at a lecture on healthy lifestyles: "It is important not to gain too much weight, to eat fresh vegetables and fruit regularly and to go to bed on time". A man in his late eighties whispered to me: "During World War II, we ate rats, we ate cats, we ate raw sugar beet, and they come here to tell us how to survive? How old do they want us to become?" During this lecture, and in many other instances, people cast glances and made faces at each other. The consensus among the larger group of visitors was that they had to endure such lectures as it was community centre policy, necessary to maintain municipal funding. To maintain their restaurant community, they had to accept being lectured to and taught how to improve their lives. Many of my respondents, however, believed that they had much to teach the social workers in return: "They may have their grades and diplomas, but I have my experiences", one told me. "Therefore no one can tell me what to do or how to behave. I could teach them!"

Other activities that evoked a sense of "groupness" (Brubaker 2004) among all visitors included those aiming to bridge differences with those whom I will call ethnic, racial and religious "others". To attract residents "of all kinds", the manager of the community centre organized activities ranging from Brazilian night, a meal serving Surinamese food, inviting Muslim youngsters to prepare an *iftar* meal[2] and showing films on diversity in contemporary Dutch society. However, ethnic minority residents generally did not attend these "special nights", despite the efforts of the community organizers to "welcome them and make them feel at home".

On one evening, the manager introduced speakers from an organization founded to create a "new sense of us" – designed to include immigrants and their descendants in the Dutch national identity while encouraging the native Dutch to embrace diversity. The spokeswoman (of German origin) introduced the organization's aims, all the while emphasizing the importance of "widening our worldviews and learning from differences". She then showed a short film in which highly educated minority citizens espoused the project of "embracing diversity". At the end of the film, a woman of Surinamese descent speaks directly to the camera: "To create a new sense of us, I suggest that all those who signed the petition to maintain Black Pete should immediately follow a naturalization program".

Black Pete (*Zwarte Piet*) is the by now infamous blackface figure in the Dutch tradition of *Sinterklaas*. Black Pete, the black servant of the white "Good Holy Man" (*de Goedheiligman*), is performed by white people in blackface, replete with big red lips, golden earrings and more often than not, displaying comically infantile behaviour. While Black Pete has become controversial due to pressure from black Dutch citizens and a report from a United Nations working group, almost 2 million (out of 16 million) Dutch citizens signed a petition to defend the "tradition" of the blackface Pete. Their main argument – that *Sinterklaas* is a children's celebration and has nothing to do with race or racism – hinges on the lack of conscious racist intent. Critics, however, point out that it is not the intent but the impact of the blackface figure that makes it racist.[3]

The black woman in the film expressing her disapproval of those who had signed the petition was like a bomb going off in the community centre. Dinner guests began shouting, hitting the table with their spoons, telling me and each other that there was nothing racist about Black Pete, that they could not believe that black people were "even making a fuss about *that*". While the lectures on health and lifestyle had only encouraged muted expressions of togetherness, the outburst of collective emotion now reaffirmed the strong bond and sense of solidarity among the white Dutch visitors. All agreed that the black woman had gone too far. Instead of bridging differences and increasing mutual understanding and adaptation between native Dutch residents and "ethnic and racial others", the film aroused a strong sense of distinctiveness. According to the many visitors, I spoke with that night, "those black people" did not understand a thing about Black Pete and *Sinterklaas*. "They" did not share "our" traditions and culture so "why should we follow a naturalization program instead of them?!" The attempts of community organizers to encourage mutual integration and adaptation had evoked its opposite, namely an increased sense of us against them. Although the regular visitors felt united through their shared emotions and feelings of being treated unfairly, this was clearly not the kind of social cohesion the organizers had hoped for.

More generally, many white participants at the community centre (and one of the three people of Surinamese descent) regularly demonized ethnic, racial and religious others who, in their view, should adapt to *them* and Western society rather than the other way around. Confirmation and reaffirmation of common concerns regarding the danger and abnormality of "foreigners", "Islam", "Moroccans" and "black people" turned out to be non-negotiable when it came to becoming part of the restaurant community. For the three people of colour who were regulars at the restaurant, inclusion in the community entailed adopting and expressing these same ideas. The elderly Surinamese-Dutch woman was willing and able to become part of the in-group by echoing the same ideas. To make her position clear, she stated at her table:

> Well, I think all this talk about Black Pete is rubbish. You know, children in Suriname, they like it. It isn't the elderly Surinamese people around here who are making trouble, it's the younger generation. They start talking about discrimination. But it's a children's celebration, it's about giving presents.

The middle-aged man of Surinamese descent, sitting at the same table together with his younger sister, made clear that they did not share these views: "It's because Black Pete is called a servant, that can be perceived as denigrating", the man explained to his tablemates. The elderly woman of Surinamese descent immediately countered: "Well, I think that's ridiculous!" The other tablemates loudly supported her, and the man and his sister kept quiet for the rest of the meal. Later that night, he told me:

> I feel excluded here ... I'm excluded from contacts ... having contact with other people is difficult here ... But, it's my own shortcoming ... I'm not able ... I'm not able to put myself in their shoes. Their world is so different from mine. They're Dutch, you know. Yeah, but I just ... I just accept it as it is. That's what I'm good at. Yeah ... that's what I'm good at.

The key point for the analysis of the ethnographic material here is that the dynamics of social interaction that I observed do not support the findings of, for example, Crul (2016) or Wessendorf (2014) that residents in majority-minority cities (including the white native residents) start to experience ethnic and racial diversity as the new normal in public and semi-public spaces, such as schools and neighbourhood centres. At least in the setting that I observed, top-down attempts by the municipality and the community centre's leaders to teach the white working-class diversity did not lead to greater acceptance of, or ease with, members of different ethnic and racial groups but ended up strengthening hostile sentiments towards them. The forceful attempts of the manager to bridge ethnic and racial differences and increase mutual understanding resulted in collective acts of resistance among the white Dutch and the exclusion of those who did not comply to Dutch cultural norms.

Discourses of (in)tolerance and othering

In what follows, I will discuss two – seemingly opposite – discourses that were used by the manager and social workers involved, to distinguish between themselves and their working-class visitors: a discourse of tolerance combined with a discourse of othering. At the same time, the visitors used a discourse of othering combined with a discourse of intolerance to distinguish themselves from so-called foreigners As the material below shows, both combinations of discourses helped maintain institutionalized boundaries between the white middle-class social workers and their white working-class visitors, as well as between white Dutch people (including the management and visitors), and coloured, non-Dutch residents.

The various activities at the centre I have described that were initiated by the manager and social workers were at times underpinned by mixed messages from them. On the one hand, the social workers relied on a discourse of tolerance towards differences – "we are all different and can learn from each other". Aware of the prejudices and worldviews of those who came to the centre, the manager told me he had to organize bridging activities to teach the white working-class tolerance towards ethnic diversity:

> It is this segment of the population. When you're so straightforward, when you don't have any education, when you're not used to dealing with matters in a profound way, then, at a certain moment you start repeating yourself, you stick to your own account simply to make things understandable. (...) If we wouldn't organize activities like these, they wouldn't get in touch with it; they must learn how to deal with diversity.

On the other hand, and while deploying their discourse of tolerance, the manager as well as the social workers carefully distanced themselves from what they referred to as "this segment of the population". Despite their good intentions, the manager and social workers used a discourse of othering to distinguish between "us" (tolerant, educated, middle-class people) and "them" (the narrow-minded, less educated, white working-class visitors at the center). As became apparent in the centre's activities, tolerance was preached for ethnic, racial and religious differences – but not for class differences.

The mixed and contradictory messages were picked up by my white working-class respondents. They knew that middle-class moral standards and norms of conduct portrayed them as different, pathological and other (cf. Wekker 2017). The mixed discourse of tolerance and othering thus had an unforeseen – yet profound – effect on the working-class visitors at the community centre. In an attempt to establish respectability (cf. Skeggs 1997; Scharff 2008), they collectively resisted the assumption underpinning the organized activities that *they* were the ones whose lifestyles and conduct needed improvement. As the following passage and my field notes suggest, many white working-class visitors to the restaurant preferred pointing to the pathologically bad morality of foreigners rather than bridging differences and embracing diversity:

> We, the Dutch people aren't aggressive. (...) But when I say something to a Moroccan, I'm drawn into a fight immediately. That's just not right. (...) And there are more of these people than we might think. It's not just two neighbors,

it's half of the neighborhood! (...) And we don't go out onto the streets to fight for our own space, you know. (...) I mean, Hitler slaughtered a whole bunch of people, and ... well, that's not the way to do it, of course. (...) I guess, we just have to live with it. (Interview with Piet)[4]

At one table, Bob asked the other visitors: "What do you all think about the American who was beheaded by Islamic State? Your opinions please?" This led to a heated conversation. One woman said: "I think it's in their blood. These people from the East, they just have to kill." Another woman added: "Yeah, I know. It's been a blood thirsty bunch of people, for as long as I can remember." Yet another woman said that she couldn't believe that "these people" are religious. The elderly woman of Surinamese descent began a detailed explanation of how the Islamic State gets its weapons, and why Jews should never have gone to Israel. "I say," another woman interjected, "it's all the same: Israelites and Palestinians, one bunch of blood-thirsty people." Everyone nods their approval. (...) Then a man says something about a new mosque that's going to be built in Amsterdam. Bob starts shouting: "Shut all the mosques down! Shut them all down and send all the Muslims back to their own country!" (Research diary)

Discussion and gossip about these "bad others" played a central role during community dinners, contributing to a sense of togetherness and self-esteem among the white Dutch residents.

In sum, the class distinctions drawn by the social workers and manager – between themselves and their white working-class charges – were primarily based on the latter's unwillingness to tolerate ethnic, racial and religious differences. By emphasizing the importance of tolerance as a means to distinguish between social classes, both class and ethnic boundaries were accentuated rather than bridged.

A related issue is the mechanism through which white working-class visitors at the community centre sought to resist the management's assumptions that they were pathological and a threat to social integration.

As we have seen, talking about ethnic, racial and religious others created a cohesive bond among the white Dutch visitors to the community centre. To put it another way, they felt connected and better about themselves as a group by comparing themselves to an "other". This mechanism, where one group is valorized with the purpose of distancing and delegitimizing another group, is known as *ethnic leveraging* (e.g. Bertossi 2012; Winter 2014).

Although the white Dutch visitors did not see themselves as part of an overall in-group of friends – and were sometimes even unwilling to mix with other "co-ethnics" who came to the centre – an overarching moral community seemed to emerge through the mechanism of ethnic leveraging. Paradoxically, this was in part a response to the management's forceful attempts to bridge differences. Visitors were eager to defend themselves against the implication that they needed to be educated to be more tolerant. They repeatedly claimed that they were not racists, that they did not need to be taught about diversity, and, above all, that it was the Muslims and black people who should be held accountable for the decline of their neighbourhood and Dutch society as a whole. "It is not our lifestyle that has to be improved", many told me. As a result, it became almost impossible for "ethnic, racial and religious others" to become part of the restaurant community and for the manager to change the ideas and conduct of the white native Dutch residents visiting the centre. Despite the attempts to invite and welcome minority residents, the overarching in-group of white native Dutch visitors was able to maintain its barriers to outsiders, thanks to their regular meetings and collective resistance to the management of the community restaurant. Unwillingly and unintentionally, the neighbourhood restaurant facilitated the empowering of white working-class visitors and the exclusion of ethnic, racial and religious others.

These findings are congruent with the work of many scholars who have shown that a sense of community among one group of residents inherently involves the exclusion of others (Elias and Scotson 1994; Hage 2000; Besnier 2009; Binken et al. 2012). Cohesive in-groups with strong bonding social capital can reinforce hatred, violence and aggression against others as they lose their capacity to deploy bridging social capital and become isolated from others:

> Strong moral bonds within a group in some cases may actually serve to decrease the degree to which members of that group are able to trust outsiders and work effectively with them. (...) At best, this prevents the group from receiving beneficial influences from the outside environment; at worst, it may actively breed distrust, intolerance, or even hatred for and violence towards outsiders. (Fukuyama 2001, 14)

Thus, ironically, in demographically super-diverse contexts, the creation of strong cohesive local communities can actually impede the emergence of the tolerance of cosmopolitan values that in many accounts super-diversity is supposed to promote.

Conclusion

Super-diversity as coined by Vertovec (2007) was initially meant to be a descriptive term to refer to "a recognition of complexities that supersede previous patterns and perceptions of migration-driven diversity" (Meissner and Vertovec 2015, 542). The super-diversity concept, however, has limits in describing social transformations on the ground, especially as it has been elaborated and used by a number of scholars concerned with super-diversity's social implications. This article has addressed this latter strand of the literature that seeks to understand how super-diversity has transformed social relationships in everyday life and thus, in the process, has added new theoretical, and at times ideological, features to the concept.

While this article has focused on a single community centre in one Amsterdam neighbourhood, the analysis, I believe, has broader implications. Unlike many scholars (Wessendorf 2014; Geldof 2015; Crul 2016) who have adopted the super-diversity concept, this study has shown that the demographic realities of super-diversity do not necessarily result in social realities where residents experience ethnic and racial diversity as normal.

This research has shown that at the everyday level of practice and experience, residents in super-diverse areas can actively resist the increasing diversity that comes with changing demographics. Ethnic and racial diversity here is not seen as normal, but rather used as a tool for educated social workers to distinguish themselves from the white working class and for the white working class to establish group cohesion and respectability by elevating themselves above ethnic and racial others.

As I have shown, class distinctions and ethnic leveraging were crucial in the establishment and reproduction of a white local community in a demographically super-diverse setting. To resist the forceful attempts of middle-class social workers to "teach them diversity", white working-class visitors to the community centre restaurant affirmed their own worth against the foil of ethnic, racial and religious "others"; a mechanism that reinforced barriers for residents of non-Dutch descent who sought to become part of the center community.

Some ethnic minority groups – in the case of the Amsterdam neighborhood, the white ethnic Dutch – have found ways to resist adaptation and assimilation into an "amalgam of ethnic minorities", contrary to what Crul's (2016) analysis of super-diversity would lead us to expect. Moreover, I found that forceful and ideological state-supported attempts to help a super-diverse social reality come into being evoked its very opposite: the reinforcement and accentuation of boundaries between ethnic groups.

The role of class and ethnic leveraging, I would argue, needs to be considered more carefully when adopting Vertovec's descriptive super-diversity concept. The impact of class distinctions and related processes of ethnic leveraging may be decisive in understanding the limitations facing community organizers as they seek to create a convivial super-diverse social reality that corresponds with super-diverse demographic features. Ultimately, it is clear is that as a descriptive tool super-diversity does not provide solid theoretical grounds to understand why and how social relations in such demographic situations unfold in certain ways. This is in effect the challenge for the future. What increasing migration-driven diversity means in everyday life and how it affects social interactions remain open questions to be further empirically interrogated and theoretically elaborated. By taking into account the distinction between the realm of demographics and of social life, as well as intersections of class, race and ethnicity, we can help to further advance our understanding of super-diversity and its many implications.

Notes

1. This is the literal meaning of the commonly used word "allochthon", which was deployed in Dutch public discourse and public policy since the 1970s. The term was used to refer to the first, second and third generation of citizens with a migrant background living in the Netherlands. The word has recently become highly debated for its suggestion of ethnic minority groups being "less legitimate Dutch citizens" (*tweederangs burgers*). This resulted in the abandoning of the term by the Dutch government in November 2016. See also: https://english.wrr.nl/publications/investigation/2017/06/26/summary-migration-and-classification-towards-a-multiple-migration-idiom
2. The evening meal during *Ramadan*, when Muslims end their daily fast at sunset.
3. See Duyvendak (2014); cf. Wekker (2016).
4. All names used in this article are pseudonyms.

Acknowledgements

The author expresses her gratitude to Jan Willem Duyvendak and Nancy Foner, who patiently read and commented on all her previous drafts. Furthermore, the author owes many thanks to David Takeo Hymans, for his beautiful language editorial work and his detailed comments. Last, but not least, the author is intensely grateful for the willingness and openness of her respondents to accept her in their midst.

Disclosure statement

No potential conflict of interest was reported by the author.

Funding

The author would like to thank the research group Political Sociology of the University of Amsterdam for their intellectual and financial support.

References

Bertossi, C. 2012. "The Performativity of Colour Blindness: Race Politics and Immigrant Integration in France, 1980–2012." *Patterns of Prejudice* 46 (5): 427–444.
Besnier, N. 2009. *Gossip and the Everyday Production of Politics*. Honolulu: University of Hawaii Press.
Binken, S., L. Zuyderwijk, J. Burgers, and D. Van der Wilk. 2012. *Openbare ruimte als professionele opgave en alledaagse omgeving*. The Hague: Platform 31.
Blommaert, J., and P. Varis. 2011. "Enough Is Enough: The Heuristics of Authenticity in Superdiversity." *Tilburg Papers in Culture Studies* 2: 1–13.
Brubaker, R. 2004. *Ethnicity Without Groups*. Cambridge: Harvard University Press.

Creese, A., and A. Blackledge. 2010. "Towards a Sociolinguistics of Superdiversity." *Zeitschrift für Erziehungswissenschaft* 13 (4): 549–572.
Crul, M. 2016. "Super-diversity vs. Assimilation: How Complex Diversity in Majority-Minority Cities Challenges the Assumptions of Assimilation." *Journal of Ethnic and Migration Studies* 42 (1): 54–68.
Crul, M. R. J., J. Schneider, and F. Lelie. 2013. *Superdiversiteit: een nieuwe visie op integratie*. Amsterdam: VU University Press.
Duarte, J., and I. Gogolin, eds. 2013. *Linguistic Superdiversity in Urban Areas: Research Approaches* (Vol. 2). Amsterdam: John Benjamins Publishing.
Duyvendak, J. W. 2014. "Are all Dutch Racists? A Country's Struggle with a Black-face Tradition." http://www.gc.cuny.edu/CUNY_GC/media/CUNY-Graduate-Center/PDF/Voices%20of%20the%20GC/Are-All-Dutch-Racists.pdf
Duyvendak, J. W., and F. Wekker, eds. 2016a. "Homing the Dutch: Politics and the Planning of Belonging." Special issue, *Home Cultures* 13 (2).
Duyvendak, J. W., and F. Wekker. 2016b. "At Home in the City? The Difference Between Friends and Amicability." In *Urban Europe: Fifty Tales of the City*, edited by V. Mamadouh and A. Van Wageningen, 23–30. Amsterdam: Amsterdam University Press.
Elias, N., and J. L. Scotson. 1994. *The Established and the Outsiders*. London: Sage.
Fukuyama, F. 2001. "Social Capital, Civil Society and Development." *Third World Quarterly* 22 (1): 7–20.
Geldof, D. 2015. *Superdiversity in the Heart of Europe. How Migration Changes our Society*. Leuven: Acco.
Hage, G. 2000. *White Nation: Fantasies of White Supremacy in a Multicultural Society*. New York: Routledge.
Meissner, F. 2015. "Migration in Migration-Related Diversity? The Nexus Between Superdiversity and Migration Studies." *Ethnic and Racial Studies* 38 (4): 556–567.
Meissner, F., and S. Vertovec. 2015. "Comparing Super-Diversity." *Ethnic and Racial Studies* 38 (4): 541–555.
Minkler, M., ed. 2012. *Community Organizing and Community Building for Health and Welfare*. New Brunswick: Rutgers University Press.
Padilla, B., J. Azevedo, and A. Olmos-Alcaraz. 2015. "Superdiversity and Conviviality: Exploring Frameworks for Doing Ethnography in Southern European Intercultural Cities." *Ethnic and Racial Studies* 38 (4): 621–635.
Phillimore, J. 2015. "Delivering Maternity Services in an Era of Superdiversity: The Challenges of Novelty and Newness." *Ethnic and Racial Studies* 38 (4): 568–582.
Phillips, T. 2008. *Superdiversity: Televisions Newest Reality*. London: Equate. https://www.coe.int/t/dg4/cultureheritage/mars/source/resources/references/others/48%20-%20Superdiversity%20Television's%20newest%20reality%20-%20Philipps%202008.pdf.
Ram, M., T. Jones, P. Edwards, A. Kiselinchev, L. Muchenje, and K. Woldesenbet. 2013. "Engaging with Super-Diversity: New Migrant Businesses and the Research–Policy Nexus." *International Small Business Journal* 31 (4): 337–356.
Scharff, C. M. 2008. "Doing Class: a Discursive and Ethnomethodological Approach." *Critical Discourse Studies* 5 (4): 331–343.
Sepulveda, L., S. Syrett, and F. Lyon. 2011. "Population Superdiversity and new Migrant Enterprise: The Case of London." *Entrepreneurship & Regional Development* 23 (7–8): 469–497.
Simpelaar, L. 2016. "Wederzijdse Integratie: It Takes Two to Tango." *Maatwerk* 17 (3): 32–32.

Skeggs, B. 1997. *Formations of Class and Gender: Becoming Respectable*. London: Sage.
Spoonley, P. 2015. "New Diversity, Old Anxieties in New Zealand: The Complex Identity Politics and Engagement of a Settler Society." *Ethnic and Racial Studies* 38 (4): 650–661.
Veldboer, L., R. Kleinhans, and J. W. Duyvendak. 2002. "The Diversified Neighbourhood in Western Europe and the United States." *Journal of International Migration and Integration/Revue de l'integration et de la migration internationale* 3 (1): 41–64.
Vertovec, S. 2007. "Super-Diversity and its Implications." *Ethnic and Racial Studies* 30 (6): 1024–1054.
VROM. 2007. *Actieplan krachtwijken. Van Aandachtswijk naar Krachtwijk*. The Hague: Ministerie voor Volkshuisvesting, Ruimtelijke Ordening en Milieu.
VROM. 2009. *Stad en wijk verweven. Schakelen, verbinden, verankeren in de stad*. The Hague: Ministerie voor Volkshuisvesting, Ruimtelijke Ordening en Milieu.
Wekker, G. 2016. *White Innocence: Paradoxes of Colonialism and Race*. Durham, NC: Duke University Press.
Wekker, F. 2017. *Top Down Community Building and the Politics of Inclusion*. New York: Palgrave/Pivot Series.
Wessendorf, S. 2010. *Commonplace Diversity: Social Interactions in a Super-diverse Context* (Working Paper 10–11). Göttingen: MMG. http://pubman.mpdl.mpg.de/pubman/item/escidoc:1126645/component/escidoc:2057868/WP_10-11_Wessendorf_Commonplace-Diversity.pdf.
Wessendorf, S. 2014. *Commonplace Diversity: Social Relations in a Super-Diverse Context*. Basingstoke: Palgrave Macmillan.
Winter, E. 2014. "Us, Them, and Others: Reflections on Canadian Multiculturalism and National Identity at the Turn of the Twenty-First Century." *Canadian Review of Sociology/Revue Canadienne de Sociologie* 51 (2): 128–151.
Wittebrood, K., and M. Permentier. 2011. *Wonen, wijken and interventies; krachtwijkenbeleid in perspectief*. The Hague: Sociaal Cultureel Planbureau, with Fenne Pinkster.

What about the mainstream? Assimilation in super-diverse times

Richard Alba and Jan Willem Duyvendak

ABSTRACT
Super-diversity has become the conceptual touchstone for a large body of research on immigration in European societies. Evolving from the ideas sketched by Steven Vertovec in his famous 2007 essay, the concept as deployed in research has become a successor to multiculturalism. The super-diversity lens has trained attention on horizontal processes of "living together" in very diverse settings, like some urban neighbourhoods where no group holds the majority status. However, we argue here that for a fuller understanding of integration, we need the vertical dimension of social power. This dimension is manifest through the mainstream, which permeates many institutions (including local ones such as schools) and becomes visible in the cultural adjustments made by members of immigrant-origin minorities, particularly among those who aspire to social mobility. The power axis represented by the mainstream is not strictly dependent on the demographic distribution of ethnic groups, given that white natives remain very powerful even when they are a numerical minority. At the same time, the character of the mainstream may be altered to some extent by the entry of individuals with non-white minority origins. To illustrate these ideas, we offer the examples of the "culturalization of citizenship" in the Netherlands and the social locations of young people of mixed background in the US.

Introduction

Over the last decade, the concept of "super-diversity" has captured multiple intellectual worlds in Western Europe, becoming a touchstone for social scientists, policymakers, urban planners, and social workers, alike. The concept, which originated with a 2007 essay by Steven Vertovec, refers to "a worldwide diversification of migration channels, differentiations of legal statuses, diverging patterns of gender and age, and variance in migrants' human capital" (Meissner and Vertovec 2015, 541). Today, any European scholar addressing issues of migration, integration, and (ethnic) diversity who does not explicitly take into account the notion of super-diversity runs the risk of being reproached for neglecting the "new multicultural condition of the twenty-first century" (Meissner and Vertovec 2015, 542).

Super-diversity challenges conventional migration studies by "moving beyond ... the 'ethno-focal lens'" (Meissner and Vertovec 2015, 542). This refocusing supersedes multicultural approaches, particularly strong in the UK, which were mainly concerned with migrant populations from the former colonies and the so-called guest workers, who originally had been contracted to work in Western Europe. Vertovec has observed that multicultural policies "had as their overall goal the promotion of tolerance and respect for collective identities"; but since the influx of immigrants in the 1990s, "new, smaller, less organized, legally differentiated and non-citizen immigrant groups have hardly gained attention or a place on the public agenda" (2007, 1027–1028). Instead of focusing solely on the country of origin and ethnicity of immigrants and the second generation, the super-diversity concept highlights the need to recognize the complexity of migration processes and the range of shifting variables involved in integration patterns in order to adequately address the needs of individual immigrants and their descendants and to better understand the dynamics of their inclusion or exclusion (Vertovec 2007, 1039).

Super-diversity can be viewed first of all as an observation – a profound one – and thus as a description of a novel phenomenon, "a term coined to portray changing population configurations particularly arising from global migration flows over the past thirty-odd years" (Meissner and Vertovec 2015, 542). One of the key implications of the notion of super-diversity concerns societal conditions in the early twenty-first century: It conveys a notion of diversity as the new normal for Western societies, an inescapable circumstance affecting not only migrants but also members of native majorities. Meissner and Vertovec (2015, 550) see a super-diversity analytic lens as leading potentially to "a greater recognition of *diversity as normalcy*" (Meissner and Vertovec 2015, 550; *italics added*). Meissner (2015, 557) goes on to emphasize how ordinary diversity has become:

> More and more researchers have been moving away from seeing ethnic diversity as exceptional. In their studies they have identified that, by and large, practices of living with tremendous ethnic diversity have actually become so normal in the everyday lives of their research subjects that this aspect of differentiation has become somewhat ordinary. (2015, 557)

One of the most consequential strands of research inspired by the notion of super-diversity pursues the idea of the normalcy of diversity into quotidian social life, the universal tapestry of human experience. The major finding reveals a conviviality that appears to reflect a degree of levelling and everyday acceptance of ethnic difference. In super-diverse contexts, people seem to get along rather well (Padilla, Azevedo, and Olmos-Alcaraz 2015, 623). Suzanne Wessendorf (2014), in her much cited work on Hackney, explains that this conviviality is not necessarily based on the active appreciation of differences but more on the ability simply to deal with them by not problematizing differences that are "out there". The linkage of conviviality to super-diversity leads to a view of super-diverse areas as increasingly level playing fields, where everyone, the native majority included, has become a minority and no one ethnic group is dominant. Following this logic, Crul, Schneider, and Lelie (2013) argue "that everybody will adapt to everybody". From this perspective, the hegemony of the native majority appears to be receding to the margins; the nature of integration is being altered profoundly.

In this paper, we focus on the question of whether the new view of integration arising from super-diversity research will prove adequate in the contemporary immigration societies of North America and Western Europe. In so doing, we heed the call to "critically interrogate, refine and extrapolate" the notion of "super-diversity" (Meissner and Vertovec 2015, 542). We recognize that super-diversity originally, in the work by Steven Vertovec, was not so much concerned with issues of integration,[1] but nevertheless it is being used to generate insights into the complexity of immigrant trajectories in a super-diverse world, with a plethora of distinct intersections of such variables as ethnic origin, religion, gender, family status, and legal situation. Inevitably, then, super-diversity has implications for integration. We try to specify where super-diversity has something important to contribute. But we are also concerned about what we see as the concept's blind spot, namely, differences in social power, broadly construed, that affect integration. Others have seen that blind spot in terms of the disregard of social-class inequalities or racism (Back and Sinha 2016). To clarify what we are concerned with, we introduce the concept of mainstream assimilation. We then give some examples of how the mainstream matters for integration and assimilation, looking in particular at the contemporary Netherlands and US, two countries that, for historical reasons, exemplify different boundaries between the mainstream and major immigrant minorities (brighter in the Netherlands, blurrier in the US). In conclusion, we see a prospect for the super-diversity perspective to extend its grasp by recognizing the critical importance of the mainstream.

Majority–minority demography and horizontal relations

In its empirical reach, the super-diversity concept calls attention to settings in which diversity has become part of quotidian "normalcy". Susanne Wessendorf argues that this is true of the "super-diverse" district of Hackney in London, where diversity has become "commonplace", "habitual and part of the everyday human landscape" (Wessendorf 2014, 3). Padilla, Azevedo, and

Olmos-Alcaraz (2015) refer to "hybrid spaces", where "heterogeneity ... is experienced on a daily basis" and "difference/otherness is internalized", possibly being "transformed into a quotidian positive feature".

Two aspects seem fundamental to such findings. One is demographic: Super-diversity corresponds with the absence of a visible numerical majority of some kind, whether it be ethno-racial or something else, a group that has both strength of numbers and a degree of establishment, allowing it to set the dominant social and cultural tone, one that must at least be heeded by others, if not adapted to by them. The other is a tendency of this research to focus on what might be called "horizontal" interpersonal relations, exchanges where any inherent authority possessed by one participant (as there would be, for instance, in an interaction involving a teacher and the parent of a student) is at a minimum. Wessendorf's (2014) field observations of Hackney, for instance, involve interactions among several or more people in shops, playgrounds, a knitting club, and an IT class, and at a public party at a housing estate.

Of these two dimensions, the demographic one tends to be seen as more definitive. Crul (2016) bases his influential analysis of super-diversity largely on numbers:

> My first criterion for a city or neighbourhood to be labelled super-diverse is that there *no* longer is an ethnic majority group that is dominant based on its *demographic majority* position. ... The second characteristic of a super-diverse city or neighbourhood is that in this majority–minority context, both *number and size* of different ethnic groups must be substantial. (2016, 2, *italics added*)

Along the same lines, he argues that the demographic context determines the pressure newcomers feel to assimilate:

> The idea of assimilation or integration becomes at any rate more complex in a situation where there is no longer a clear majority group into which one is to assimilate or integrate. The pressure to assimilate, coming from the – old – majority group, is less strong if not backed by sheer numbers *in everyday life*. The group into which one assimilates in the *concrete situation* of a neighbourhood or a school is, as a result, more and more unlikely to be the old majority group but rather an amalgam of people of different ethnic backgrounds, migration cohorts, migration statuses and socio-economic positions. (Crul 2016, 4, *italics added*)

We accept that there may be something distinctive about majority–minority areas. As Crul's argument suggests, they provide many social contexts in which the mainstream majority is no longer visible, or at least no longer seems dominant. In this sense, the daily experiences of many minority residents do not seem to require adjustments (or, at least, not many) to the mainstream. There is a *proximity principle* at work in the argument: mutual adjustment depends on the people encountered as neighbours, at school, in the market, or on the street. Indeed, when individuals with native-majority backgrounds appear in these settings, they too may even adjust their behaviour to fit with the others they meet, thus apparently assimilating (at least for a time and in some respects) to a minority group (Jiménez 2017). Situations like these lend themselves to the creative cultural syncretism that often appears in migration settings. As Philip Kasinitz points out: "We all know that there are times and spaces where cultural creativity comes into flower, and cities with diverse populations and cosmopolitan outlooks tend to be fertile grounds for artistic achievement" (2014, 283).

However, we caution that this picture of mutual adjustment among diverse individuals who share a rough equality cannot be extended to all super-diverse settings. In recent years, a team of researchers at the University of Amsterdam has been pursuing such questions as: do citizens consider "diversity" as a normal fact of life? Is diversity for them the new normalcy? Most of our research has taken place in Western Europe, particularly in the Netherlands. And what we found suggests something opposite to what one would expect from the super-diversity thesis: citizenship itself has become politicized and "culturalized" in some Western countries, while space for diversity has decreased instead of increased, let alone come to be considered "normal" (Duyvendak, Geschiere, and Tonkens 2016).

This problematization of cultural and religious differences is not only happening at the level of national discourse but in neighbourhoods as well. As Paul Mepschen concludes in his recent PhD dissertation on the "culturalization of everyday life" in a multi-ethnic neighbourhood in Amsterdam New West:

> The contemporary global city is characterized by a powerful focus on locality, belonging and identity "fixture".... Dutch "culturalism" produces an increased awareness of the proximity and alterity of others. The resulting focus on "autochthony" is a process of boundary-making between those who belong and those who are construed as guests or strangers. (Mepschen 2016; see also article in this special issue)

Very few people seem to be *indifferent to difference*; the emergence and reinforcement of exclusionary articulations of belonging – so central to the "culturalization of citizenship" – create *increasing* physical awareness of the cultural, corporeal alterity of others, and not a lack thereof. The powerful emergence of autochthony in the Netherlands stands in contrast to Wessendorf's observations regarding Hackney. Autochthony denotes a bright, powerful boundary between those who come from elsewhere and those who can claim to be "born of the soil" and thus the nation as their home (cf. Duyvendak 2011).[2] This boundary between "autochthonous" and "allochthonous" residents plays a key role in everyday discourse in Amsterdam New West and many other super-diverse neighbourhoods in the Netherlands, and is intimately entwined with political and public discourses that impose meaning upon everyday life.

So what about the mainstream?

All of the North American and Western European societies that have taken in massive immigrations since the mid-twentieth century possess dominant native white majorities and stark power differentials between this majority (which is still a demographic majority on the national plane) and immigrant minorities. The concept of the mainstream provides a way of understanding how the power of the native majority is expressed in relation to minorities and generates the specific conditions that shape integration.

Two interlocking aspects of the mainstream reveal the power of the native majority. One is institutional: The mainstream encompasses a core set of societal institutions, such as the education system, the economy, the polity, and the media, whose leading positions are occupied by members of the native majority or by others who have met their standards for acceptance (Alba and Nee 2003, 12). These institutions broadcast mainstream standards and values to all parts of the society, and they also possess a critical gatekeeping role. Thus, the gatekeeping that controls access to improvements in educational credentials and jobs for immigrants and the second generation is generally in the hands of individuals who employ mainstream criteria, as it occurs through institutions such as schools that reflect the mainstream's culture and standards. (The exception – a rare case – is when a minority group has successfully established its own sub-economy; and usually this offers just truncated ladders of mobility.) For this reason, one can speak of "dominant formal and informal ways of doing and thinking" in a society, which reflect the most consequential parts of the mainstream.

Another aspect of the mainstream consists of the social and cultural settings – not just formal institutions – where the members of the native majority, even when they are working class, feel "at home" (Alba 2009). This aspect emphasizes the more subjective and emotional side of being part of the mainstream. Feeling at home not only means that the setting is familiar, safe, and predictable but that one feels in control as well: one belongs, and one believes (perhaps incorrectly) one has the power to define who else belongs (Duyvendak 2011). This conception highlights also that the use the singular "mainstream" is a matter of convenience because the mainstream can be itself internally diverse, differentiated by region, religion and social class, to name but a few dimensions. Moreover, although the presence of the native majority identifies the settings that are part of the mainstream, these milieus need not be ethno-racially exclusive (though, obviously, some may be). That is, members of immigrant minorities can and do participate in them also, whether in work environments, neighbourhoods, or sports teams; and the interaction across boundaries is greater when some degree of social compatibility exists. In the usual case, such compatibility requires more adjustment, whether achieved by past assimilation or present efforts, by individuals from minority backgrounds than by those in the majority. This asymmetry reflects differences in social power, especially the potential for exclusion by the majority.

This more social-demographic aspect of the mainstream is the more encompassing: it overlaps with the institutional one insofar as institutions can be constituted by assemblages of social settings, such as offices and social relations among personnel (institutions also require rules and procedures, which are not implied). Nevertheless, any operationalization of the socio-demographic conception demands recognition of certain practical limits that are hard to specify with complete precision. There has to be a socio-economic floor to the mainstream – for instance, we should not count the homeless or desperately poor in it, even if they belong to the native majority. And some in this majority – such as the adherents of certain religious groups, for example, the Amish and Ultra-orthodox Jews – shun the mainstream society and should also not be reckoned as part of it. But we believe that the native-majority working class belongs in it because integration, which often requires multiple generations to run its course, can begin with integration with the working-class part of the mainstream. The very fact that, more recently, parts of the white working class claim not to feel at home in their "own" land anymore (Hochschild 2016) illustrates our argument: they were used to be self-evidently part of the mainstream, it was their country, and now they feel threatened in their mainstream status.

Super-diverse areas such as those described by Wessendorf can co-exist to some extent alongside the mainstream, but they cannot avoid exposure to it, even its intrusion. Certainly, it is much more difficult for some residents to gain access to the mainstream in highly segregated cities, for example, certain US cities that suffer from high black and Hispanic segregation. But even in segregated neighbourhoods, minority citizens know very well what the mainstream is, who controls the resources and power, has the power to arrest, etc. In Europe, where segregation overall is less pronounced, the mainstream is even less distant.

Indeed, institutions of the larger society, schools most obviously, reach into super-diverse areas. Even when they accommodate in significant ways the specificities of the backgrounds of their non-majority students, schools still teach a curriculum infused with the mainstream – e.g. the history of the larger society – and they do so, with very rare exceptions, in the mainstream language. The findings of Crul (2016, 12) exemplify how in different European countries mainstream institutions and settings shape the lives of the second generation:

We see how differences between Swedish and German institutional arrangements in education for the second generation are crucial because of the resulting differences in partner choice and in the pace of change in gender roles among the lower and higher educated.

This is exactly how mainstream institutions work: dominant societal norms – regarding, for example, education and men's and women's participation on the labour market – are translated and "embodied" in local institutions, even in highly diverse neighbourhoods. The very existence of mainstream institutions turns children of diverse backgrounds into Swedish or Dutch citizens, with all their national peculiarities. Proximate institutions and settings represent norms, values, practices, etc., that have formidable reach and shape children's subjectivities and life chances.

The mainstream should not be viewed as inherently static, a point that is quite visible in countries with long histories of immigration. The US mainstream has been altered – in superficial and profound ways – by the inclusion of the descendants of the immigrant waves of the past and present. For instance, the assimilation of Jewish and Catholic second and third generations after the Second World War was accompanied by an expansion of the American core identity, which became "Judeo-Christian", whereas previously it had been "white Christian" and vociferously not Catholic (Alba 2009). This was a profound change, given the importance of religious identities since colonial times in North America. Nevertheless, change was asymmetric – the descendants of the early twentieth century European migrants changed far more than did the mainstream. Indeed, they even refashioned their religious identities to a considerable extent, with the rise of Reform Judaism, at mid-century a Protestant-like denomination, and the individualization of Catholic faith, including a new willingness to reject specific Church teachings, such as birth control, that were seen as incompatible with contemporary family life, as well as an exodus from the parochial school system.

The Dutch mainstream: the culturalization of Dutch membership

In Western Europe, many policymakers and citizens apparently do not embrace diversity as a normal fact of life. Quite the contrary: over the past decade, Western European countries have heatedly debated how much and what kind of cultural differentiation is acceptable in the public domain. It is questionable to what extent citizens, and particularly native-majority residents of diverse neighbourhoods, consider the diversity they witness around them as "normal".

In the Netherlands, powerful discourses, which reverberate throughout the political world, cast Muslim immigrants as a threat to social cohesion and national identity. The building of mosques, the call to prayer, religious symbols such as the headscarf, gender inequality, the alleged refusal to embrace LGBT rights, and Islam-inspired political extremism are all popular subjects in politics and the media, often portrayed as threatening Dutch culture.

In the background of these discussions and debates are important discursive changes that emphasize the need for immigrants to adopt "Western" (or Judeo-Christian or "Dutch") values and the right of the "natives" to define their country's identity (see Geschiere 2009; Kesic and Duyvendak 2016a; van Reekum 2014). This *culturalization of citizenship* (Duyvendak, Geschiere, and Tonkens 2016) would not have been possible, however, without an important development that is easily overlooked because of the country's political divisions: the majority population of the Netherlands has rapidly become more culturally *homogeneous*. After a period of intense cultural polarization during the "long sixties", the majority has developed remarkably uniform, progressive ideals.[3] Almost the entire political spectrum now supports similar values on gender, family, sexuality, abortion, euthanasia, drugs policies, and so on.

The culturalization of citizenship and the homogenization of the native majority – the virtual consensus within the majority population that immigrants should share "national" values – has important consequences for the space for diversity. This "progressive" consensus requires policy to enforce the acculturation of those who are assumed to fall outside of it. Since the "native" culture is seen as under threat, its "traditional" cultural heritage has to be protected (for instance in the form of a "canon" as part of the history school curriculum and the lessons taught to newcomers in citizenship courses; see Kesic and Duyvendak 2016b).

The cultural consensus among the native Dutch goes hand in hand with a dismissal of other sets of values. Hence, the advancement of liberal moral and social values is tied to the belief, trumpeted by vocal politicians, that everyone must adhere to them. Debate in Dutch politics now focuses less on the substance of certain topics (e.g. homosexual marriage) than on the procedural question of how to deal with people who do not share the relevant "modern" values. This question polarizes the political spectrum as nothing else. So whereas cultural polarization on moral traditionalism has declined since 1970, polarization on the majority's moral authority has grown (compare de Koster and van der Waal 2006; Houtman et al. 2008).

This is also apparent in the programmes of Dutch political parties: The data clearly show that the decline of support for traditional moral values has fuelled a new polarization over the importance of individual freedom and cultural pluralism. Among the supporters of the ethnic majority's moral authority, we see the desire for uniformity and community, and preference for ethnocentrism and a shared understanding of the Netherlands as "home" (Duyvendak 2011, Chapter 4). All in all, the majority population of the Netherlands has come to define cultural diversity as a growing problem, brightening the boundaries between natives and immigrants (who remain immigrants forever, even into the 3rd generation). And the Netherlands is clearly not the only country in Europe where this is happening.

It is not only that on the discursive, cognitive level the idea is forcefully rejected that "everybody adapts to everybody" (dismissed as old-fashioned "multiculturalism"). The processes sketched above also reflect the *emotional* aspects of citizenship, which has evolved from a status or practice into a deep sentiment. Citizens are subjected to new "feeling rules" (Hochschild 2003, 82). Belonging, or feeling at home, has become a requirement (Morley 2001). Particularly at the national level, new feeling rules are applied to immigrants who are increasingly expected to demonstrate feelings of attachment, belonging, connectedness, and loyalty to their new country. Because feelings as such cannot easily be perceived, certain actions become their symbolic stand-ins (Verkaaik 2010). For example, having dual nationality has come to represent lack of loyalty to Dutch culture in the eyes of a majority of Dutch politicians.

These emotional aspects not only play out at the national level. As Mepschen and many others have shown, relations at the local level have become extremely tense and emotional: there is a lot of territorial and emotional boundary-making going on, based on resistance (and not on indifference) to differences. Recently, this emotional investment in a bright boundary intruded in a remarkable way into public life, when the liberal-conservative Prime Minister, Mark Rutte, scolded a small band of Dutch Turkish youth for harassing a TV news team in their neighbourhood, telling the youth to "fuck off" and to leave the country ("pleur op"). The coarse language, unheard of from a European national leader speaking about fellow citizens at a news conference, emphasized Rutte's view of the great distance separating these immigrant-background youth from mainstream respect.

The very fact that the Dutch mainstream is not readily opening up to Muslim migrants does not imply that they are not affected by it. They are, in contradictory ways. Some assimilate into the mainstream, or at least make impressive progress in terms of education, work, and income. The second generation is often more liberal than its parents, another sign of ongoing integration (Maliepaard and Alba 2016). However, the harsh xenophobic discourse in Dutch political and public debate causes many migrants and their children to have difficulty identifying as Dutch (Slootman and Duyvendak 2015) and therefore to feel excluded from the mainstream.

The US mainstream: signs of an expansion

If we now turn to the US, we find evidence of a rather different story, one of blurring boundaries, at least for some: that is, an expansion of the mainstream shows some similarities to, but also some differences from, the post-Second World War expansion that brought the descendants of Jewish and Catholic immigrants, mainly from Ireland and from southern and eastern Europe, en masse into the mainstream.

A number of social forces contributed in the mid-twentieth century to the mass entry of previously excluded groups into the mainstream. Their shifting generational distribution – the young adults from these groups then belonged mainly to the second and third generations – combined with the cutoff of immigration since the 1920s brought about rapid Americanization and the weakening of mother tongues. The educational attainments of low-status groups like the Italians soared in the post-war period (assisted, one should add, by the state-sponsored expansion of higher education); and large-scale occupational mobility ensued (Alba 2009; Perlmann 2005). The development of suburbs and homeownership encouraged young ethnic families to forsake urban enclaves for mixed communities. As a consequence of these processes, rates of interethnic and interreligious marriage climbed sharply (Alba and Nee 2003).

This mass assimilation was stoked by the unusual prosperity and reduced inequality of the post-War period. In addition, the issue of legal status among immigrant parents was much less consequential than today (Ngai 2003). Assimilation in the post-war period was driven in large part by a prodigious expansion of opportunity – for instance, the higher educational sector of the US grew fivefold in the 1940–70 period – which allowed massive non-zero-sum mobility. That is, numerous ethnics of the second and third generation could move upwards without challenging the opportunities available to already established groups. As a vast literature has established, inequality is much higher today, and social mobility more constrained.

One can presume therefore that the scale of mainstream expansion is much less today than in the earlier, unusual period. Nevertheless, assimilation processes still operate. One structural force that promotes them is demographic shift (Alba 2009). It has led to a widening of entry into higher occupational tiers by non-whites, as the number of whites who can compete for positions there declines.

The growing diversity in the top tiers of the workforce emerges in sharp profile from an analysis by Alba and Yrizar-Barbosa (2016). They show that, over time and as new cohorts enter economic life, whites' onetime dominance of the top quartile of jobs (as ranked by the average pay to specific occupations) is eroding. The fraction of these jobs held by non-Hispanic whites slipped from nearly 90 per cent in the oldest cohort (56–65 years old) in 2000 to about 70 per cent in the youngest one (26–35 years old) of 2010. These changes have come about largely because of the retirement of cohorts where whites monopolized the best jobs and the altered demographic composition of cohorts that are maturing and entering the workforce.

The groups that are benefitting most from this growing diversity at the top are of immigrant origin – Asians, both immigrant and native born, and native-born Latinos. Black Americans have also seen some gains, but these are modest compared to those of the other groups.

Concomittently, as socio-economic parity between whites and some minorities rises, and demographic shifts also encourage higher rates of interaction between them, the level of mixed unions increases. Recent analyses of census data have revealed that the overall rate of intermarriage among new unions is about 17 per cent, representing a steep increase in marriage across the major lines of race and Hispanic origin over the last several decades (Livingston and Brown 2017). This increase is normalizing intermarriage in some parts of the country. That rising intermarriage is indeed connected with mainstream expansion is shown above all in the characteristics of the children of these unions.

The evidence concerning these children – individuals with mixed ethno-racial backgrounds, who consequently have family connections to two different groups – is telling. These children now represent a substantial fraction of the American youth population (Alba, Beck, and Sahin 2017) – 14–15 per cent of the infants now born in the US. And the great majority of them, about three-quarters, come from mixed majority–minority families – that is, one of their parents is non-Hispanic white, and the other is non-white or Hispanic.

The social contexts in which these children grow up are diagnostic for the integrative character of mixed unions, as are their identities, social affiliations, and partner choices as adults. An examination of the income and residential characteristics of the families of mixed infants indicates that, on the whole, the families that mix one majority with one minority parent resemble much more all-white families than they do the all-minority families that share the same minority origin. But mainstreaming is not just a matter of developing characteristics like those of all-white families, but also being located in similar residential spaces and, by implication, having white families as neighbours. Families that have a white mother and a black father, which make up the great majority of white–black unions, are the exception to these generalizations. The families that meld two minority origins look very much like other minority families.

If we examine the adult characteristics of individuals from mixed majority–minority family backgrounds – and, admittedly, the evidence is sparser here – we again find a picture consistent with integration into the white mainstream for most, with those of partly black ancestry the prominent exception. In terms of social identities, the data support the idea that for the most part these identities are more fluid and contingent than are the identities of individuals with unmixed backgrounds (see Alba, Beck, and Sahin 2017; Lee and Bean 2010; Pew Research Center 2015). For individuals who are partly white but not black, this fluidity often "tilts white", in the sense that they appear to incline more to the white side of their ancestry than to the minority side – importantly, in their sense of acceptance by others. For those who are partly black, it tilts in the other direction. This pronounced divide among those from mixed backgrounds reveals one very bright boundary in American society: the still powerful stigmatization of African heritage (Alba and Foner 2015).

The social worlds of individuals with white and non-black minority parentage also tilt white. For example, individuals whose parentage is partly white marry mostly all-white partners. In the case of individuals who are white and either American Indian or Asian, about 70 per cent do (Miyawaki 2015). Even in the case of adults who are partly white and partly black, a majority takes white partners.

This mixing speaks to a potent form of conviviality, which brings families from different sides of an ethno-racial divide together, at least for important symbolic occasions such as weddings and funerals. Yet it is also deeply coloured by power differentials, in which the less powerful adapt to the most powerful. African-Americans' experiences with bright boundaries strongly resemble those of Dutch Muslims. They experience the exclusionary impact of a very real mainstream on a day-to-day basis, resulting in very low percentages of intermarriage for these groups with mainstream natives.

Experiencing (super)diversity I: assimilation diversifies immigrants

Super-diversity researchers focus particularly on the increasing diversity in everyday lives of the immigrants themselves (Vertovec 2007). That is, immigrants to Western countries have become more diverse in terms of age, gender, country of origin, ethnicity, language, religious background, and migration channels, resulting in an increased variety of legal statuses, along with more diverse forms and levels of human capital. Some of these differences are present upon arrival, some are produced by family reunification and marriage, and others have to do with the passing of time in the receiving country. Some of these differences have a temporary character; others are more permanent.

What should be acknowledged though is that a portion of this diversification is actually produced by mainstream assimilation, in other words by the adaptations some immigrants and their children make to the mainstream in order to improve their opportunities, understood in the broadest sense. As we have already noted, Crul and his co-authors demonstrate that at least some members of immigrant-origin minority groups eventually adapt to the dominant norms, values, and practices of receiving societies, changes that are often associated with the experience of upward mobility channelled through mainstream institutions. Indeed, these scholars observe that the socially mobile members of the Moroccan and Turkish second generations are generally the most progressive members of their groups, thus bringing some mainstream values into their homes and communities. Not surprisingly, ambitious members of the second generation, who recognize that the gatekeepers impacting their chances to rise employ mainstream standards for assessing talent, accommodate themselves to an important degree to the mainstream culture (Alba and Nee 2003), especially since, in general, this does not require wholesale abandonment of their familial and ethnic cultures.

The heterogeneity introduced by assimilation grows over time because of the mobility and assimilation experienced by some – but not all – children of immigrants (on Mexicans in the US, see Agius Vallejo 2012; Jiménez 2010; Vasquez 2011). Its lack of uniformity is a hallmark, as assimilation introduces or exacerbates differences and inequalities among immigrants and their children, which range from different language competencies (in the mainstream language and the mother tongue) to different levels of educational credentials and occupational qualifications in the receiving society. How do the members of immigrant-origin groups experience increased internal diversification, caused by the assimilation of some? On the one hand, we know that this can produce painful forms of difference, for example incomprehension between children and parents who have received very different educations (Slootman 2014). On the other hand, we also know from the literature that differences among immigrants caused by the assimilation of some can be broadly welcomed: parents are proud that their children move up and into the mainstream, even when they move out of the neighbourhood, stop speaking the homeland language and embrace the norms and values of the country of arrival. More research is needed to better understand the appreciation by immigrants of diversity produced by assimilation processes.

Thus, the *experience of increased diversity* within immigrant-origin groups is an important aspect of super-diversity, one that raises critical questions. When it comes to the new variabilities introduced by immigration itself, a safe assumption is that, while some are really experienced by immigrants and their children as differences (particularly the linguistic, ethnic, and religious ones), others are probably not experienced in this way at all. They may well in fact be experienced as getting back to normal: alongside male immigrants, there are now also female immigrants; alongside the young and middle-aged, there are older people and children; alongside the lower-educated, there are now many with higher educations. What may appear as "super-diverse" in the eyes of migration scholars could be experienced as a return to regular, non-deviant, and therefore non-diverse situations by immigrants themselves.

Experiencing (super)diversity II: assimilation diversifies the mainstream

It is, however, not only the immigrant population that seems to recognize its experiences in the notion of super-diversity. Many in the native majority consider their country as increasingly diverse as well, and not all of them are pleased with this development. Here, it is important once more to stress that the processes of immigrant and second-generation assimilation partly cause the experience of diversity in the mainstream: individuals of immigrant background now live almost everywhere (not only in the poor neighbourhoods of the big cities), have various educational backgrounds, and move into diverse professions. All citizens of Western countries are now very much aware that immigrant minorities form an important part of their societies. But does this awareness – driven by both demographic changes and processes of assimilation – necessarily tell us something about how these new groups are experienced and appreciated by natives? Writing on super-diversity often seems to imply that the majority will get used to these differences, particularly where the majority group becomes a numerical minority itself. But the earlier examples of the Netherlands and the US suggest that the outcomes of diversity are variable and contingent, especially for the boundary strategies employed by the majority group and for the intimacy of the social relations that develop across the majority–minority boundary.

In the Netherlands, the growing diversity that appears in mainstream settings is connected frequently with a brightening of this boundary, at least from the perspective of the majority, whose members consider some groups of newcomers to embody the antithesis of Dutchness. Many in the majority see "adapting" as surrendering to non-natives and do not want the boundaries to blur. Even though the processes of assimilation are implicated in the increasing frequency of interactions between the native population and (successful) immigrants and their children, many in the Dutch majority focus on what they see as the eruption of diversity in their daily lives and give less attention to the commonalities created by assimilation. Particularly when certain group characteristics are culturalized and politicized, individuals from certain immigrant backgrounds are viewed and treated as "different", even when they themselves think and feel that they conform to the mainstream (Slootman and Duyvendak 2015).

In the US, this pattern also appears, as the white nativistic assertiveness during the 2016 election shows. When it comes to the growing diversity within the families of the mainstream majority, however, the evidence is strong that boundary blurring is occurring at the same time that some degree of socially acknowledged diversity is maintained. To begin with, many Americans – about a third – now acknowledge having a "close" relative from an ethno-racial group other than their own (Wang 2012). Moreover, many of those coming from mixed majority–minority homes (again, with the exception of many black–white individuals) feel accepted by their white relatives and, more generally, by whites (Pew Research Center 2015). These feelings appear to indicate that they perceive little or no disparity in their treatment at the hands of the majority. At the same time, a substantial portion asserts at times the minority sides of their heritage, in the form of professing mixed identities, for example. Such identities are preferred by most white-Asian individuals and, though the evidence is more tentative, by individuals who are Anglo and Mexican, it appears (Pew Research Center 2015; Vasquez 2014). Very likely, these mixed identities are linked to everyday expressions of ethnicity that are relatively muted and easily shared, just as was the case for European Americans. After all, individuals in mixed family networks have strong incentives to get along with one another.

Assimilation therefore produces experiences of diversity within the mainstream, but these experiences are not uniform. In some contexts, people do not grow indifferent towards each other's differences. On the contrary, they remain aware and even wary of (alleged) differences. In such cases, it may appear that the "mainstream" is expanding since newcomers share comparable socio-economic positions and socio-cultural convictions with the native group; but the appearance can be an illusion. In other contexts, the mainstream does actually expand, as social, cultural, and relational boundaries between groups and between individuals blur, producing feelings of mutual acceptance. Thus, it remains an open empirical question how and to what extent the mainstream changes by expanding. Often, newcomers can only really become part of the mainstream when differences have already become relatively small. In this sense, mainstreams are far from super-diverse.

Yet, in one respect, the experience of diversity does seem to produce similar outcomes in the Netherlands and the US: Those in the native majority have become more aware of their distinctiveness (Jiménez 2017). Whereas once their equation of the nation with their own group identity was automatic and unself-conscious, in both countries it has been troubled by the undeniability of growing diversity. In the Netherlands, it has taken on as a result a pronounced defensive character; in the US, this is true also for portions of the native white population. This effect of growing diversity is profound in both societies and of uncertain outcome in the long run, and a crucial question remains as to whether, and to what extent, the recognition of the presence of "others" eventually generates more tolerance or intensifies intolerance (or does both at the same time).

To conclude

Super-diversity, which in the last decade has swept through the social sciences studying immigration in Western Europe, offers a lens that yields some new insights but also misses something critically important: the mainstream. The point of departure for the idea is the observation of a thorough-going change in the immigrant-origin populations in Europe, as the single axis of national origin has been replaced by a tangle of multiple axes, from age and generation to legal status. We argue that super-diversity, at least to judge by the research it has so far inspired, seems best attuned to the "normalized" everyday diversity that sometimes characterizes horizontal interpersonal interactions in micro-settings with a very substantial immigrant presence.

The super-diversity lens has so far been less able to capture the vertical phenomena that reflect the social power of the native majority. This may be partly because observing them requires a lens operating on a macro scale, rather than a micro one. Since one of the goals of the super-diversity idea in its original formulation by Vertovec is to offer guidance to social service practitioners, the mainstream institutions that interact with immigrants have not been entirely left out of its field of vision. But the emphasis is on the need for these institutions to adapt to the new super-diverse condition; neglected is the power they exert to bring about adaptations by the immigrant and their children.

When we take macro-processes into consideration, we see that in countries of Western Europe such as the Netherlands the native majority draws sharper immigrant/native boundaries than before. Although the Netherlands has been often misunderstood as a "multicultural paradise" (Duyvendak et al. 2013; Duyvendak and Scholten 2012), culturalized and homogenized versions of citizenship have grown hegemonic there over the past decade(s), as they have in many West European countries. The new ethnic hierarchies and sensitivities linked to this nativist turn have not been taken into account by many super-diversity scholars.

Yet, despite the boundary intensification, many immigrants and their children still assimilate according to mainstream standards in terms of both conduct and convictions, though this is not always enough to bring them truly into the mainstream. This assimilation, when its implications are understood, points to ways that the ideas of super-diversity could benefit from recognizing the power of the mainstream. For, as we have argued, the processes of assimilation produce internal diversification and experiences of increased diversity among immigrant-origin groups; and they lie behind some of what is "lived" as pluralization by the hyper-sensitive native majority as well. Such experiences may be another reason why the term "super-diversity" resonates so strongly: not because immigrants are no longer forced to assimilate given the new normalcy of diversity, but *as a consequence* thereof.

Notes

1. In this paper, we use the terms "integration" and "assimilation" as approximate synonyms, although we recognize that there are some conceptual differences between them (see Alba and Foner 2015, chap. 1).
2. As we write this paper, an important Dutch advisory body has recommended that the government scrap the autochtonous/allochthonous distinction (de Volkskrant 2016). However, its use is widespread in the populace, and aligned there with common distinctions between "white" and "black". Whether a government decision will make it fade from popular use is doubtful.
3. According to the Euro-barometer, European Social Survey, European Values Study, International Social Survey Program, and the Continuous Tracking Survey, as recapitulated in various studies.

Disclosure statement

No potential conflict of interest was reported by the authors.

References

Agius Vallejo, Jody. 2012. *Barrios to Burbs: The Making of the Mexican-American Middle Class*. Palo Alto, CA: Stanford University Press.

Alba, Richard. 2009. *Blurring the Color Line: The New Chance for a More Integrated America*. Cambridge: Harvard University Press.

Alba, Richard, Brenden Beck, and Duygu Basaran Sahin. 2017. "The U.S. Mainstream Expands – Again." *Journal of Ethnic and Migration Studies*, doi:10.1080/1369183X.2017.1317584.

Alba, Richard, and Nancy Foner. 2015. *Strangers No More: The Challenges of Integration in North America and Western Europe*. Princeton, NJ: Princeton University Press.

Alba, Richard, and Victor Nee. 2003. *Remaking the American Mainstream: Assimilation and Contemporary Immigration*. Cambridge: Harvard University Press.

Alba, Richard, and Guillermo Yrizar-Barbosa. 2016. "Room at the Top? Minority Mobility and the Transition to Demographic Diversity in the US." *Ethnic and Racial Studies* 39: 917–938.

Back, Les, and Shamser Sinha. 2016. "Multicultural Conviviality in the Midst of Racism's Ruins." *Journal of Intercultural Studies* 37: 517–532.

Crul, Maurice. 2016. "Super-Diversity Vs. Assimilation: How Complex Diversity in Majority – Minority Cities Challenges the Assumptions of Assimilation." *Journal of Ethnic and Migration Studies* 42: 54–68.

Crul, Maurice, Jens Schneider, and Frans Lelie. 2013. *Superdiversiteit: Een Nieuwe Visie op Integratie*. Amsterdam: VU University Press.

Duyvendak, Jan Willem. 2011. *The Politics of Home. Nostalgia and Belonging in Western Europe and the United States*. Basingstoke: Palgrave Macmillan.

Duyvendak, Jan Willem, Peter Geschiere, and Evelien Tonkens, eds. 2016. *The Culturalization of Citizenship. Belonging and Polarization in a Globalizing World*. Basingstoke: Palgrave Macmillan.

Duyvendak, Jan Willem, Rogier van Reekum, Fatiha El-Hajjari, and Christophe Bertossi. 2013. "Mysterious Multiculturalism. The Risks of Using Model-Based Indices for Making Meaningful Comparisons." *Comparative European Politics* 11: 599–620.

Duyvendak, Jan Willem, and Peter Scholten. 2012. "Deconstructing the Dutch Multicultural Model: A Frame Perspective on Dutch Immigrant Integration Policymaking." *Comparative European Politics* 10 (3): 266–282.
Geschiere, Peter. 2009. *The Perils of Belonging: Autochthony, Citizenship, and Exclusion in Africa and Europe.* Chicago, IL: University of Chicago Press.
Hochschild, Arlie. 2003. *The Commercialization of Intimate Life.* Berkeley: University of California Press.
Hochschild, Arlie. 2016. *Strangers in Their Own Land: Anger and Mourning on the American Right.* Berkeley: University of California Press.
Houtman, Dick., Peter Achterberg, Anton Derks, and Jeroen van der Waal. 2008. "A Decline in Class Voting? Class Voting and Cultural Voting in the Postwar Era (1956–1990)." In *Farewell to the Leftist Working Class*, edited by Dick Houtman, Peter Achterberg, and Anton Derks, 71–89. New Brunswick: Transaction.
Jiménez, Tomás. 2010. *Replenished Ethnicity: Mexican Americans, Immigration, and Identity.* Berkeley: University of California Press.
Jiménez, Tomás. 2017. *The Other Side of Assimilation: Immigration and the Changing American Experience.* Berkeley: University of California Press.
Kasinitz, Philip. 2014. "Immigrants, the Arts, and the 'Second-Generation Advantage' in New York." In *New York and Amsterdam. Immigration and the New Urban Landscape*, edited by Nancy Foner, Jan Rath, Jan Willem Duyvendak, and Rogier van Reekum, 263–286. New York: NYU Press.
Kesic, Josip, and Jan Willem Duyvendak. 2016a. "Nationalism Without Nationalism? Dutch Self-Images among the Progressive Left." In *The Culturalization of Citizenship*, edited by Jan Willem Duyvendak, 49–71. London: Palgrave Macmillan.
Kesic, Josip, and Jan Willem Duyvendak. 2016b. "Anti-Nationalist Nationalism: The Paradox of Dutch National Identity." *Nations and Nationalism* 22 (3): 581–597.
de Koster, Willem, and Jeroen van der Waal. 2006. "Moreel Conservatisme en Autoritarisme Theoretisch en Methodisch Ontward. Culturele Waardeoriëntaties in de Politieke Sociologie." *Mens & Maatschappij* 81: 121–141.
Lee, Jennifer, and Frank Bean. 2010. *The Diversity Paradox: Immigration and the Color Line in Twenty-First Century America.* New York: Russell Sage Foundation.
Livingston, Gretchen, and Anna Brown. 2017. *Intermarriage in the U.S. 50 Years After Loving v. Virginia.* Washington, DC: Pew Research Center.
Maliepaard, Mieke, and Richard Alba. 2016. "Cultural Integration in the Muslim Second Generation in the Netherlands: The Case of Gender Ideology." *International Migration Review* 50: 70–94.
Meissner, Fran. 2015. "Migration in Migration-related Diversity? The Nexus Between Superdiversity and Migration Studies." *Ethnic and Racial Studies* 38: 556–567.
Meissner, Fran, and Steven Vertovec. 2015. "Comparing Super-Diversity." *Ethnic and Racial Studies* 38: 541–555.
Mepschen, Paul. 2016. *Everyday Autochthony: Difference, Discontent and the Politics of Home in Amsterdam.* PhD, University of Amsterdam.
Miyawaki, Michael. 2015. "Expanding Boundaries of Whiteness? A Look at the Marital Patterns of Part-white Multiracial Groups." *Sociological Forum* 30: 995–1016.
Morley, David. 2001. "Belongings: Place, Space and Identity in a Mediated World." *European Journal of Cultural Studies* 4: 425–448.
Ngai, Mae. 2003. *Impossible Subjects: Illegal Aliens and the Making of Modern America.* Princeton, NJ: Princeton University Press.

Padilla, Beatriz, Joana Azevedo, and Antonia Olmos-Alcaraz. 2015. "Super-diversity and Conviviality: Exploring Frameworks for Doing Ethnography in Southern European Intercultural Cities." *Ethnic and Racial Studies* 38: 621–635.

Perlmann, Joel. 2005. *Italians Then, Mexicans Now: Immigrant Origins and Second-Generation Progress, 1890–2000*. New York: Russell Sage Foundation.

Pew Research Center. 2015. *Multiracial in America: Proud, Diverse and Growing in Numbers*. Washington, DC: Pew Research Center.

van Reekum, Rogier. 2014. *Out of Character: Debating Dutchness, Narrating Citizenship*. PhD, University of Amsterdam.

Slootman, Marieke. 2014. *Soulmates: Reinvention of Ethnic Identification Among Higher Educated Second Generation Moroccan and Turkish Dutch*. PhD, University of Amsterdam.

Slootman, Marieke, and Jan Willem Duyvendak. 2015. "Feeling Dutch: The Culturalization and Emotionalization of Citizenship and Second-Generation Belonging in the Netherlands." In *Fear, Anxiety, and National Identity: Immigration and Belonging in North America and Western Europe*, edited by Nancy Foner and Patrick Simon, 147–168. New York: Russell Sage Foundation.

Vasquez, Jessica. 2011. *Mexican Americans Across Generations: Immigrant Families, Racial Realities*. New York: New York University Press.

Vasquez, Jessica. 2014. "The Whitening Hypothesis Challenged: Biculturalism in Latino and Non-Hispanic White Intermarriage." *Sociological Forum* 29: 386–407.

Verkaaik, Oskar. 2010. "The Cachet Dilemma: Ritual and Agency in New Dutch Nationalism." *American Ethnologist* 37: 69–82.

Vertovec, Steven. 2007. "Super-Diversity and Its Implications." *Ethnic and Racial Studies*. 30: 1024–1054.

de Volkskrant. 2016. "Overheid Schrapt 'Allochtoon' per Direct uit Vocabulaire." November 1.

Wang, Wendy. 2012. *The Rise of Intermarriage: Rates, Characteristics Vary by Race and Gender*. Washington, DC: Pew Research Center.

Wessendorf, Susanne. 2014. *Commonplace Diversity: Social Relations in a Super-diverse Context*. Basingstoke: Palgrave Macmillan.

ə OPEN ACCESS

Talking around super-diversity

Steven Vertovec

ABSTRACT
The concept of super-diversity has been widely evoked – sometimes in highly misleading ways. Based on a survey of 325 publications across multiple disciplines, this special issue endword piece presents a typology of ways of understanding super-diversity. This includes addressing super-diversity as: a contemporary synonym of diversity, a backdrop for a study, a call for methodological reassessment, a way of simply talking about more ethnicity, a multidimensional reconfiguration of social forms, a call to move beyond ethnicity, and a device for drawing attention to new social complexities. Indeed, I believe the latter – the search for better ways to describe and analyze new social patterns, forms and identities arising from migration-driven diversification – is perhaps the most driving reason for expanding interests and uses, however varied, surrounding the concept of super-diversity.

These days, there is a substantial amount of talking *around* super-diversity. There is also talk *about* super-diversity. Across a range of social scientific terrains, the concept of super-diversity is variably invoked, referenced, concocted or criticized as an idea, setting, condition, theory or approach. Sometimes such talking is really about the concept; that is, discussions ensue with reference to its original meaning or intention. Other times, super-diversity is merely a prompt around which the talk is actually about something else – a springboard to present a set of related research findings, a segue to another topic, or indeed a false starting point, misnomer or sheer strawman. Such divergence is surely OK – indeed, that's what happens to many scholarly ideas, concepts and theories. Once a notion is "out there", its development takes on a life of its own. Multiple understandings, misunderstandings and misuses arise – and such conceptual evolution (including mutation) mostly moves social science forward.

This is an Open Access article distributed under the terms of the Creative Commons Attribution License (http://creativecommons.org/licenses/by/4.0/), which permits unrestricted use, distribution, and reproduction in any medium, provided the original work is properly cited.

But listeners should be offered more clarity concerning the ways a concept is being talked about or around. A caricatured concept does no one any good. In the following brief essay, I outline some of the ways super-diversity has been talked about and around, including some ways represented by contributions to this special issue.

I start with a necessary re-cap of the concept and its original intention. "Super-diversity" was intended to give a name to changing patterns observed in British migration data. It was clear in various statistics (presented in the original article), that, over a period of twenty years or so, the UK had witnessed not just new movements of people reflecting more countries of origin (entailing multiple ethnicities, languages and religions), but – along with these patterns, and differentially reflecting or comprising the new country-of-origin flows, there have been shifts in:

> differential legal statuses and their concomitant conditions, divergent labour market experiences, discrete configurations of gender and age, patterns of spatial distribution, and mixed local area responses by service providers and residents. The dynamic interaction of these variables is what is meant by "super-diversity". (Vertovec 2007, 1025)

Super-diversity is a summary term proposed also to point out that the new migration patterns not only entailed variable combinations of these traits, but that their combinations produced new hierarchical social positions, statuses or stratifications. These, in turn, entail: new patterns of inequality and prejudice including emergent forms of racism, new patterns of segregation, new experiences of space and "contact", new forms of cosmopolitanism and creolization (including what's more recently discussed in terms of conviviality and multiculture), and more.

In these ways, I have always advocated super-diversity as (merely) a concept and approach about new migration patterns. It is not a theory (which, for me, would need to entail an explanation of how and why these changing patterns arose, how they are interlinked, and what their combined effects causally or necessarily lead to). However, for all sorts of reasons, since 2007 super-diversity has been taken up by a wide variety of scholars from an array of disciplines and fields, in myriad (sometimes helpful, sometimes obfuscating, sometimes brilliant) ways and for multiple (sometimes poignant, sometimes curious) purposes. The same can be said of the various ways super-diversity has been used in policy circles – in relation to integration, health, social services and education – and in public debates among NGOs and think-tanks, media outlets and internet forums – concerning issues such as immigration, diversity and urban development [for a fuller discussion of the many understandings of super-diversity, see the online lecture "Super-diversity as concept and approach" at www.mmg.mpg.de].

Since the publication of the *Ethnic and Racial Studies* article "Super-diversity and its implications" in 2007, the term "super-diversity" has been picked up across a surprising range of disciplines and fields. There is certainly no consensus on its meaning "out there". Hence, it is disingenuous if not outright wrong to suggest, as some have done, that "super-diversity scholars" mean such-and-such (for instance, "happy conviviality") by the term. The multiple meanings of "super-diversity" are evident in a limited exercise that traced ways that the term has been invoked or employed in academic literature. Together with a research assistant, Wiebke Unger, I acquired 325 publications between 2008 and 2014 through broad online searches for the term. The results of the review were interesting and telling.

Uses of super-diversity: a typology

Firstly, there is considerable disciplinary spread of articles referring to super-diversity. These go well beyond the expected ones – Sociology, Anthropology, Geography and Political Science as well as the multidisciplinary fields of Migration and Ethnic Studies – to include Linguistics and Socio-Linguistics, History, Education, Law, Business Studies, Management, Literature, Media Studies, Public Health, Social Work, Urban Planning and Landscape Studies. Moreover, while the original article described phenomena in London and the UK, the term has been used subsequently to describe social, cultural and linguistic dynamics in such widespread contexts as Brussels, Venice, New York, Jerusalem, the Baltic states, Italy, Cyprus, Egypt, Nigeria, French Guiana, Zimbabwe, Hong Kong, Hokkaido, Oaxaca, villages of south-west Slovakia, the German state of Brandenburg, the border province of Limburg, Manenberg township in Cape Town, and Enshi in China.

Across all of these disciplines and research contexts, we can see at least seven ways that the concept of super-diversity has been used (so far) [Note: this typology is certainly not intended as particularly scientific: it is based on my reading of the ways that various authors have used the concept of super-diversity. The authors themselves may well context my reading].

Very much diversity

(1) Some social scientists have understood super-diversity as a term that is basically synonymous with "diversity", or perhaps meaning *very much diversity*. This has included attention to more pronounced kinds and dimensions of social differentiation – particularly cultural identities. A few examples are works that refer to super-diversity in terms of: ways of thinking about difference (Baycan and Nijkamp 2012; Mavroudi 2010), "diversity, or what recently has been called 'superdiversity'" (Hüwelmeier 2011, 450), "emerging cultural and demographic diversity" (Svenberg, Skott, and Lepp 2011, 2), "multiple dimensions of differentiation" (Kandylis,

Maloutas, and Sayas 2012, 268), "significant demographic change and diversification" (Aspinall and Song 2013, 548) and "classification encompassing dozens of different cultures and nationalities" (Aspinall 2009, 1425).

Backdrop to a study

(2) A very common way that super-diversity has been used in many articles is merely as a *backdrop to a study*. That is, scholars invoke super-diversity as a new condition or setting, and then carry on with describing whatever set of research findings they wish to present (that more often than not don't really have much directly to do with super-diversity). In this way, we have seen copious, scene-setting statements about "'super-diverse' places" (Osipovič 2010, 212), "superdiverse circumstances" (Jørgensen 2012, 57), "a stage of 'super-diversity'" (Colic-Peisker and Farquharson 2011, 583), "the superdiverse condition" (Neal et al. 2013, 309), "super-diverse realities" (Juffermans 2012, 33), "a super-diverse society" (Hawkey 2012, 175), "a 'super-diverse' world" (Jacquemet 2011, 494), "this time of 'super-diversity'" (Catney, Finney, and Twigg 2011, 109) and an "era of super-diversity" (Burdsey 2013).

Raising super-diversity is also sometimes a way of setting up a strawman argument. As we have seen a number of times in this special issue, this includes dubious argumentative strategies such as commencing an article by pointing to Wessendorf's (2014) book *Commonplace Diversity*, suggesting it portrays super-diversity as the ubiquitous new normal (and a happy one at that), assuming therefore that this is what the super-diversity concept means writ large, and then proceeding to describe some instance in which diversity has not brought normalcy and happiness – or to point out the obvious, that racism or class remains important – and that therefore super-diversity is a poor or misguided concept. Such arguments entail a gross misrepresentation of super-diversity as well as Wessendorf's data and proposition (for one who actually reads the book, it is clear that Wessendorf underlines the specificity of Hackney, stresses that racism and class tensions are ever present, and that – despite a "normalized" perception of multiple differences in certain public places – people remain quite separate in their private spheres).

Methodological reassessment

(3) Also by way of setting up a study or argument, the changing, multidimensional patterns referred to as super-diversity, and the intersectional approach it calls for, have also been underlined by scholars in order to urge a *methodological reassessment* of their respective field or discipline. Here, for example, Blommaert (2013, 6) has stressed

the paradigmatic impact of super-diversity: it questions the foundations of our knowledge and assumptions about societies, how they operate and function at all levels, from the lowest level of human face-to-face communication all the way up to the highest levels of structure in the world system.

Leone (2012, 189) notes that in key migrant-receiving societies, "it is increasingly found that the conceptual framework of 'cultural integration', predominant thus far in social research and policy making about social cohesion and harmony, is largely unsatisfactory in dealing with the challenges of the so-called super-diverse cities".

Appeals for conceptual and methodological re-tooling have been strong in social policy fields. For instance, the conditions of super-diversity have prompted assessments that "policies and discourses need updating in order to match and facilitate new multicultural realities" (Colic-Peisker and Farquharson 2011, 583). Yildiz and Bartlett (2011) make a similar case regarding super-diversity and public services, especially surrounding health, just as Phillimore (2013) does for housing, while Newall, Phillimore, and Sharpe (2012, 22) argue that

> The complexity associated with superdiverse populations, combined with lack of funds or political will to develop specialist services, means it will not be easy to improve migrant women's experiences of maternity in the UK unless universal maternity services are better equipped to meet the needs of all women.

In the field of Education, Guo (2010) puts forward super-diversity to criticize existing approaches to lifelong learning.

However, perhaps no other field or discipline has employed super-diversity for methodological reassessment more than Socio-linguistics. This is illustrated by Kell (2013, 8) who writes that,

> Superdiversity, thus, seems to add layer upon layer of complexity to sociolinguistic issues. Not much of what we were accustomed to methodologically and theoretically seems to fit the dense and highly unstable forms of hybridity and multimodality we encounter in fieldwork data nowadays. Patching up will not solve the problem; fundamental rethinking is required.

Creese and Blackledge (2010, 550) also recognize the new configurations of super-diversity and call "to shift the gaze to the linguistic, focusing on the ways in which the new diversity becomes the site of negotiations over linguistic resources". They elaborate:

> The ways in which people negotiate access to resources in increasingly diverse societies are changing in response to other developments, and we argue that the new diversity is not limited to "new" migrants who arrived in the last decade, but includes changing practices and norms in established migrant (and non-migrant) groups, as daughters and sons, grand-daughters and grand-sons, great-grand-daughters and great-grandsons of immigrants (and non-migrants) negotiate their place in their changing world.... [W]e propose

that looking at these phenomena through a sociolinguistic lens is key to a developed understanding of superdiverse societies. (Ibid.)

The call is taken up by Arnaut (2012, 11), who uses the concept of super-diversity as a platform to foster a "critical sociolinguistics of diversity" (CSD), an approach that first,

> must set off from super-diversity's transgressive moment, which consists of discarding the false certainties of multiculturalism and its endorsement of established differences and hierarchies.... The second step consists in CSD embracing the radical unpredictability that comes with the melt-down of the diversity measurement system which super-diversity has provoked.

Accordingly, an array of sociolinguists (one conference on the sociolinguistics of super-diversity included 300 researchers) have pushed methodological and theoretical boundaries concerning such intriguing notions as linguistic landscapes, translanguaging, "digital super-diversity", multiple discursive practices, multiple subject positions, sociolinguistic economies and the polycentricity of semiotic resources.

More ethnicity

(4) In a much more limited and, at times, unimaginative way, many writers invoke "super-diversity" merely to mean *more ethnicity* – meaning that new migration processes have brought more ethnic groups to a nation or city than in the past. This is certainly not the intention of the super-diversity concept, but it is prevalent among scholars who draw upon super-diversity to call attention to: global movements of people (Roberts 2010), ever wider range of new migrant groups (Nathan and Lee 2013), people from more countries (Syrett and Lyons 2007), migration from more remote corners of the world (Drinkwater 2010), new diversity of migrant origins (Antonsich 2012), growth in the percentage of population born abroad (Hollingworth and Williams 2010), or the plurality of minorities (Hill 2007). Most of these studies do not take into account the multidimensional nature of categories, shifting configurations and new social structures that these entail. Hence, the "more ethnicities" understanding of super-diversity is highly misapplied.

Multidimensional reconfiguration

(5) The previous type of usage in the literature surveyed is countered by articles that are truer to the original meaning of the concept. These are works elaborating descriptions and analyses of *a multi-dimensional reconfiguration* of various social forms. One such piece is by Dahinden (2009) concerning the emergence of super-diversity, coupled with heightened transnationalism, as it fundamentally affects social networks and cognitive

classifications among migrants. Other publications note how new super-diverse configurations raise the need to take multiple variables into account when trying to measure diversity (Longhi 2013), or call attention to how a combination of variables and attributes are variously combined and used by migrants as different forms of capital (Vershinina, Barrett, and Meyer 2009), or recognize how a confluence of factors shape the life chances of ethnic minorities (Stubbs 2008), or bring a critique of the ways older categories may be getting in the way of understanding minority communities' achievements as well as needs (Hollingworth and Mansaray 2012) and may affect strategies for recruitment in social and advocacy services (Richardson and Fulton 2010). In these important contributions, the call for a super-diverse approach has been productively taken up.

Beyond a focus on ethnicity

(6) Yet other scholars have drawn upon the multidimensionality of super-diversity to augment their desire to move *beyond a focus on ethnicity* as the sole or optimal category of analysis surrounding migrants. In this way, social scientists have used the concept to emphasize that: ethnic groups are not the optimal units of analysis (Cooney 2009) and may actually mask more significant forms of differentiation (Fomina 2006); ethnic boundaries are increasingly blurred (Lobo 2010; Pecoud 2010); there are internal divisions within ethnic groups (Glick Schiller and Çağlar 2009); other "strands of identity" that people experience are equally or more important than their identity (Schmidt 2012); ethnicity must be cross-tabulated with other categories to get truer picture of contemporary diversity (Aspinall 2011); multiple "modes of differentiation" come into play from context to context (van Ewijk 2011); and ethnicity-only approaches in social policy are inadequate for addressing needs (Bauböck 2008; Crawley 2010). Overall, super-diversity has been used to emphasize the inherent complications of classifying people (Aspinall 2009; Song 2009; Wimmer 2009).

New or other complexities

(7) Finally, there are numerous academics who, although invoking the concept of super-diversity, actually draw attention to something rather different (though often not wholly unrelated) to what was originally intended: *new or other complexities*. Within this type, scholars have referred to super-diversity with regard to at least three fields of new or other complexity. (a) One concerns *globalization and migration*, in which writers discuss issues like "the complexity of new migration and non-linear trajectories of migrants" (McCabe, Phillimore, and Mayblin 2010, 19), how "migrants have become more transitory and more diverse not only in

terms of their origins, but also in their motives, intentions and statuses within destination countries" (McDowell 2013, 19), how "International migration has become 'liquid'" (Engbersen, Snel, and de Boom 2010, 117) and even how, relatedly, "there are now many sources for ideas and commodities, not simply from Europe or the US or from East to west" (Nolan, MacRaild, and Kirk 2010, 11).

(b) Another field of complexity concerns *ethnic categories and social identities*. Here, super-diversity has prompted renewed interest in: "the origins of people, their presumed motives for migration, their 'career' as migrants (sedentary versus short-term and transitory), or their sociocultural and linguistic features [that] cannot be presupposed" (Jacquemet 2011, 494); "individuals and groups who themselves are superdiverse … across a wide range of variables" (Leppänen and Häkkinen 2012, 18); "socially and culturally complex individuals who cannot be pigeonholed in particular ways and are not necessarily segregated into closed-off communities" (Ros i Solé 2013, 327); "a new, 'super-diverse' terrain in which 'old' structural indicators are less salient to social identities" (Francis, Burke, and Read 2014, 2); the "blurring of distinctions" (Newton and Kusmierczyk 2011, 76) or the situation in which "clear-cut categories of difference (race, ethnicity, culture, religion) are no more: notions of Whiteness and Blackness, and minority categories as constructed in the postcolonial context and in the premises of multiculturalism, are blurred" (Hatziprokopiou 2009, 24); "encounters which undermine held stereotypes" (Osipovič 2010, 171); the ways "cultural traditions become manifold or hazy" (Koch 2009); how "it is descriptively inadequate to assume fixed relations between ethnicity, citizenship, residence, origin, language, profession, etc. or to assume the countability of cultures, languages, or identities" (Juffermans 2012, 33); the "complexity of multiple, fluid, intersectional identifications" (Dhoest, Nikunen, and Cola 2013, 13) and, consequently, how "'super-diversity' requires an analysis of racism not in a dichotomous or top-down frame but as differentially positioning and constituting different groups and individuals" (Erel 2011, 705).

(c) A final mode of complexity seen to be stemming from the concept of super-diversity concerns *new social formations*. Here, a variety of articles address issues such as: "new hierarchies and power relations within the migrant group" (Erel 2009, 10); "trends [that] have diversified the varied forms of contestation of belonging, including new dynamics of spatial segregation and cross-cultural contacts" (Matejskova 2013, 46); "complex new 'meaningful exchanges'" (Butcher 2010, 510) that can lead to "greater interaction, to the evolution of culture, and to the development of convivial and cosmopolitan identities" (Taylor-Gooby and Waite 2014, 272); how "daily life worlds are increasingly diverse, a process which affects both native and migrant populations ... . Institutional monoculturalism and life world super-diversity thus end up coexisting" (Dietz 2013, 27); the ways "superdiversity, and its superimposition of diverse networks, brings groups together with very different frames of reference" (Bailey 2013, 203); and,

> phenomena of globally expanded mobility, which entail new and increasingly complex social formations and networking practices beyond traditional affiliations. Although one could formerly assume the existence over a longer span of time of relatively stable communities of practice, these have become more temporary given the conditions of super-diversity. (Busch 2012, 505)

The breakdown of these 325 articles into 7 usages of super-diversity by discipline or multidisciplinary field is represented in Figure 1. It is immediately interesting to see that no discipline or field is wholly associated with a particular usage. The spread of meanings, uses and understandings of super-diversity is now likely even broader, since at the time of writing this essay, Google Scholar indicates that the original ERS article of 2007 has been cited 2,731 times, while the 2006 COMPAS Working Paper on super-diversity, on which the 2007 article is based, has been cited over 500 times. Overall, I present this typology not just as an exercise in tracing how the concept of super-diversity has travelled and transformed, but to curb or show the futility of some writers' attempts to simplify super-diversity and its meaning (for instance, as the new, happy normal) "in the literature".

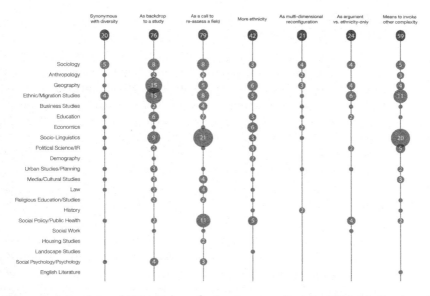

Figure 1. A typology of 325 articles referring to super-diversity, 2008–14: Number of articles by discipline/field and type.

Super-diversity, the USA and Europe

The editors of this special issue have asked why super-diversity seems to have had more uptake among European than American scholars. As pointed out earlier in the limited review of works citing super-diversity, the concept has been applied by scholars worldwide to numerous contexts and scales, including the USA. But indeed, there appears to have been less usage among American social scientists about American contexts. What might be some reasons for this?

I do not agree that American scholars have used other terms to do the "work" done by the super-diversity concept and approach. They editors suggest that the concept and approach of intersectionality is already existing and in wide use in the USA – but that is the situation in Europe as well. Intersectionality and super-diversity are not really addressing the same thing. Rarely in the USA or Europe has intersectionality referred to migration patterns and outcomes. As mentioned above, super-diversity was coined as a concept to single out and tie together certain migration data patterns. I further suggested that understanding the patterns of super-diversity calls for an approach to research that could simultaneous take into account the compound effects of multiple variables or characteristics. This is of course the inherent approach signalled by the concept of intersectionality. But since (at the time I wrote the original article, at least) intersectionality literature was concentrated on the race–gender–class complex, I called for something focused exclusively on migration-related categories. However, the concepts of intersectionality and super-diversity indeed share a call for recognizing the composite effects of social categories.

The study of urban ethnic politics, which has quite a legacy in the USA, is also not an appropriate substitute for super-diversity's subject matter. The study of ethnic politics favours large, organized groups with outspoken representatives; it often largely overlooks new and small migrant populations with precarious, temporary and changing legal statuses. Further, there has been far less attention in the USA to the intersection of nationalities and legal statuses, for instance (important exceptions include Massey and Bartley 2005; there are, of course, important works dealing with undocumented migrants' status – such as Menjívar and Abrego 2012 – but this is represents only a part of what super-diversity is intended to address). Perhaps less interest in the USA arises because there are far few legal statuses and conditions in the USA as compared with European and other countries (see Beine et al. 2016). But this is not a terribly satisfying reason.

The editors importantly underline a key factor possibly explaining less attention to the concept of super-diversity in the USA, namely a preponderance of methodological group-ism, crucially shaped by specific categories of race (cf. Wimmer 2015). A great deal of diversity discussions of any kind are framed by specific terms of race, but a great deal of American social scientific analysis, particularly involving statistics, depends on core, official ethnoracial classifications (as does much public discourse). Josh DeWind of the American Social Science Research Council (SSRC) explains,

> An issue that has plagued immigration studies, is that most of the social identity categories that are used analytically, are also categories that are used or have their origin in usage by states to manage populations. Many studies are limited to such categories of state censuses, for example, to define racial and ethnic groups that often use more nuanced, overlapping, and contextually distinct categories. Academics then have used state categories to frame studies of immigrant group incorporation and mobility, even if members of the groups define themselves as distinct on the basis of language, religion, class or the like. Measuring the "mobility" of Latinos, for example, compared to that of "Asians" is for many members of those groups meaningless, as these categories obscure significant differences between rich and poor, and educated and uneducated members of the groups .... What is good for administration may not be good for explanation.
>
> So if studies of "diversity" begin with given categories, rather than utilizing categories that are directly appropriate to the analysis, then the categories end up being more of a problem than being useful or they get in the way of understanding. (in Vertovec 2015, 5)

The dilemma described by DeWind is by no means wholly representative of American scholarship, but it is likely one fact hampering more complex descriptions and multidimensional analyses of migration-driven diversification. Relatedly, although concerns with *racism* remain high, many European studies of migrants and ethnic minorities – also reflecting respective country-based official statistics – have engaged less with racial categories than with ones of nationality.

Questions of American vs. European approaches still do not address a basic question: in recent times wherever based, why has there been so much assorted attention, and such varied readings and uses, of super-diversity? For my part, I believe that social scientists are avidly seeking ways of describing and talking about increasing and intensifying complexities in social dynamics and configurations at neighbourhood, city, national and global levels. Sometimes these are addressed in light of changing migration patterns, but as we have seen, now super-diversity is being invoked with reference to other complex social developments. As academics, we are still struggling to describe new, ever more complicated trends, processes and outcomes. Addressing "the superdiversity of cities and societies of the 21st century", the late Beck (2011, 53) suggested that the rise of such dynamics are "both inevitable (because of global flows of migration, flows of information, capital, risks, etc.) and politically challenging". However, he said,

> It is in this sense that over the last decades the cultural, social and political landscapes of diversity are changing radically, but we still use old maps to orientate ourselves. In other words, my main thesis is: *we do not even have the language*

through which contemporary superdiversity in the world can be described, conceptualized, understood, explained and researched. [Ibid., italics in original]

Through such attempts at describing and analysing new complexities, we are ever better at developing what Nando Sigona has called "ways of looking at a society getting increasingly complex, composite, layered and unequal" (www.nandosigona.worldpress.com). I believe that this is best done when scholars talk about, not just around, concepts like super-diversity.

Disclosure statement

No potential conflict of interest was reported by the author.

References

Antonsich, M. 2012. "Exploring the Demands of Assimilation Among White Ethnic Majorities in Western Europe." *Journal of Ethnic and Migration Studies* 38 (1): 59–76.
Arnaut, K. 2012. "Super-diversity: Elements of an Emerging Perspective." *New Diversities* 14 (2): 1–16.
Aspinall, P. J. 2009. "The Future of Ethnicity Classifications." *Journal of Ethnic and Migration Studies* 35 (9): 1417–1435.
Aspinall, P. J. 2011. "The Utility and Validity for Public Health of Ethnicity Categorization in the 1991, 2001 and 2011 British Censuses." *Public Health* 125 (10): 680–687.
Aspinall, P. J., and M. Song. 2013. "Is Race a 'Salient …' or 'Dominant Identity' in the Early 21st Century: The Evidence of UK Survey Data on Respondents' Sense of Who They Are." *Social Science Research* 42 (2): 547–561.
Bailey, A. J. 2013. "Migration, Recession and an Emerging Transnational Biopolitics Across Europe." *Geoforum* 44: 202–210.
Bauböck, R. 2008. "Beyond Culturalism and Statism. Liberal Responses to Diversity, Eurosphere." Online Working Paper No. 6: 1–34.
Baycan, T., and P. Nijkamp. 2012. "A Socio-economic Impact Analysis of Urban Cultural Diversity: Pathways and Horizons." In *Migration Impact Assessment. New Horizons*, edited by P. Nijkamp, J. Poot, and M. Sahin, 175–202. Cheltenham: Edward Elgar.
Beck, Ulrich. 2011. "Multiculturalism or Cosmopolitanism: How Can We Describe and Understand the Diversity of the World?" *Social Sciences in China* 32 (4): 52–58.
Beine, M., A. Boucher, B. Burgoon, M. Crock, J. Gest, M. Hiscox, P. McGovern, H. Rapoport, J. Schaper, and E. Thielemann. 2016. "Comparing Immigration Policies: An Overview from the IMPALA Database." *International Migration Review* 50 (4): 827–863.
Blommaert, J. 2013. *Ethnography, Superdiversity and Linguistic Landscapes: Chronicles of Complexity*. Bristol: Multilingual Matters.
Burdsey, D. 2013. "'The Foreignness Is Still Quite Visible in this Town': Multiculture, Marginality and Prejudice at the English Seaside." *Patterns of Prejudice* 47 (2): 95–116.
Busch, B. 2012. "The Linguistic Repertoire Revisited." *Applied Linguistics* 33 (5): 503–505.
Butcher, M. 2010. "Navigating 'New' Delhi: Moving Between Difference and Belonging in a Globalising City." *Journal of Intercultural Studies* 31 (5): 507–524.
Catney, G., N. Finney, and L. Twigg 2011. "Diversity and the Complexities of Ethnic Integration in the UK: Guest Editors' Introduction." *Journal of Intercultural Studies* 32 (2): 107–114.

Colic-Peisker, V., and K. Farquharson. 2011. "Introduction: A New Era in Australian Multiculturalism? The Need for Critical Interrogation." *Journal of Intercultural Studies* 32 (6): 579–586.
Cooney, M. 2009. "Ethnic Conflict Without Ethnic Groups: A Study in Pure Sociology." *British Journal of Sociology* 60 (3): 473–492.
Crawley, H. 2010. "Moving Beyond Ethnicity: The Socio-Economic Status and Living Conditions of Immigrant Children in the UK." *Child Indicators Research* 3 (4): 547–570.
Creese, A., and A. Blackledge. 2010. "Towards a Sociolinguistics of Superdiversity." *Zeitschrift für Erziehungswissenschaft* 13 (4): 549–572.
Dahinden, J. 2009. "Are We All Transnationals Now? Network Transnationalism and Transnational Subjectivity: The Differing Impacts of Globalization on the Inhabitants of a Small Swiss City." *Ethnic and Racial Studies* 32 (8): 1365–1386.
Dhoest, A., K. Nikunen, and M. Cola 2013. "Exploring Media Use Among Migrant Families in Europe." *Observatorio*. doi:10.7458/obs002013663.
Dietz, G. 2013. "A Doubly Reflexive Ethnographic Methodology for the Study of Religious Diversity in Education." *British Journal of Religious Education* 35 (1): 20–35.
Drinkwater, S. 2010. "Immigration and the Economy." *National Institute Economic Review* 213 (1): R1–R4.
Engbersen, G., E. Snel, and J. de Boom. 2010. "'A Van Full of Poles': Liquid Migration from Central and Eastern Europe." In *A Continent Moving West? EU Enlargement and Labour Migration from Central and Eastern Europe*, edited by R. Black, G. Engbersen, M. Okólski, and C. Pantîru, 115–140. Amsterdam: Amsterdam University Press.
Erel, U. 2009. *Migrant Women Transforming Citizenship: Life Stories from Britain and Germany*. Farnham: Ashgate.
Erel, U. 2011. "Reframing Migrant Mothers as Citizens." *Citizenship Studies* 15 (6–7): 695–709.
Fomina, J. 2006. "The Failure of British Multiculturalism: Lessons for Europe." *Polish Sociological Review* 4 (156): 409–424.
Francis, B., P. Burke, and B. Read. 2014. "The Submergence and Re-emergence of Gender in Undergraduate Accounts of University Experience." *Gender and Education* 26 (1): 1–17.
Glick Schiller, N., and A. Çağlar. 2009. "Towards a Comparative Theory of Locality in Migration Studies: Migrant Incorporation and City Scale." *Journal of Ethnic and Migration Studies* 35 (2): 177–202.
Guo, S. 2010. "Migration and Communities: Challenges and Opportunities for Lifelong Learning." *International Journal of Lifelong Education* 29 (4): 437–447.
Hatziprokopiou, P. 2009. "Strangers as Neighbors in the Cosmopolis: New Migrants in London, Diversity, and Place." In *Branding Cities. Cosmopolitanism, Parochialism and Social Change*, edited by S. Donald, E. Kofman, and C. Kevin, 14–27. New York: Routledge.
Hawkey, K. 2012. "History and Super Diversity." *Education Sciences* 2 (4): 165–179.
Hill, A. 2007. "The Changing Face of British Cities by 2020." *The Observer*, December 23.
Hollingworth, S., and A. Mansaray. 2012. *Language Diversity and Attainment in English Schools: A Scoping Study*. London: The Institute for Policy Studies in Education (IPSE), London Metropolitan University.
Hollingworth, S., and K. Williams. 2010. "Multicultural Mixing or Middle-class Reproduction? The White Middle Classes in London Comprehensive Schools." *Space and Polity* 14 (1): 47–64.
Hüwelmeier, G. 2011. "Socialist Cosmopolitanism Meets Global Pentecostalism: Charismatic Christianity Among Vietnamese Migrants After the Fall of the Berlin Wall." *Ethnic and Racial Studies* 34 (3): 436–453.

Jacquemet, M. 2011. "Crosstalk 2.0: Asylum and Communicative Breakdowns." *Text & Talk* 31 (4): 147.

Jørgensen, J. N. 2012. "Ideologies and Norms in Language and Education Policies in Europe and Their Relationship with Everyday Language Behaviours." *Language, Culture and Curriculum* 25 (1): 57–71.

Juffermans, K. 2012. "Exaggerating Difference: Representations of the Third World Other in Pl Aid." *Intercultural Pragmatics* 9 (1): 23–45.

Kandylis, G., T. Maloutas, and J. Sayas. 2012. "Immigration, Inequality and Diversity: Socio-ethnic Hierarchy and Spatial Organization in Athens, Greece." *European Urban and Regional Studies* 19 (3): 267–286.

Kell, C. 2013. "Ariadne's Thread: Literacy, Scale and Meaning Making Across Space and Time." London: Working Papers in Urban Language & Literacies 118, Kings College London.

Koch, G. 2009. "Intercultural Communication and Competence Research Through the Lens of an Anthropology of Knowledge." *Forum Qualitative Sozialforschung* 10 (1), Art. 15.

Leone, M. 2012. "Hearing and Belonging: On Sounds, Faiths, and Laws." In *Transparency, Power and Control: Perspectives on Legal Communication*, edited by V. K. Bhatia, C. A. Hafner, L. Miller, and A. Wagner, 183–197. Farnham: Ashgate.

Leppänen, S., and A. Häkkinen. 2012. "Buffalaxed Superdiversity: Representations of the Other on Youtube." *New Diversities* 14 (2): 17–33.

Lobo, M. 2010. "Interethnic Understanding and Belonging in Suburban Melbourne." *Urban Policy and Research* 28 (1): 85–99.

Longhi, S. 2013. "Impact of Cultural Diversity on Wages, Evidence from Panel Data." *Regional Science and Urban Economics* 43 (5): 797–807.

Massey, Douglas S., and Katherine Bartley. 2005. "The Changing Legal Status Distribution of Immigrants: A Caution." *International Migration Review* 39 (2): 469–484.

Matejskova, T. 2013. "The Unbearable Closeness of The East: Embodied Micro-economies of Difference, Belonging, and Intersecting Marginalities in Post-socialist Berlin." *Urban Geography* 34 (1): 30–35.

Mavroudi, E. 2010. "Nationalism, the Nation and Migration: Searching for Purity and Diversity." *Space and Polity* 14 (3): 219–233.

McCabe, A., J. Phillimore, and L. Mayblin. 2010. "Below the Radar: Activities and Organisations in the Third Sector: A Summary Review of the Literature." Third Sector Research Centre Paper 29, University of Birmingham.

McDowell, Linda. 2013. *Working Lives: Gender, Migration and Employment in Britain, 1945–2007*. London: John Wiley & Sons.

Menjívar, Cecilia, and Leisy J. Abrego. 2012. "Immigration Law and the Lives of Central American Immigrants." *American Journal of Sociology* 117 (5): 1380–1421.

Nathan, M., and N. Lee. 2013. "Cultural Diversity, Innovation, and Entrepreneurship: Firm-level Evidence from London." *Economic Geography* 89 (4): 367–394.

Neal, S., K. Bennett, A. Cochrane, and G. Mohan. 2013. "Living Multiculture: Understanding the New Spatial and Social Relations of Ethnicity and Multiculture in England." *Environment and Planning C: Government and Policy* 31 (2): 308–323.

Newall, D., J. Phillimore, and H. Sharpe. 2012. "Migration and Maternity in the Age of Superdiversity." *Practising Midwife* 15 (1): 20–23.

Newton, J., and E. Kusmierczyk. 2011. "Teaching Second Languages for the Workplace." *Annual Review of Applied Linguistics* 31: 74–92.

Nolan, M., D. M. MacRaild, and N. Kirk. 2010. "Transnational Labour in the Age of Globalization." *Labour History Review* 75 (1): 8–19.

Osipovič, D. 2010. "Social Citizenship of Polish Migrants in London: Engagement and Non-engagement with the British Welfare State." Doctoral thesis, University College London.
Pecoud, A. 2010. "What Is Ethnic in an Ethnic Economy?" *International Review of Sociology* 20 (1): 59–76.
Phillimore, J. 2013. "Housing, Home and Neighbourhood Renewal in the Era of Superdiversity: Some Lessons from the West Midlands." *Housing Studies* 28 (5): 682–670.
Richardson, K., and Fulton, R., 2010. "Towards Culturally Competent Advocacy: Meeting the Needs of Diverse Communities." Better Health Briefing Paper 15. Kidderminster: British Institute of Race Equality in Advocacy Services.
Roberts, C. 2010. "Language Socialization in the Workplace." *Annual Review of Applied Linguistics* 30: 211–227.
Ros i Solé, C. 2013. "Cosmopolitan Speakers and Their Cultural Cartographies." *The Language Learning Journal* 41 (3): 326–339.
Schmidt, G. 2012. "'Grounded' Politics: Manifesting Muslim Identity as a Political Factor and Localized Identity in Copenhagen." *Ethnicities* 12 (5): 603–622.
Song, M. 2009. "Is Intermarriage a Good Indicator of Integration?" *Journal of Ethnic and Migration Studies* 35 (2): 331–348.
Stubbs, S. 2008. "In Place of Drums and Samosas: In a 'Super Diverse' Britain, the Key to Social Cohesion is Not a New British 'Identity' but Tackling Poverty and Inequality." *The Guardian*, May 13.
Svenberg, K., C. Skott, and M. Lepp. 2011. "Ambiguous Expectations and Reduced Confidence: Experience of Somali Refugees Encountering Swedish Health Care." *Journal of Refugee Studies* 24 (4): 690–705.
Syrett, S., and M. Lyons. 2007. "Migration, New Arrivals and Local Economies." *Local Economy* 22 (4): 325–334.
Taylor-Gooby, P., and E. Waite. 2014. "Toward a More Pragmatic Multiculturalism? How the UK Policy Community Sees the Future of Ethnic Diversity Policies." *Governance* 27 (2): 267–289.
van Ewijk, A. R. 2011. "Diversity Within Police Forces in Europe: A Case for the Comprehensive View." *Policing* 6 (1): 76–92.
Vershinina, N., R. Barrett, and M. Meyer. 2009. "Polish Immigrants in Leicester: Forms of Capital Underpinning Entrepreneurial Activity." Leicester Business School Occasional Papers 86.
Vertovec, Steven. 2007. "Super-Diversity and Its Implications." *Ethnic and Racial Studies* 30 (6): 1024–1054.
Vertovec, Steven. 2015. "Introduction: Formulating Diversity Studies." In *Routledge International Handbook of Diversity Studies*, edited by Steven Vertovec, 1–20. London: Routledge.
Wessendorf, Susanne. 2014. *Commonplace Diversity: Social Relations in a Super-diverse Context*. Basingstoke: Palgrave.
Wimmer, Andreas. 2009. "Herder's Heritage and the Boundary-making Approach: Studying Ethnicity in Immigrant Societies." *Sociological Theory* 27 (3): 244–227.
Wimmer, Andreas. 2015. "Race-centrism: A Critique and a Research Agenda." *Ethnic and Racial Studies* 38 (13): 2186–2205.
Yildiz, C., and A. Bartlett. 2011. "Language, Foreign Nationality and Ethnicity in an English Prison: Implications for the Quality of Health and Social Research." *Journal of Medical Ethics* 37 (10): 637–640.

Index

Note: **Bold** page numbers refer to tables; *italic* page numbers refer to figures and page numbers followed by "n" denote endnotes.

Acosta-García, Raúl 56
aggression 84, 100
Ahmed, Sarah 67, 72
Alba, Richard 4, 9, 12, 13, 74, 115
allochthons 11, 74, 75, 78, 82–4, 102n1, 109
America, multi-ethnic: cross-Atlantic perspectives 39; cultural and social differences 36; data and methods 39–43; demographic characteristics of sample 40, **41**; diversity and intergroup relations 36; from diversity to super-diversity in everyday life 49–50; family and theme codes 40; inequality, processes of 36; intergroup relations 38–9; interviews 40–1; multi-dimensionality of diversity 36; multi-group and cross-site analysis 36; native parentage experience diversity 36; sampling methods 40, 42; secondary analyses of qualitative data 42; stayers, leavers and returners 40; young adulthood, diversity and transition 37–8, 43–9
American Social Science Research Council (SSRC) 135
Amsterdam: autochthonous and allochthonous residents 74–5; cultural and religious differences 109; discourse of displacement 75–80; Dutch social engineering 92–4; "Muslim district" 86n2; "newness and novelty" 89; original city dwellers 85; public housing tradition 75; strangers in community centre 94–7; super-diversity and culturalization of citizenship 72–5; (in)tolerance and othering, discourses of 97–100
Aptekar, Sofya 10
Arnaut, K. 130
assimilation: diversifies immigrants 117–18; diversifies mainstream 119–20; experience of increased diversity 118; immigrant and second-generation 119; in Netherlands 119, 120; in US 119–20
Astoria 59; immigration-driven diversity 59; super-diverse community garden 58–62
asylum seekers 17; dispersal policies 20; legal statuses 20; and refugees 20
autochthones 11, 12n2, 72, 74–5, 79–80, 80, 82–5, 109
Azevedo, Joana 56

baby boomer generation 37
Back, Les 9
Bakewell, O. 22–3, 29
Bartlett, A. 129
Baumann, Gerd 73
Berg, Mette Louise 56
Berrey, Ellen 67
Blackledge, A. 129
Blackness, notions of 132
black/white divide 4–5
Blommaert, J. 128
Boccagni, Paolo 67
Borer, Michael 58
Borgen, Linda 40
Bourdieu, P.: economic, cultural and social capital, differentiation between 19; social capital, notion of 23
Brazilian migrants 29

INDEX

Carr, Patrick 40
Catholic faith 112
chain migrations 18, 22
Chinese immigrant 60
class 3, 4, 49, 65, 91, 102; and cultural boundaries 72; distinctions and ethnic leveraging 101; and educational status/ethnicity 4; inequalities 61
co-ethnic networks 20, 21, 26–9, 99; cultural values and religious beliefs 18; high educational backgrounds 27; social control 28
coexistence, in diverse neighbourhoods 57
"colonial matrices of power" 67
"common Dutchman" 82
commonplace diversity 8, 9, 91
Commonplace Diversity (Wessendorf) 128
community-building practices 94
concentration neighborhoods 78
conceptual evolution (mutation) 125
contact hypothesis 7
cosmopolitanism 6, 56, 126
Creese, A. 129
creolization 56, 126
crime 49, 78, 92, 93
"critical sociolinguistics of diversity" (CSD) 130
Crul, Maurice 97, 107, 108, 111, 117
cultural capital: definition 19; ethnic differences 20; pioneer migration 30; research participants 22, 27, 29; social network formation 19, 30
cultural essentialism 72, 73
cultural identities 127
culturalization of citizenship 72–4, 109, 113
"culturalization of everyday life" 74, 109
cultural syncretism 109
culture, notion of 7, 36, 73–4, 85, 96, 118, 132
"culture of civility" 38

Dahinden, J. 130
Dekker, R. 23, 25
demographic diversity 2–6, 8, 11, 13, 37, 59, 73, 74, 89–102, 108, 127–8
demolition plans 76–81
development areas 78
DeWind, Josh 135
differentiation mechanism 74
digital super-diversity 130
discourse of displacement 67, 71–85, 83
discourse of diversity 62

diversification of diversity 3, 7, 13, 55, 73
divide-and-rule manner 11
domestic violence 92, 93
dominant Labor Party (PvdA) 83
"doomsday scenarios" 78
Dutch mainstream: cultural consensus 113–14; cultural nationalism and racism 85; "feeling rules" 114; membership, culturalization of 113; in Netherlands 112–13; virtual consensus 113; in Western Europe 112
Duyvendak, Jan Willem 9, 12

economic capital 19
economic migrants 17
education: advanced 37; backgrounds 9, 18, 19, 23, 25–7, 30–1, 119; formal 19, 26; higher 19, 67, 115, 118; levels of 28, 45, 118; status 4
"embracing diversity" 96
Engbersen, G. 23
ethnic absolutism 72
ethnic differences 14, 20, 36, 107
ethnic diversity 1, 4–5, 5, 7–10, 36–8, 46, 73, 106
ethnic (immigrant-origin) groups 4
ethnicity 8, 12, 54, 56–7, 59, 63, 91, 92, 102, 117; and diversity 74; of immigrants 106; "modes of differentiation" 131; more ethnic groups 130; nationality 19, 30, 31; and religion 23; shaping settlement 18
ethnic leveraging 92, 99, 101
ethnic minorities 3, 10, 78, 90, 94, 101, 131, 135
ethnic origin 4, 107
ethnography: of Dutch social engineering 92–4; on London's borough of Hackney 7
ethnoracial diversity 35, 36
ethno-racial groups 2, 10, 119
European immigrant 59, 60
European style super-diversity 7
everyday encounters 55, 57–8, 60–2
everyday interactions: effects of super-diversity 7–12; ethnographic study of 66
exclusion 97, 106; of ethnic, racial and religious others 100; politics 71; practices of 63, 65, 67

Facebook 25
"failed multiculturalism" 6
family migration 22

INDEX

family relations/close friendships 23
fear 6, 27, 28, 77, 78, 80, 93
Fenstermaker, Sarah 57, 58
Foner, Nancy 38
foreigners 91, 96, 98
Fortier, Anne-Marie 57
foundation contacts 24–6
foundation networks 23, 24
Freedom Party 72
frustration 81
Furstenberg, Frank, Jr. 40

Garfinkel, Harold 57
gender 2–5, 11, 21, 30, 37, 39–42, 54–6, 59, 61, 63, 66, 67n1, 91, 105, 107, 112, 113, 117
generation 3; baby boomer 37; parental 36, 37, 38, 48–9, 50, 114–15; second 9, 10, 36–8, 40–1, 45–7, 50, 60, 106, 110–12, 114, 118–19; third 102n1, 112, 115
Gidley, Ben 57
Gilroy, Paul 57
Glazer, Nathan 4, 5
globalization 72, 131–2
Goffman, Erving 58, 65
green urbanism 60
"groupness," sense of 95
guest workers 82, 91, 106
Guo, S. 129

Haas, H. de 22, 28
Hackney: commonplace diversity 8, 74, 107; ethnography on London's borough of 7
Hall, Suzanne M. 55, 57
hard boundary multiculturalism 6
Hartmann, Douglas 40
hatred 100
heterogeneity 118; networks 93; of urban experience 73
high-skilled professionals, migration of 22
Hmong refugees 42
Holdaway, Jennifer 40
"horizontal" interpersonal relations 108
housing corporation officials 80
hybrid spaces 108
hyper-sensitive native majority 121

Immigrant Second Generation 40
immigration 17; and public discourse of tolerance 10; settlement 19–20; status 49, 54

inclusion 64, 106; of descendants 112; of four research sites 41; trace patterns of 58
individual migrants 18
inequality: and discrimination 57; gender 113; and prejudice 54, 126; socio-economic and racial 57
insecurity 77, 92
integration 38, 106; and assimilation 107, 122n1; and cohesion 31, 92; cultural 129; issues of 107; of migrants 23, 74
interdisciplinary collaboration 36
interethnic friendships, development of 8–9, 115
intergroup prejudice 7
intergroup relations 38–9; "city as context" framework 38; "culture of civility" 38; importance of local context 38; "integration context theory" 38; "particular New York way" 38
intergroup social relations 8
internet 25, 27, 126
interpersonal relations 9, 108
intersectionality approach 5, 7, 66, 134
interviews 20, 36, 40, 42, 50, 56, 60, 63, 66, 75, 84, 93–4, 99
intolerance, discourse of 6, 97–8, 100, 120

"Judeo-Christian"/"Dutch" values 11, 112

Kasinitz, Philip 40, 109
Kefalas, Maria 40
Kell, C. 129
Kosta, Ervin 40
Kubal, A. 22

language 2; diversity 67; high cultural capital 27; importance of 25; knowledge of English 29, 30, 54; Spanish 54
legal status 2, 3, 13, 17, 18, 20, 22, 29–31, 39, 54, 91, 105, 115, 117, 121, 126, 134
Lelie, Frans 107
Leone, M. 129
linguistic landscapes 130
local community 65, 93, 101
London: beyond co-ethnic networks 26–9; foundation contacts 24–6; pioneer migrants and social networks 21–3; research participants 20
Louis Couperusbuurt 76, 77

macro-processes 13, 121
mainstream: assimilation, concept of 107; emotional investment 114; institutional 110; religious identities 112; singular 110; social and cultural settings 110; social-demographic aspect 111
majority-minority cities 97; demography and horizontal relations 107–10
Makoni, Sinfree 55
Malinke-speaking Muslims 25
Marcouch, Ahmed 86n2
Martinez, Miranda 62
Martínez-Ortiz, Esperanza 56
Mayorga-Gallo, Sarah 67
Meissner, Fran 54, 56, 66, 72, 89–90, 106
Mepschen, Paul 11, 114
methodological nationalism 18, 26
migrant settlement 19, 23, 30–1
migration movements 18, 106; early adopter or group migration stage 22; initial or pioneer stage 22; mature or mass migration stage 22; scholarship 18; social relations 18; strong ties and weak ties 23
mixing strategy 94–5
"modes of differentiation" 131
Mollenkopf, John 5, 40
Moroşanu, L. 18, 27, 31
Mortimer, Jeylan 40
Moynihan, Daniel Patrick 4
multiculturalism 5–6; failed 6; hard boundary 6; soft boundary 6
multidimensionality 131
multi-group, multi-site sample 40
"Muslim district" 86n2
Muslims: immigrants 112–13; intolerance of homosexuals 6; migrants 114

Ndhlovu, Finex 57, 67
Neal, S. 56
neighbourhood restructuring plans, perception of 82
Netherlands: "autochthonous" and "allochthonous" residents 109; emergence of autochthony 109; multicultural paradise 121
Newall, D. 129
"new sense of us" 95–6
new social formations 132–3
New York City-regulated community garden system 59–60
"no majority" cities, creation of 4
non-profit organization 62

"northern model" 4
NVivo 20

"old ethno-racial majority" 91
Olmos-Alcaraz, A. 56
Olympic Games, 2012 67
oppression, practices of 55, 66, 67
"ordinary Amsterdammers" 82
"ordinary people," notion 72, 79, 82, 83, 85
Orthodox Jewish intolerance of feminists 6
"othered" cultures 74
other-than-ethnic factors 19, 31

Padilla, Beatriz 56, 107–8
parental generation 36, 37, 38, 48–9, 49, 50, 114–15
Partij van de Allochtonen (the party of allochthones) 83
people with disabilities 54
petty crime 78
Phillimore, J. 129
pioneer migration 21; co-ethnics 31; feedback mechanisms 22; higher financial and cultural capital 30; highly educated pioneers 31; limited social capital 23; methodological nationalism 22; and social networks 21–3; in twenty-first century London 19
policy makers 54, 80, 89
Polish migrants 23
political structure 13
polycentricity of semiotic resources 130
poverty 77, 92, 93
power: balance in urban settings 90; between blacks and whites 5; and inequality 53–67; in super-diverse community garden 58–62
Protestant-like denomination 112
proximity principle 108
public housing 10, 60, 76, 78–81, 85
Putnam, R.D. 7, 23

racial diversity 65, 90, 91, 97, 101
racism 3, 4, 9, 14, 35, 49, 54, 74, 102, 126; domination 57; inequalities 10, 61
Ramadan 102n2
refugees 20, 25, 27–30, 42–3
religion 5, 7, 10, 12, 17–18, 18, 23, 25–6, 30–1, 36, 42, 45, 54, 59, 92, 107, 126, 132, 135
research participants 18–22, 24–5, 27–31
residential neighbourhoods 37, 46

INDEX

restructuring plans 82–3
Romanians, social networks in London 27
Rumbaut, Ruben 40
Rutte, Mark (Dutch Prime Minister) 71, 114
Ryan, L. 23, 29, 31

scheefwonen, discourse of 81–2
Schinkel, Willem 74
Schneider, J. 107
second generation 9, 10, 36–8, 37, 40–1, 45–7, 50, 60, 106, 110–12, 114, 118–19
Second World War 19, 20, 35
segregation 4–5, 56, 77, 111, 126, 132
Sen, Amartya 6
settlement 18; of individual migrants 18; patterns, variations in 19; and social network formation 20; stages of 26
sexuality 3, 11, 42, 59, 63, 91, 113
sexual orientation 2, 5, 54
Sharpe, H. 129
Sigona, Nando 56, 136
Sinha, Shamser 9
Skerry, Peter 5
slavery 4, 9
"*Slotermeer verandert*" (Slotermeer is changing) 76
Small, Mario 58
social anxiety 77
social capital 19; bridging or bonding 31; definition 19; use of 23
social class 2, 39, 99, 107, 110
social cohesion 6, 23, 77, 92, 96, 112, 129
social diversity 8, 43, 84
social interaction 37, 56, 58, 61, 91, 94, 97, 101
social marginalization 78
social network formation 30; cultural capital 30; migration and migrant settlement 18; patchworking 31
social power 107, 111, 121
social relations 9; educational backgrounds 30; pioneer migrants 18
social welfare system 42
social work 1, 12, 20, 67, 92–5, 97–9, 101, 105, 127
societal mainstream, existence of 13
socio-economic status 10, 54, 59
sociolinguistic economies 130
Socrates Sculpture Park 62–3
soft boundary multiculturalism 6
"southern model" 4

SSRC *see* American Social Science Research Council (SSRC)
strict black/white segregation 4
structural racism 66–7
student migration 22
super-diversity: American *vs.* European approaches 135; of Atlantic 3–7; "collective intermingling" 56; community garden, power in 58–62; definition 2; discipline or multidisciplinary field 133, *133*; and "diversity turn" 56; effects of 7–12; ethnic categories and social identities 132; ethnicity 131; ethnoracial 7; few cautions 66–7; fleeting interactions 62–6; intergroup relations 7; methodological leverage 56–8; methodological reassessment 128–30; more ethnicity 130; multi-dimensional nature of diversity 54–5; multidimensional reconfiguration 130–1; new configurations 129; new or other complexities 131–3; prejudice and exclusion 56; re-centring power and inequality; social scientists 54; USA and Europe 134–6; uses of 127–33; very much diversity 127–8
Swartz, Teresa 40
symbolic interactionism 57, 58, 63, 66

third generation 102n1, 112, 115
togetherness 94–6, 99
tolerance, discourse of 97; and othering 98; social classes 99
translanguaging 130
Tran, Van C. 9

Uitermark, Justus 78
undocumented migrant 19, 20, 24, 134
undocumented persons 17
unemployment 78, 92, 93
Unger, Wiebke 127
United Kingdom: analysis of multiculture 57; asylum dispersal policies 20; Brazilian migrants in 29; multiculture analysis in 57; refugees in 27
urban culturalism 55, 58–9; analysis of interactions 64
urban development 126
urban diversity 17; in United States 3–4
urban ethnic politics 4, 134
urban neighborhoods 2
urban regeneration and renewal 78

INDEX

US mainstream: exclusionary impact 117; expansion, signs of 114–15; generational distribution 115; interethnic and interreligious marriage 115; intermarriage 116; mass assimilation 115; mixed majority–minority family backgrounds 116–17; mixed unions 116; workforce 115–16

Valentine, Gill 57
Vertovec, Steven 1, 2, 13, 14, 39, 54, 56, 67, 89, 100, 101, 105, 107, 121; concept of super-diversity 90; descriptive tool 89–90
violence 100; domestic 92, 93

Warikoo, Natasha 67
Wekker, Fenneke 8, 11–12
welfare organizations 89
Wessendorf, Suzanne 2, 7, 8, 9, 29, 74–5, 91, 97, 107, 108, 111, 128
West, Candace 58

Western Garden Cities 85
whiteness 74; ideas about 82, notions of 77, 132
Wilson, Helen 56
working-class: migrants 30; neighbourhoods 77, 91–2; residents 79, 92–4; visitors 92, 94, 95, 97–101
work schemes 17

Yildiz, C. 129
young adulthood, diversity and transition 43–9; background and upbringing 43; in college settings 43–4; dating, relationships and marriage 47–8; in friendship networks 47; intergenerational differences 48–9; in residential neighbourhoods 46; in workplace 45–6
youth delinquency 93
Youth Development Study 40
youth programme 64
Yrizar-Barbosa, Guillermo 115

Printed in Great Britain
by Amazon